Stand Out Basic

Lesson Planner

Second Edition

Rob Jenkins

Staci Johnson

HEINLE
CENGAGE Learning

Australia • Brazil • Japan • Korea • Mexico • Singapore • Spain • United Kingdom • United States

HEINLE
CENGAGE Learning™

**Stand Out Basic: Lesson Planner,
Second Edition**
Rob Jenkins, Staci Johnson

Editorial Director: Joe Dougherty

Publisher, ESL and Dictionaries: Sherrise Roehr

Acquisitions Editor: Tom Jefferies

VP, Director of Content Development:
   Anita Raducanu

Development Editor: John Hicks

Associate Media Development Editor:
   Jonelle Lonergan

Director of Product Marketing: Amy T. Mabley

Senior Field Marketing Manager:
   Donna Lee Kennedy

Product Marketing Manager: Katie Kelley

Senior Content Project Manager: Maryellen
   Killeen

Content Project Manager: Dawn Marie Elwell

Senior Print Buyer: Mary Beth Hennebury

Development Editors: Kasia McNabb,
   Judi Lauber

Project Manager: Tunde Dewey

Composition: Pre-Press PMG

Cover and Interior Design: Studio Montage

Illustrators: James Edwards; S.I. International

Cover Art: ©Lisa Henderling/Getty Images

© 2008 Heinle, Cengage Learning

For product information and technology assistance, contact us at
Cengage Learning Customer & Sales Support, 1-800-354-9706

For permission to use material from this text or product,
submit all requests online at **www.cengage.com/permissions**
Further permissions questions can be emailed to
permissionrequest@cengage.com

ISBN 13: 978-1-4240-0255-9
ISBN 10: 1-4240-0255-9

Lesson Planner with Activity Bank CD-ROM and Audio CD
ISBN 13: 978-1-4240-1927-4
ISBN 10: 1-4240-1927-3

Heinle
20 Channel Center Street
Boston, MA 02210
USA

Cengage Learning is a leading provider of customized learning solutions with office locations around the globe, including Singapore, the United Kingdom, Australia, Mexico, Brazil, and Japan. Locate your local office at
international.cengage.com/region

Cengage Learning products are represented in Canada by Nelson Education, Ltd.

Visit Heinle online at **elt.heinle.com**
Visit our corporate website at **www.cengage.com**

Credits appear on page 174, which constitutes a continuation of the copyright page

Printed in China
3 4 5 6 7 15 14 13 12 11

ACKNOWLEDGMENTS

Elizabeth Aderman
New York City Board of Education, New York, NY

Lisa Agao
Fresno Adult School, Fresno, CA

Sharon Baker
Roseville Adult School, Roseville, CA

Lillian Barredo
Stockton School for Adults, Stockton, CA

Linda Boice
Elk Grove Adult Education, Elk Grove, CA

Chan Bostwick
Los Angeles Unified School District, Los Angeles, CA

Debra Brooks
Manhattan BEGIN Program, New York, NY

Anne Byrnes
North Hollywood-Polytechnic Community Adult School, Sun Valley, CA

Rose Cantu
John Jay High School, San Antonio, TX

Toni Chapralis
Fremont School for Adults, Sacramento, CA

Melanie Chitwood
Miami-Dade College, Miami, FL

Geri Creamer
Stockton School for Adults, Stockton, CA

Stephanie Daubar
Harry W. Brewster Technical Center, Tampa, FL

Irene Dennis
San Antonio College, San Antonio, TX

Eileen Duffell
P.S. 64, New York, NY

Nancy Dunlap
Northside Independent School District, San Antonio, TX

Gloria Eriksson
Grant Skills Center, Sacramento, CA

Marti Estrin
Santa Rosa Junior College, Santa Rosa, CA

Lawrence Fish
Shorefront YM-YWHA English Language Program, Brooklyn, NY

Victoria Florit
Miami-Dade College, Miami, FL

Sally Gearheart
Santa Rosa Junior College, Santa Rosa, CA

Rhoda Gilbert
New York City Board of Education, New York, NY

Debbie Glass
Merced Adult School, Merced, CA

Laurie Hartwick
Lawrence High School/Adult Learning Center, Lawrence, MA

Kathleen Jimenez
Miami-Dade College, Miami, FL

Nancy Jordan
John Jay High School Adult Education, San Antonio, TX

Renee Klosz
Lindsey Hopkins Technical Education Center, Miami, FL

David Lauter
Stockton School for Adults, Stockton, CA

Patricia Long
Old Marshall Adult Education Center, Sacramento, CA

Daniel Loos
Seattle Community College, Seattle, WA

Maria Miranda
Lindsey Hopkins Technical Education Center, Miami, FL

Karen Moore
Stockton School for Adults, Stockton, CA

George Myskiw
Malcolm X College, Chicago, IL

Dr. Betty Payne
Montgomery College, Rockville, MD

Heidi Perez
Lawrence Public Schools Adult Learning Center, Lawrence, MA

Marta Pitt
Lindsey Hopkins Technical Education Center, Miami, FL

Sylvia Rambach
Stockton School for Adults, Stockton, CA

Eric Rosenbaum
BEGIN Managed Programs, New York, NY

Laura Rowley
Old Marshall Adult Education Center, Sacramento, CA

Stephanie Schmitter
Mercer County Community College, Trenton, NJ

Amy Schneider
Pacoima Skills Center, Pacoima, CA

Sr. M. B. Theresa Spittle
Stockton School for Adults, Stockton, CA

Andre Sutton
Belmont Adult School, Los Angeles, CA

Jennifer Swoyer
Northside Independent School District, San Antonio, TX

Marcia Takacs
Coastline Community College, Fountain Valley, CA

Claire Valier
Palm Beach County School District, West Palm Beach, FL

Sarah Young
Arlington Education and Employment Program (REEP), Arlington, VA

Rob Jenkins

I love teaching. I love to see the expressions on my students' faces when the light goes on and their eyes show such sincere joy of learning. I knew the first time I stepped into an ESL classroom that this was where I needed to be and I have never questioned that resolution. I have worked in business, sales, and publishing, and I've found challenge in all, but nothing can compare to the satisfaction of reaching people in such a personal way.

Staci Johnson

Ever since I can remember, I've been fascinated with other cultures and languages. I love to travel and every place I go, the first thing I want to do is meet the people, learn their language, and understand their culture. Becoming an ESL teacher was a perfect way to turn what I love to do into my profession. There's nothing more incredible than the exchange of teaching and learning from one another that goes on in an ESL classroom. And there's nothing more rewarding than helping a student succeed.

We are so happy that instructors and agencies have embraced the lesson planning and project-based activities that we introduced in the first edition and are so enthusiastically teaching with **Stand Out**. It is fantastic that so many of our colleagues are as excited to be in this profession as we are. After writing over 500 lesson plans and implementing them in our own classrooms and after personal discussions with thousands of instructors all over the United States and in different parts of the world, we have found ourselves in a position to improve upon our successful model. One of the most notable things in the new edition is that we have continued to stress integrating skills in each lesson and have made this integration more apparent and obvious. To accomplish any life skill, students need to incorporate a combination of reading, writing, listening, speaking, grammar, pronunciation, and academic skills while developing vocabulary and these skills should be taught together in a lesson! We have accomplished this by extending the presentation of lessons in the book, so each lesson is more fully developed. You will also notice an extended list of ancillaries and a tighter correlation of these ancillaries to each book. The ancillaries allow you to extend practice on particular skill areas beyond the lesson in the text. We are so excited about this curriculum and know that as you implement it, you and your students will *stand out*.

Our goal is to give students
challenging opportunities
to be successful in their
language-learning experience
so they develop confidence
and become independent,
lifelong learners.

Rob Jenkins
Staci Johnson

ABOUT THE SERIES

The **Stand Out** series is designed to facilitate *active* learning while challenging students to build a nurturing and effective learning community.

The student books are divided into eight distinct units, mirroring competency areas most useful to newcomers. These areas are outlined in CASAS assessment programs and different state model standards for adults. Each unit in *Stand Out Basic* is then divided into five lessons, a review, and a team project. Lessons are driven by performance objectives and are filled with challenging activities that progress from teacher-presented to student-centered tasks.

SUPPLEMENTAL MATERIALS

- The *Stand Out Basic Lesson Planner* is in full color with 60 complete lesson plans, taking the instructor through each stage of a lesson from warm-up and review through application.
- The *Stand Out Basic Activity Bank CD-ROM* has an abundance of customizable worksheets. Print or download and modify what you need for your particular class.
- The *Stand Out Basic Grammar Challenge* is a workbook that gives additional grammar explanation and practice in context.
- The *Stand Out Basic Assessment CD-ROM with ExamView®* allows you to customize pre- and post-tests for each unit as well as a pre- and post-test for the book.
- The listening script can be found in the back of the student book. CDs are available with focused listening activities described in the Lesson Planner.

STAND OUT BASIC LESSON PLANNER

The *Stand Out Basic Lesson Planner* is a new and innovative approach. As many seasoned teachers know, good lesson planning can make a substantial difference in the classroom. Students continue coming to class, understanding, applying, and remembering more of what they learn. They are more confident in their learning when good lesson planning techniques are incorporated.

We have developed lesson plans that are designed to be used each day and to reduce preparation time. The planner includes:

- Standard lesson progression (Warm-up and Review, Introduction, Presentation, Practice, Evaluation, and Application)
- A creative and complete way to approach varied class lengths so that each lesson will work within a class period.

- 180 hours of classroom activities
- Time suggestions for each activity
- Pedagogical comments
- Space for teacher notes and future planning
- Identification of SCANS and CASAS standards

USER QUESTIONS ABOUT *STAND OUT*

- **What are SCANS and how do they integrate into the book?**
  SCANS is the Secretary's Commission on Achieving Necessary Skills. SCANS was developed to encourage students to prepare for the workplace. The standards developed through SCANS have been incorporated throughout the **Stand Out** student books and components.

  Stand Out addresses SCANS a little differently than do other books. SCANS standards elicit effective teaching strategies by incorporating essential skills such as critical thinking and group work. We have incorporated SCANS standards in every lesson, not isolating these standards in the work unit, as is typically done.

- **What about CASAS?** The federal government has mandated that states show student outcomes as a prerequisite to receiving funding. Some states have incorporated the **C**omprehensive **A**dult **S**tudent **A**ssessment **S**ystem (CASAS) testing to standardize agency reporting. Unfortunately, since many of our students are unfamiliar with standardized testing and therefore struggle with it, adult schools need to develop lesson plans to address specific concerns. **Stand Out** was developed with careful attention to CASAS skill areas in most lessons and performance objectives.

- **Are the tasks too challenging for my students?**
  Students learn by doing and learn more when challenged. **Stand Out** provides tasks that encourage critical thinking in a variety of ways. The tasks in each lesson move from teacher-directed to student-centered so the learner clearly understands what's expected and is willing to "take a risk." The lessons are expected to be challenging. In this way, students learn that when they work together as a learning community, anything becomes possible. The satisfaction of accomplishing something both as an individual and as a member of a team results in greater confidence and effective learning.

- **Do I need to understand lesson planning to teach from the student book?** If you don't understand lesson planning when you start, you will when you finish! Teaching from **Stand Out** is like a course on lesson planning, especially if you use the Lesson Planner on a daily basis.

Stand Out does *stand out* because, when we developed this series, we first established performance objectives for each lesson. Then we designed lesson plans, followed by student book pages. The introduction to each lesson varies because different objectives demand different approaches. **Stand Out's** variety of tasks makes learning more interesting for the student.

- **What are team projects?** The final lesson of each unit is a **team project**. This is often a team simulation that incorporates the objectives of the unit and provides an additional opportunity for students to actively apply what they have learned. The project allows students to produce something that represents their progress in learning. These end-of-unit projects were created with a variety of learning styles and individual skills in mind. The team projects can be skipped or simplified, but we encourage instructors to implement them, enriching the overall student experience.

- **What do you mean by a customizable Activity Bank?** Every class, student, teacher, and approach is different. Since no one textbook can meet all these differences, the *Stand Out Activity Bank CD-ROM* allows you to customize **Stand Out** for your class. You can copy different activities and worksheets from the CD-ROM to your hard drive and then:

  - change items in supplemental vocabulary, grammar, and life skill activities;

  - personalize activities with student names and popular locations in your area;

  - extend every lesson with additional practice where you feel it is most needed.

- **Is *Stand Out* grammar-based or competency-based?** **Stand Out** is a competency-based series; however, students are exposed to basic grammar structures. We believe that grammar instruction in context is extremely important. Grammar structures are periodically identified as principal lesson objectives. Students are first provided with context that incorporates the grammar, followed by an explanation and practice. At this level, we expect students to learn basic structures but we do not expect them to acquire them. It has been our experience that students are exposed several times within their learning experience to language structures before they actually acquire them. For teachers who want to enhance grammar instruction, the *Activity Bank CD-ROM* and/or the *Grammar Challenge* workbooks provide ample opportunities.

The six competencies that drive **Stand Out** are basic communication, consumer economics, community resources, health, occupational knowledge, and lifelong learning (government and law replace lifelong learning in Books 3 and 4).

- **Are there enough activities so I don't have to supplement?** **Stand Out** stands alone in providing 180 hours of instruction and activities, even without the additional suggestions in the Lesson Planner. The Lesson Planner also shows you how to streamline lessons to provide 90 hours of classwork and still have thorough lessons if you meet less often. When supplementing with the *Stand Out Activity Bank CD-ROM*, the *Assessment CD-ROM* with Exam*View®*, and the *Stand Out Grammar Challenge* workbook, you gain unlimited opportunities to extend class hours and provide activities related directly to each lesson objective. Calculate how many hours your class meets in a semester and look to **Stand Out** to address the full class experience.

Stand Out is a comprehensive approach to adult language learning, meeting needs of students and instructors completely and effectively.

CONTENTS

	Numeracy/ Academic Skills	EFF	SCANS	CASAS
Pre-Unit	• Writing numerals 1-9 • Writing telephone numbers • Dictation • Focused listening • Class application • Test-taking skills	• Speak so others can understand • Listen actively	Many SCAN skills are incorporated in this unit with an emphasis on: • Listening • Speaking • Writing • Sociability • Acquiring and evaluating information • Interpreting and communicating information	1: 0.1.1, 0.1.4, 0.2.1 2: 0.1.1, 0.1.4, 0.2.1 3: 0.1.5, 7.4.7 R: 7.4.1, 7.4.2, 7.4.3
Unit 1	• Writing numerals 1-31 • Writing dates • Focused listening • Teamwork skills • Reviewing • Evaluating • Developing study skills	• Speak so others can understand • Listen actively • Cooperate with others	Many SCAN skills are incorporated in this unit with an emphasis on: • Basic skills • Acquiring and evaluating information • Interpreting and communicating information • Seeing things in the mind's eye • Sociability	1: 0.1.1, 0.2.1 2: 0.1.2, 0.2.1, 1.1.3, 4.8.7 3: 0.1.2, 0.2.1 4: 0.1.2, 0.2.1, 1.1.3, 4.8.7 5: 0.1.2, 0.2.1, 2.3.2 R: 0.1.1, 0.2.1, 7.4.1, 7.4.2, 7.4.3 TP: 0.1.1, 0.2.1, 4.8.1
Unit 2	• Interpreting a bar graph • Telling time • Focused listening • Scheduling • Reviewing • Evaluating • Developing study skills	• Read with understanding • Convey ideas in writing • Speak so others can understand • Listen Actively • Cooperate with others • Observe critically • Take responsibility for learning	Many SCAN skills are incorporated in this unit with an emphasis on: • Acquiring and evaluating information • Organizing and maintaining information • Interpreting and communicating information • Basic skills • Reflect and Evaluate	1: 0.1.4 2: 0.1.5 3: 0.1.5 4: 0.2.1, 0.2.4, 2.3.1 5: 0.1.2, 0.2.1, 1.1.3, 2.3.3 R: 0.1.5, 2.3.1, 2.3.2, 2.3.3, 7.4.1, 7.4.2, 7.4.3 TP: 0.1.5, 2.3.1, 2.3.2, 2.3.3, 4.8.1

Contents

CONTENTS

• Grammar points that are explicitly taught   ◇ Grammar points that are presented in context   △ Grammar points that are being recycled

	Numeracy/Academic Skills	EFF	SCANS	CASAS
Unit 3	• Using U.S. measurements: pounds, gallons • Working in a group • Focused listening • Skimming • Categorizing and organizing information • Teamwork skills • Reviewing • Evaluating • Developing study skills	• Read with understanding • Convey ideas in writing • Speak so others can understand • Listen actively • Cooperate with others • Take responsibility for learning • Reflect and evaluate	**Many SCAN skills are incorporated in this unit with an emphasis on:** ◊ Acquiring and evaluating information ◊ Organizing and maintaining information ◊ Interpreting and communicating information • Allocating human resources • Basic skills • Seeing things in the mind's eye	**1:** 1.3.8 **2:** 1.3.8 **3:** 1.1.1, 1.3.8 **4:** 1.3.8 **5:** 1.3.8 **R:** 1.3.8, 7.4.1, 7.4.2, 7.4.3 **TP:** 1.88, 4.8.1
Unit 4	• Using U.S. measurements: clothing sizes • Maintaining inventories • Counting U.S. money • Calculating totals • Writing checks • Asking for information ' • Focused listening • Test-taking skills • Reviewing • Evaluating • Developing study skills	• Read with understanding • Convey ideas in writing • Speak so others can understand • Listen actively • Cooperate with others • Observe critically • Use math • Take responsibility for learning • Reflect and evaluate • Observe critically • Guide others	**Many SCAN skills are incorporated in this unit with an emphasis on:** • Acquiring and evaluating information • Organizing and maintaining information • Interpreting and communicating information • Basic skills • Allocating money • Serving clients and customers	**1:** 1.3.9 **2:** 1.1.9, 1.2.1, 1.3.9 **3:** 1.1.9, 1.2.1, 1.3.9 **4:** 1.1.6, 1.3.9, 4.8.1, 6.1.1 **5:** 1.1.9, 1.2.1, 1.3.9, 4.8.3 **R:** 1.1.9, 1.2.1, 1.3.9, 7.4.1, 7.4.2, 7.4.3 **TP:** 1.3.9, 4.8.1
Unit 5	• Interpreting a bar graph • Creating a bar graph • Test-taking strategies • Focused listening • Dictation • Reviewing • Evaluating • Developing study skills	• Read with understanding • Convey ideas in writing • Speak so others can understand • Listen actively • Cooperate with others • Observe critically • Take responsibility for learning • Reflect and evaluate • Solve problems and make decisions	**Many SCAN skills are incorporated in this unit with an emphasis on:** • Acquiring and evaluating information • Organizing and maintaining information • Interpreting and communicating information • Basic skills • Creative thinking • Participating as a member of a team	**1:** 1.3.7, 7.2.3 **2:** 1.4.1, 1.4.2, 1.9.4 **3:** 1.1.3, 2.2.3, 2.2.5, 6.7.2 **4:** 0.1.2, 0.2.4 **5:** 1.1.3, 1.9.1, 1.9.4, 2.2.1, 2.2.2, 2.5.4 **R:** 2.2.3, 7.4.1, 7.4.2, 7.4.3 **TP:** 2.2.3, 4.8.1

Correlations to the latest state-specific standards are on our website.

CONTENTS

• Grammar points that are explicitly taught   ◊ Grammar points that are presented in context   △ Grammar points that are being recycled

	Numeracy/ Academic Skills	EFF	SCANS	CASAS
Unit 6	• Focused listening • Test-taking skills • Reviewing • Evaluating • Developing study skills	• Read with understanding • Convey ideas in writing • Speak so others can understand • Listen actively • Cooperate with others • Observe critically • Take responsibility for learning • Reflect and evaluate • Advocate and influence	**Many SCAN skills are incorporated in this unit with an emphasis on:** • Acquiring and evaluating information • Organizing and maintaining information • Interpreting and communicating information • Basic skills • Self-management • Responsibility	**1:** 3.1.1, 3.1.3 **2:** 0.1.2, 0.2.1, 3.1.1 **3:** 2.3.1, 3.1.2, 3.3.1 **4:** 3.1.1 **5:** 3.1.3 **R:** 3.1.1, 3.1.2, 3.1.3, 3.3.1 **TP:** 1.3.9, 4.8.1
Unit 7	• Focused listening • Making graphs • Reviewing • Evaluating • Developing study skills	• Read with understanding • Convey ideas in writing • Speak so others can understand • Listen actively • Cooperate with others • Advocate and influence • Resolve conflict and negotiate • Observe critically • Take responsibility for learning • Reflect and evaluate	**Many SCAN skills are incorporated in this unit with an emphasis on:** • Acquiring and evaluating information • Organizing and maintaining information • Interpreting and communicating information • Basic skills • Self-management	**1:** 0.2.1, 4.1.8 **2:** 0.1.6, 4.8.1 **3:** 4.1.3, 4.1.8, 4.4.4 **4:** 4.4.4 **5:** 4.4.4, 4.8.1, 4.8.3 **R:** 4.1.3, 4.1.8, 4.4.1, 4.8.1, 4.8.3, 7.4.1, 7.4.2, 7.4.3 **TP:** 2.2.3, 4.8.1.
Unit 8	• Identifying quantities and sizes • Calculating totals • Reading telephone numbers • Interpreting a bar graph • Focused listening • Test-taking skills • Organizational skills • Reviewing • Evaluating • Developing study skills	• Read with understanding • Convey ideas in writing • Speak so others can understand • Listen actively • Cooperate with others • Resolve conflict and negotiate • Observe critically • Take responsibility for learning • Reflect and evaluate	**Many SCAN skills are incorporated in this unit with an emphasis on:** • Acquiring and evaluating information • Organizing and maintaining information • Interpreting and communicating information • Basic skills • Self-management	**1:** 0.2.1, 0.2.2, 7.1.4 **2:** 1.1.6, 1.2.1, 1.3.1, 1.6.4, 7.1.4 **3:** 2.1.1, 2.2.1, 7.1.4 **4:** 0.2.1, 3.5.9, 6.7.2, 7.1.1, 7.1.2, 7.1.4 **5:** 4.1.1, 4.4.4, 7.1.1, 7.1.4 **R:** 7.4.2, 7.4.3 **TP:** 2.2.3, 4.8.1

Contents   **xiii**

Welcome to Stand Out, Second Edition

Stand Out works.

And now it works even better!

Built from the standards necessary for adult English learners, the second edition of *Stand Out* gives students the foundation and tools they need to develop confidence and become independent, lifelong learners.

- **Grammar** Charts clearly explain grammar points, and are followed by personalized exercises.
- **Pronunciation** activities are integrated through the program.

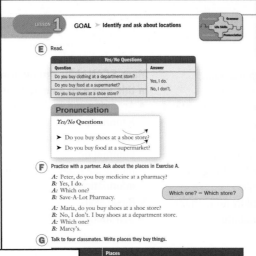

- Clearly defined **goals** provide a roadmap of learning for the student.
- State and federally required **life skills and competencies** are taught, helping students meet necessary benchmarks.

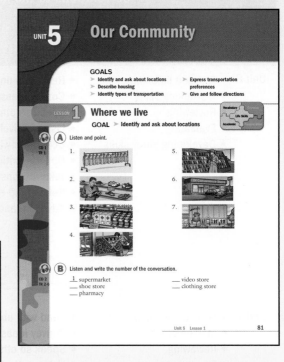

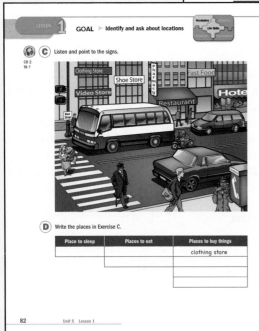

- A variety of **examples from real life**, like bank checks, newspaper ads, money, etc. help students learn to access information and resources in their community.

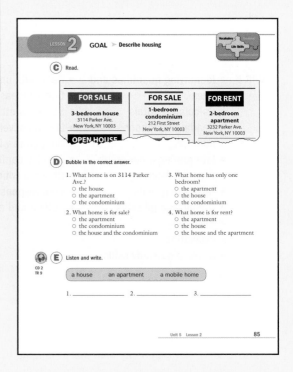

- Key **vocabulary** is introduced visually and orally.

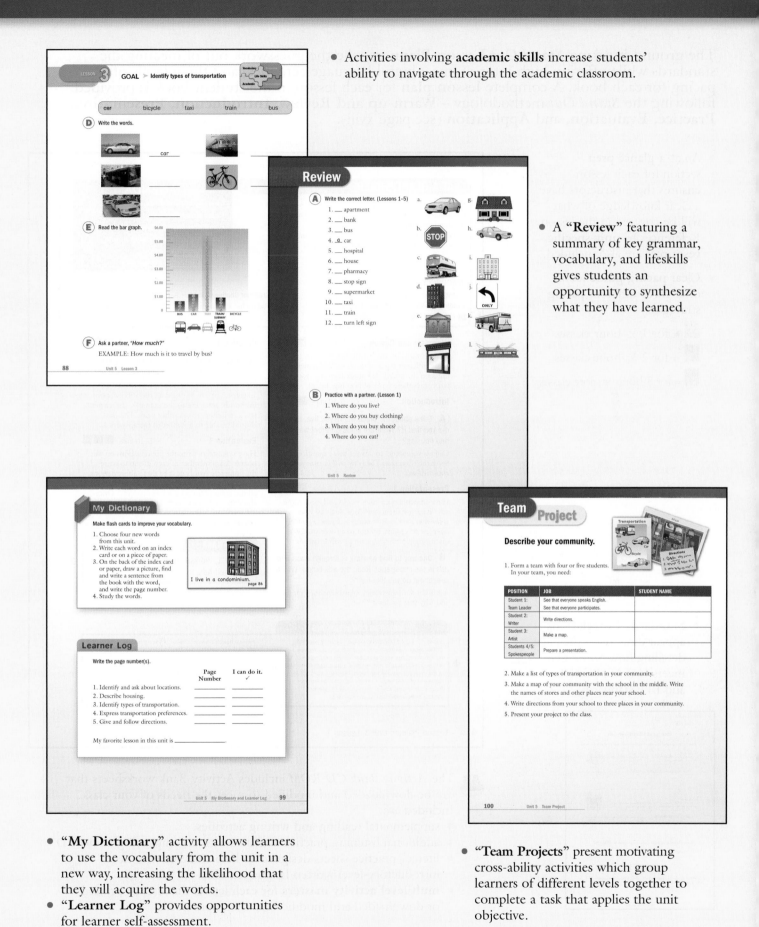

- Activities involving **academic skills** increase students' ability to navigate through the academic classroom.

- A **"Review"** featuring a summary of key grammar, vocabulary, and lifeskills gives students an opportunity to synthesize what they have learned.

- **"My Dictionary"** activity allows learners to use the vocabulary from the unit in a new way, increasing the likelihood that they will acquire the words.
- **"Learner Log"** provides opportunities for learner self-assessment.

- **"Team Projects"** present motivating cross-ability activities which group learners of different levels together to complete a task that applies the unit objective.

The ground-breaking *Stand Out* **Lesson Planners** take the guesswork out of meeting the standards while offering high-interest, meaningful language activities, and three levels of pacing for each book. A complete **lesson plan** for each lesson in the student book is provided, following the *Stand Out* methodology – **Warm-up and Review, Introduction, Presentation, Practice, Evaluation,** and **Application** (see page xviii).

- An **at-a-glance prep** section for each lesson ensures that instructors have a clear knowledge of what will be covered in the lesson. References to **unit-specific resources** are also included.

- Clear **pacing guide** icons offer three different pacing strategies.

  ▪ = for 1 ½-hour classes

  ▪ = for 2 ½-hour classes

  ▪ = for 3-hour or more classes

- **Standards Correlations** appear directly on the page, detailing how *Stand Out* meets CASAS, SCANS, and EFF standards.

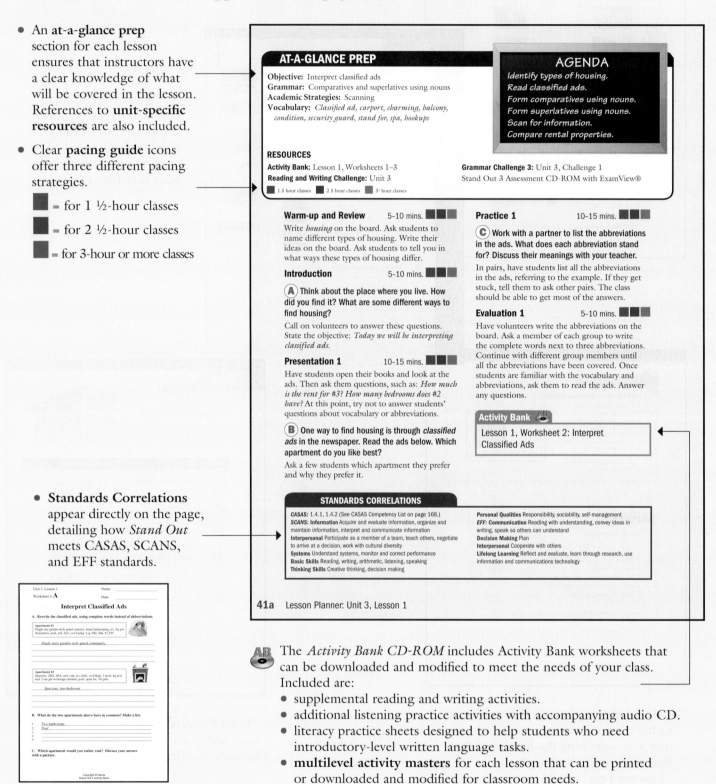

AT-A-GLANCE PREP

Objective: Interpret classified ads
Grammar: Comparatives and superlatives using nouns
Academic Strategies: Scanning
Vocabulary: *Classified ad, carport, charming, balcony, condition, security guard, stand for, spa, hookups*

RESOURCES
Activity Bank: Lesson 1, Worksheets 1–3
Reading and Writing Challenge: Unit 3
Grammar Challenge 3: Unit 3, Challenge 1
Stand Out 3 Assessment CD-ROM with ExamView®

▪ 1.5 hour classes   ▪ 2.5 hour classes   ▪ 3⁺ hour classes

AGENDA
Identify types of housing.
Read classified ads.
Form comparatives using nouns.
Form superlatives using nouns.
Scan for information.
Compare rental properties.

Warm-up and Review 5–10 mins.
Write *housing* on the board. Ask students to name different types of housing. Write their ideas on the board. Ask students to tell you in what ways these types of housing differ.

Introduction 5–10 mins.
(A) Think about the place where you live. How did you find it? What are some different ways to find housing?
Call on volunteers to answer these questions. State the objective: *Today we will be interpreting classified ads.*

Presentation 1 10–15 mins.
Have students open their books and look at the ads. Then ask them questions, such as: *How much is the rent for #3? How many bedrooms does #2 have?* At this point, try not to answer students' questions about vocabulary or abbreviations.

(B) One way to find housing is through *classified ads* in the newspaper. Read the ads below. Which apartment do you like best?
Ask a few students which apartment they prefer and why they prefer it.

Practice 1 10–15 mins.
(C) Work with a partner to list the abbreviations in the ads. What does each abbreviation stand for? Discuss their meanings with your teacher.
In pairs, have students list all the abbreviations in the ads, referring to the example. If they get stuck, tell them to ask other pairs. The class should be able to get most of the answers.

Evaluation 1 5–10 mins.
Have volunteers write the abbreviations on the board. Ask a member of each group to write the complete words next to three abbreviations. Continue with different group members until all the abbreviations have been covered. Once students are familiar with the vocabulary and abbreviations, ask them to read the ads. Answer any questions.

Activity Bank
Lesson 1, Worksheet 2: Interpret Classified Ads

STANDARDS CORRELATIONS

CASAS: 1.4.1, 1.4.2 (See CASAS Competency List on page 168.)
SCANS: Information Acquire and evaluate information, organize and maintain information, interpret and communicate information **Interpersonal** Participate as a member of a team, teach others, negotiate to arrive at a decision, work with cultural diversity **Systems** Understand systems, monitor and correct performance **Basic Skills** Reading, writing, arithmetic, listening, speaking **Thinking Skills** Creative thinking, decision making

Personal Qualities Responsibility, sociability, self-management **EFF: Communication** Reading with understanding, convey ideas in writing, speak so others can understand **Decision Making** Plan **Interpersonal** Cooperate with others **Lifelong Learning** Reflect and evaluate, learn through research, use information and communications technology

41a Lesson Planner: Unit 3, Lesson 1

Unit 3, Lesson 1   Name:
Worksheet 1 **A**   Date:

Interpret Classified Ads

A. Rewrite the classified ads, using complete words instead of abbreviations.

Apartment #1
Single story garden-style gated community, bonut landscaping, a/c, lrg pvt fncd patios, pool, crpt, frpls, cov'd prkg. Lrg 3Bd, 2Ba, $1,295.

Single story garden-style gated community,

Apartment #2
Spacious, 2BD, 2BA, new crpt, a/c, frplc, w/d hkup, 1 level, lrg pvt encl 2-car gar w/storage cabinets, pool, quiet loc. No pets.

Spacious, two-bedroom,

B. What do the two apartments above have in common? Make a list.
1. *Two bathrooms*
2. *Pool*
3.
4.
5.

C. Which apartment would you rather rent? Discuss your answer with a partner.

Copyright © Heinle
Stand Out 3 Activity Bank

The *Activity Bank CD-ROM* includes Activity Bank worksheets that can be downloaded and modified to meet the needs of your class. Included are:

- supplemental reading and writing activities.
- additional listening practice activities with accompanying audio CD.
- literacy practice sheets designed to help students who need introductory-level written language tasks.
- **multilevel activity masters** for each lesson that can be printed or downloaded and modified for classroom needs.

Presentation 2   10–15 mins. ■■■

Ask students to imagine they are moving to a new home. Tell them they need to cancel the electricity in their current home and get it turned on at their new home. Ask them how they would do this. (Call the electric company.) Ask what sort of information they would need to give to the company's representative to make this happen.

Practice 2   5–10 mins. ■■■

Tell students they will be listening to Vu call the electric company to prepare for his family's move. Direct their attention to Exercise C and tell them they will be listening for four pieces of information.

Teaching Tip

Focused listening

The purpose of teaching focused listening is to help students learn how to understand the main ideas in a conversation even when they don't understand every word.

It's important to remind students that they will not understand every word each time they do a focused listening activity. Otherwise, they may become frustrated and stop listening all together. Preparing students for the listening activity will make them much more effective listeners.

1. Explain the context of the conversation.
2. Ask students what they think they might hear.
3. Show students specifically what they are listening for.

C Vu and his family are getting ready to move. Vu calls the electric company to speak to a customer service representative. Listen to the recording and write short answers for the following information.

🎧 **Listening Script**   CD 1, Track 8

Recording: *Thank you for calling Texas Electric. Your call is very important to us. Please choose from the following options. For new service or to cancel your existing service, press 1. To report a problem with your service, press 2. If you have questions about your bill, press 3. For all other questions, press 4. (Vu presses 1.) Thank you. Just one moment.*

Representative: *Hello, my name is Kristen. How may I help you?*
Vu: *Um, yes. My family is moving next week. We need to cancel our current service and get service in our new home.*
Representative: *What is your current address?*
Vu: *3324 Maple Road.*
Representative: *Are you Vu Nguyen?*
Vu: *Yes.*
Representative: *When would you like the service turned off?*
Vu: *Next Wednesday, please.*
Representative: *And what is your new address?*
Vu: *5829 Bay Road.*
Representative: *And when would you like the service turned on?*
Vu: *This Monday, please.*
Representative: *OK. Your current service will be turned off sometime between 8 and 12 on Wednesday the 11th. Your new service will be on before 9 on Monday morning the 9th. Is there anything else I can do for you?*
Vu: *No, that's it.*
Representative: *Thank you for calling Texas Electric. Have a nice day.*
Vu: *You, too.*

🎧 **D** Listen to the recording again and answer the questions.

Prepare students for the information they are to listen for. (CD 1, Track 8)

Evaluation 2   5 mins. ■■

Go over the answers with the class.

Pronunciation

Rising and Falling Intonation

Ask students a few information questions. Ask if your voice goes up or down at the end of each question. Students should be able to recognize the rising and falling intonation. Explain that this rising and falling intonation helps the listener know that you are asking a question that requires an answer.

Go over the examples in the box in the student book, emphasizing the intonation. Have students practice by repeating after you, first as a class and then individually.

- **Teaching Tips** and **Culture Tips** provide ideas and strategies for teaching diverse learners in the classroom.

- 🎧 **Listening Scripts** from the *AudioCD* are included next to the student book page for ease-of-use.

- *Grammar Challenge* workbooks include supplemental activities for students who desire even more **contextual grammar and vocabulary practice.**

- *Reading & Writing Challenge* workbooks provide challenging materials and exercises for students who want even **more practice in reading, vocabulary development, and writing.**

- **Exam***View*® **Test Bank** allows you to create **customizable pre- and post- tests for every unit.** The questions are correlated to CASAS and state standards and include multiple choice, true/false, numeric response, matching types. Listening questions are included along with an audio CD.

The *Stand Out* Lesson Planner methodology ensures success!

Stand Out ensures student success through good lesson planning and instruction. Each of the five Lessons in every Unit has a lesson plan. Unlike most textbooks, the Lesson Planner was written before the student book materials. A lot of learning occurs with the student books closed so by writing the lesson plans first, we could ensure that each objective was clearly achieved. Each lesson plan follows a systematic and proven format:

W	**Warm-up and/or review**
I	**Introduction**
P	**Presentation**
P	**Practice**
E	**Evaluation**
A	**Application**

WARM-UP AND/OR REVIEW
The warm-up activities establish a context and purpose to the lesson. Exercises use previously learned content and materials that are familiar to students from previous lessons.

INTRODUCTION
In the introduction step, exercises focus the students' attention on the goals of the lesson by asking questions, showing visuals, telling a story, etc. Instructors should state the objective of the lesson and tell students what they will be doing. The objective should address what students are expected to be able to do by the end of the lesson.

PRESENTATION
The presentation activities provide students with the building blocks and skills they need to achieve the objectives set in the introduction. The exercises introduce new information to the students through visuals, realia, description, listenings, explanation, or written text. This is the time to check students' comprehension.

PRACTICE
Practice activities provide meaningful tasks for students to practice what they have just learned through different activities. These activities can be done as a class, in small groups, pairs, or individually. All of these activities are student centered and involve cooperative learning. Instructors should model each activity, monitor progress, and provide feedback.

EVALUATION
Evaluation ensures that students are successful. Instructors should evaluate students on attainment of the objective set at the start of the lesson. This can be done by oral, written, or demonstrated performance. At this point, if students need more practice, instructors can go back and do additional practice activities before moving onto the application.

APPLICATION
Application activities help students apply new knowledge to their own lives or new situations. This is one of the most important steps of the lesson plan. If students can accomplish the application task, it will build their confidence to be able to sue what they've learned out in the community. The Team Projects are an application of unit objectives that involves task-based activities with a product.

In addition to each lesson plan following the WIPPEA model, each Unit in *Stand Out* follows this same approach. The first lesson is always in Introduction to the Unit, introducing new vocabulary and the basic concepts that will be expanded upon in the unit. The following four lessons are the Presentations and Practices for the unit topic. Following the five lessons is a Review lesson, which allows students to do more practice with everything they already learned. The final lesson is an Application for everything they learned in the unit, a team project.

AT-A-GLANCE PREP

Objective: Greet your classmates
Grammar: *I'm* (contraction)
Pronunciation: /m/
Academic Strategy: Dictation
Vocabulary: Greeting words

RESOURCES

Activity Bank: Lesson 1, Worksheet 1
Grammar Challenge: Pre-Unit, Challenge 1

 1.5 hour classes █ 2.5 hour classes █ 3⁺ hour classes

Audio: CD 1, Tracks 1–6
Heinle Picture Dictionary: Wave, Greet, Smile, pages 40–41
Stand Out Basic Assessment CD-ROM with *ExamView®*

Preassessment *(optional)*

Use the Stand Out Basic Assessment CD-ROM with *ExamView®* to create a pretest for the Pre-Unit.

Warm-up and Review   2-5 mins.

Shake hands and introduce yourself to students as they enter the classroom. Say: *Hi,* or *Hello, I'm* _____ (your name).

Introduction   2 mins.

Write the day of the week, the date, and the lesson's agenda on the board. Say the date while pointing to it and have students repeat it. State the objective: *Today we will greet our classmates.*

Presentation 1   5 mins.

Write your name on the board. Greet a few students. Show them the American way to shake hands (curl fingers, make eye contact, etc.). Have students open their books and point to the picture of the teacher and student shaking hands.

Listen.

Play the conversations two times. After the first time, write *hello, hi, goodbye,* and *bye* on the board. Point to these words while students listen the second time.

Listening Script   *CD 1, Tracks 1–2*

1. **Mrs. Adams:** *Hello.*
   Orlando: *Hi.*

2. **Mrs. Adams:** *Goodbye.*
   Orlando: *Bye.*

Practice 1   3 mins.

Play the conversations three more times. Point to the words on the board when you hear them on the recording. Have students do the same in their books.

Listen. Repeat the words. Point to the picture.

Play the conversations three more times. Show students how to point to the people talking in the picture. Then ask students to repeat the target words in Exercise A after you say them.

Evaluation 1   3 mins.

Observe students as they point to the people in the pictures and listen for correct pronunciation of the target words.

STANDARDS CORRELATIONS

CASAS: 0.1.1, 0.1.4, 0.2.1 (See CASAS Competency List on pages 167-173.)

SCANS: Basic Skills Listening, speaking, writing
EFF: Communication Speak so others can understand

Welcome to Our Class

GOALS

➤ Greet your classmates
➤ Say and write phone numbers
➤ Follow classroom instructions

LESSON 1

Say hello!

GOAL ➤ Greet your classmates

  A Listen.

CD 1
TR 1-2

| hello | hi | goodbye | bye |

  B Listen. Repeat the words. Point to the picture.

CD 1
TR 1-2

  C Listen and point to the picture. Who is speaking?

CD 1
TR 3-4

Orlando   Mrs. Adams   Amal   Chinh

 Pronunciation

CD 1
TR 5

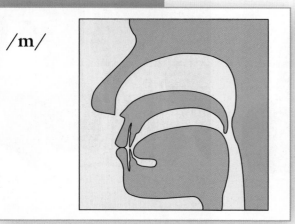

/m/

  D Listen again and read.

CD 1
TR 3-4

Mrs. Adams: Hello. I'm Mrs. Adams.
Orlando: Hi, Mrs. Adams. I'm
Orlando. Nice to meet you.
Mrs. Adams: Nice to meet you, too.
Orlando: Bye.
Mrs. Adams: Goodbye.

Chinh: Hi. I'm Chinh.
Amal: Hello, Chinh. I'm Amal.
Chinh: Nice to meet you.
Amal: Nice to meet you, too.
Chinh: Bye now.
Amal: Bye.

Presentation 2   10-15 mins. ▪▪▪▫

Say the following: *Hi, I'm _____ (your name). Nice to meet you.* Shake hands with a few students and introduce yourself again. The objective of this lesson is to have students learn *hi, hello, goodbye,* and *bye,* as well as introduce them to the contraction *I'm.* The expression *nice to meet you* is used to establish the context. If students are ready, they may also say this phrase.

Play the first conversation between Orlando and Mrs. Adams in Exercise C (CD 1, Track 3). Point to the pictures of the people talking.

Do a mini lesson on pronunciation. Some students may have difficulty pronouncing the final /m/ in *I'm.* Emphasize that it is important to close the lips to produce this sound.

Pronunciation

Final /m/

The instructor should not expect acquisition of pronunciation points after students' first exposure to them. Students may understand the concept of what is being taught; however, it is likely, especially at this level, that additional practice will be necessary for students to master the target pronunciation.

In this case, /m/ is familiar to most languages although in some languages /m/ as a final consonant is not pronounced. Make sure students can produce an /m/ sound and then apply it to *I'm.* Students may do this well in isolation, but when they try to follow the sound with their name, they may drop the /m/.

 Listening Script   CD 1, Track 5

/mmm/... /mmm/... /mmm/
(slowly with long /m/): *I'm a student.*
(slowly with long /m/): *I'm Amal.*
(normal pace): *I'm a student.*
(normal pace): *I'm Amal.*

Practice 2   7-10 mins. ▪▪▫

 C **Listen and point to the picture.**
Who is speaking?

Play the recording and ask students to point to the person speaking.

 Listening Script   CD 1, Tracks 3–4

The listening scripts match the conversations in Exercise D.

D **Listen again and read.**

Have students listen to the conversations again (CD 1, Tracks 3–4). This time have them read along with the text silently. At this point, they are only expected to learn the target vocabulary, not the entire conversation. Ask students to underline the target vocabulary from Exercise A in the two conversations, as well as the contraction *I'm.*

Evaluation 2   7-10 mins. ▪▪

Ask four students to come to the front of the class and write the target words: *hello, hi, goodbye,* and *bye.* Then erase the words from the board, ask students to close their books, and give them a quick dictation of the four words.

Teaching Tip

One-word dictation

Dictation at this level does not need to involve more than a few isolated words. However, the instructor might give the word in a sentence and then ask students to write only the target vocabulary that they hear within the sentence.

As students become more competent, they will begin to write entire sentences or paragraphs. When this occurs, they should learn to listen to a phrase or sentence and repeat it mentally before attempting to write it. Students learning a second language often find it hard to write and listen at the same time, so this strategy of dictation is important. To prepare students for more extensive dictation, say each word three times. Ask students to listen only the first time, to write the second time, and to confirm their writing the third time.

Dictation helps students remember the new vocabulary, more so than if they were to merely listen, recognize, and repeat it.

Presentation 3   15–20 mins. ■■■

Scribble your name on the board, intentionally making it hard to read. Next to your scribble, write your name again. This time, do it neatly and legibly. Ask students to tell you which example is easier to read. Use a thumbs-up to indicate *better*. As students identify which handwriting is better, circle the example they choose.

From this explanation, students will understand that some writing is more acceptable than others.

E Listen and repeat. Then, write.

Play the recording. The first time students only listen. The second time they listen and repeat each letter.

Listening Script   CD 1, Track 6

A B C D E F G H I J K L M
N O P Q R S T U V W X Y Z

Write *I'm Amal.* on the board and spell the name a few times out loud until students begin to spell it with you. Refer students to the grammar box and help them to see how the contraction works. Don't spend too much time on this contraction because it is only exposure at this point.

Write the alphabet on the board; quiz students by pointing to a letter and allowing them to call it out. Help with pronunciation, paying particular attention to the vowels. Invite a few students to the board. As you say a letter, have them point to it.

For shorter classes, ask students to do Exercise F for homework.

Practice 3   5 mins. ■

F Write.

Teaching Tip

Volunteers

The first time you invite students to the board, you may want to ask for volunteers. Once all the students understand the activity, call on some of the quieter students to respond. Getting students up in the front of the classroom is a great way to help prepare them for the classroom presentations they will be giving at the end of each unit.

Evaluation 3   5 mins. ■

Check students' work while they complete Exercise F to make sure they stay within the lines in the book.

 Refer students to *Stand Out Basic Grammar Challenge*, Pre-Unit, Challenge 1 for more practice with contractions and *I'm*.

Application   5–7 mins. ■■■

G Write your name and a classmate's name. Then, meet four more classmates.

After students write their own names and a classmate's name, ask them to read what they have written to the class. Then ask for a few volunteers to do the short conversation in front of the class. Finally, ask students to meet and greet four other students in the class.

Activity Bank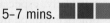

Lesson 1, Worksheet 1: Say *Hello* and *Goodbye*

GOAL ➤ **Greet your classmates**

  E Listen and repeat. Then, write.

CD 1
TR 6

Aa Bb Cc Dd Ee Ff Gg Hh Ii

Jj Kk Ll Mm Nn Oo Pp Qq Rr

Ss Tt Uu Vv Ww Xx Yy Zz

I'm Amal.

Contractions
I am = *I'm*

F Write.

hi   hi

hello   hello

goodbye   goodbye

G Write your name and a classmate's name. Then, meet four more classmates.

Hi. I'm _____(Answers will vary.)_____. (your name)

Hello. I'm _____(Answers will vary.)_____. (classmate's name)

Phone numbers

GOAL ➤ **Say and write phone numbers**

Vocabulary · Grammar · Life Skills · Academic · Pronunciation

  A Listen and point. Who is speaking?

CD 1
TR 7

  B Listen and repeat. Point to each number. Then, write all the numbers.

CD 1
TR 8

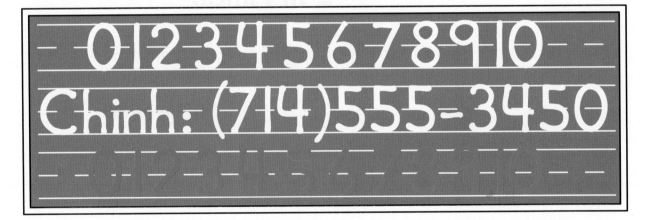

0 1 2 3 4 5 6 7 8 9 10

Chinh: (714)555-3450

0 1 2 3 4 5 6 7 8 9 10

AT-A-GLANCE PREP

Objective: Say and write phone numbers
Grammar: *am* and *is*
Academic Strategy: Focused listening
Vocabulary: Numbers

RESOURCES

Activity Bank: Lesson 2, Worksheet 1
Grammar Challenge: Pre-Unit, Challenge 2
Audio: CD 1, Tracks 7–9

▪ 1.5 hour classes ▪ 2.5 hour classes ▪ 3⁺ hour classes

AGENDA

Review names.
Learn numbers and phone numbers.
Identify spoken numbers.
Make a phone list.

Heinle Picture Dictionary: Numbers, pages 2–3;
The Telephone, pages 16–17

Warm-up and Review   10-12 mins. ▪▪▪

Write the following conversation on the board:
A: *Hello, I'm _____. What's your name?*
B: _____, __-__-__-__-__.

Show students how to insert their names in the
blanks. Have students walk around the room and
practice this conversation with ten classmates.
Then ask them to practice it again, this time
writing down the names of five people.

Introduction   2 mins. ▪▪▪

Write the day of the week, the date, and the lesson's
agenda on the board. Say the date while pointing
to it and have students repeat it. State the objective:
Today we will say and write phone numbers.

Presentation 1   5 mins. ▪▪▪

Count students off, using the numbers one to ten.
See how well students already know their numbers
by playing the game "Stand Up and Share." Ask all
students to stand. Say *two*. All the students who are
the number two should repeat the number and sit.
Repeat the activity until all students are sitting.

Listen and point. Who is speaking?

Before playing the recording, describe the
pictures using a few details. Students won't
understand all the words, but it is good
exposure. Write *phone* and/or *telephone* on the
board. Then play the recording. Have students
point at the speakers.

Listening Script   CD 1, Track 7

Chinh: *Hello?*
Amal: *Hi, Chinh. This is Amal.*
Chinh: *Hello, Amal. How are you?*
Amal: *Fine, thanks.*

Listen and repeat. Point to each number. Then, write all the numbers.

Play the recording three times. First, have
students listen and point to the numbers. The
second time, ask students to repeat each number.
Finally, have students write the numbers.

Listening Script   CD 1, Track 8

0 1 2 3 4 5 6 7 8 9 10

Practice 1   3 mins. ▪▪▪

Play the listening again (CD 1, Track 8).
Ask students to write the numbers below the
examples. Ask students to also write Chinh's
name and phone number.

Evaluation 1   3 mins. ▪▪▪

Observe students writing in their books.

STANDARDS CORRELATIONS

CASAS: 0.1.1, 0.1.4, 0.2.1 (See CASAS Competency List on
pages 167-173.)
SCANS: **Basic Skills** Writing, listening, speaking, reading
Information Acquire and evaluate information, organize and maintain
information, interpret and communicate information

EFF: **Communication** Read with understanding, convey ideas in writing,
speak so others can understand, listen actively
Interpersonal Cooperate with others

Presentation 2   12-15 mins.

Dictate a few numbers (zero to ten only) and ask students to write the numbers they hear. Ask for volunteers to come to the board and write the numbers they heard.

C   Listen to your teacher and write the numbers you hear.

Give students seven arbitrary numbers. Have them write them in the spaces provided. The numbers should be any numbers from zero to nine. It is all right to repeat numbers. You should do this as a class, allowing students to talk among themselves and check answers as they go.

D   Write your phone number.

Write *phone number* on the board. Ask students how many numbers are in a phone number. Show students how we often put parentheses around the area code and a dash (–) after the next three numbers. Have students write their own phone numbers in the space provided.

Cultural Note

Phone numbers

Phone numbers are grouped differently in different countries. This may be a new concept to students. Also, when spoken, numbers in the United States are often said one number at a time and not in combination; for example, *five-five-five* pause *three-seven-six-five*. However, it is also correct to say *five-five-five* pause *thirty-seven, sixty-five*. Write different phone numbers on the board. Say the numbers in a variety of ways. Ask students to indicate when you are speaking with correct rhythm and when you are not.

Prepare students for Exercise E by doing the example with them.

For shorter classes, ask students to do Activities F, G, and H for homework.

Practice 2   5-7 mins.

E   Listen and circle.

Play the recording and ask students to circle the correct phone number.

 Listening Script   CD 1, Track 9

1. *(714) 555-3450*
2. *(352) 555-6767*
3. *(808) 555-3456*
4. *(915) 555-3455*

Evaluation 2   5 mins.

F   Write.

Ask students to copy the numbers from Exercise E on another sheet of paper. Then ask what Chinh's phone number is. Ask students about the other numbers.

Teaching Tip

Evaluation

The evaluation stage of a lesson plan is important because this is where the instructor determines if students have mastered the concept they have just practiced. If they are still having problems with the target language, students may need additional practice activities before moving on.

GOAL ➤ **Say and write phone numbers**

C Listen to your teacher and write the numbers you hear. (Answers will vary.)

1. _____   5. _____

2. _____   6. _____

3. _____   7. _____

4. _____

D Write your phone number. (____) ____-_____ (Answers will vary.)

E Listen and circle.

CD 1
TR 9

1. Mai
2. Paulo
3. Mrs. Bank
4. Ali

1. Mai	2. Paulo	3. Mrs. Bank	4. Ali
(714) 555-7682	(352) 555-6767	(808) 555-4512	(915) 555-4576
(714) 555-3450	(352) 555-1415	(808) 555-6755	(915) 555-3466
(714) 555-7689	(352) 555-2655	(808) 555-3456	(915) 555-3455

F Write.

1. Mai's phone number is **(714) 555-3450**.

2. Paulo's phone number is (352) 555-6767.

3. Mrs. Bank's phone number is (808) 555-3456.

4. Ali's phone number is (915) 555-3455.

GOAL ➤ Say and write phone numbers

G Read the phone list.

PHONE LIST Mrs. Adam's English Class	
Name	**Phone Number**
Chinh	(714) 555–3450
Andre	(714) 555–1333
Shiro	(714) 555–9812
Concepción	(714) 555–4545
Taylor	(714) 555–1237

Be verb

I *am* …

The phone number *is* …

H Write the phone numbers.

1. Andre's phone number is ___(714) 555–1333___.

2. Shiro's phone number is ___(714) 555–9812___.

3. Concepción's phone number is ___(714) 555–4545___.

4. Taylor's phone number is ___(714) 555–1237___.

I Make a class phone list. (Answers will vary.)

PHONE LIST	
Name	**Phone Number**
(my name)	

Presentation 3   15–20 mins.

G Read the phone list.

Read the phone list with students. Check for comprehension by asking: *What is _____'s phone number?* Ask students about each person on the list.

Go over the grammar box with students. The grammar presented here is a tool needed to understand the upcoming practice. This grammar box is intended to be only exposure at this time. Students should not be expected to completely understand the concept of conjugating the verb *be* after this introduction.

For shorter classes, ask students to do Exercise H for homework.

Practice 3   10–15 mins.

H Write the phone numbers.

Students have not yet learned to form questions, but they can start by helping each other complete sentences.

This activity can be an information gap activity if you decide the students are ready. Ask students to work in pairs. Have Student A cover the phone list. Student A will read the incomplete sentences in Exercise H. Student B will read the numbers to complete the sentence and Student A will write. Then have students change roles.

Evaluation 3   2 mins.

Ask students to check their answers by looking back at the chart in Exercise G.

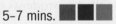 **Refer students to *Stand Out Basic Grammar Challenge*, Pre-Unit, Challenge 2 for more practice with *I am* and *it is*.**

Application   5–7 mins.

I Make a class phone list.

Some students may not have phones and others may not want to share their numbers publicly. If this is a problem, ask for volunteers to share their numbers with the class. As they share their numbers, classmates can write what they hear. See the template folder in the Activity Bank CD-ROM for a two-column template. This template can be used to make a phone list.

Activity Bank

Lesson 2, Worksheet 1: Write Phone Numbers

Instructor's Notes

_____

_____

_____

_____

_____

_____

_____

_____

_____

_____

_____

_____

_____

_____

_____

_____

_____

_____

_____

_____

_____

_____

_____

Objective: Follow classroom instructions
Grammar: Action verbs, imperatives
Pronunciation: Final /t/
Academic Strategies: Test-taking strategies, focused listening
Vocabulary: *read, write, listen, repeat*

RESOURCES

Activity Bank: Lesson 3, Worksheet 1
Grammar Challenge: Pre-Unit, Challenge 3

■ 1.5 hour classes   ■ 2.5 hour classes   ■ 3⁺ hour classes

AGENDA

Review numbers and counting.
Learn new vocabulary for classroom actions.
Take a practice test.
Show that you understand classroom instructions.

Audio: CD 1, Tracks 10–13
Heinle Picture Dictionary: Listen, Read, Write: pages 20–21

Warm-up and Review   5 mins.

Take out five pencils. Count them slowly. Repeat the exercise until students begin to count with you. Say: *Repeat.* Do the same thing with small numbers of books and sheets of paper and say: *Write the number.* Pantomime the action. Check what students write.

Introduction   2 mins.

Write the day of the week, the date, and the lesson's agenda on the board. Say the date while pointing to it and have students repeat it. State the objective: *Today we will learn to follow classroom instructions.*

Presentation 1   7-10 mins.

Establish context by asking students to look at the pictures on page P1. Ask how many people are in the pictures. Compare the class to yours. Ask how many students are in your class.

Teaching Tip

Establishing a context

The *Stand Out* approach recommends that all target language be presented in context. Context helps students connect with the vocabulary.

Here, the classroom itself establishes a good context. Help students identify items in the picture. The vocabulary may not be the objective of the lesson so no repetition is necessary, but students should begin to see a relationship between the work they do in class and their real lives.

Ⓐ Listen.

Ask students to listen to Mrs. Adams. Write the word *poster* on the board. Ask: *Where is the poster?* If students can't respond, help them find the poster in the picture.

🎧 Listening Script   CD 1, Track 10

Hello, class. Today we will discuss three important things you need to know to participate in class and to learn English. This is a poster. It says you should always listen carefully, read all instructions, and write your name on every sheet of paper. Please repeat these words—listen...read...write. Again—listen...read... write. Thank you.

Practice 1   5-7 mins.

Ⓑ Listen again and point.

Play the recording again (CD 1, Track 10) and ask students to point to the words as they hear them. Play the recording three times.

Evaluation 1   5-7 mins.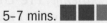

Observe students pointing.

STANDARDS CORRELATIONS

CASAS: 0.1.5, 7.4.7 (See CASAS Competency List on pages 167-173.)
SCANS: **Basic Skills** Listening, speaking, reading, writing
EFF: **Communication** Speak so others can understand, listen actively

Class work

GOAL ➤ **Follow classroom instructions**

 A Listen.

CD 1
TR 10

  B Listen again and point.

CD 1
TR 10

Classroom Instructions	
Read all instructions.	
Write your name on your papers.	
Listen carefully.	

GOAL ➤ **Follow classroom instructions**

C Write.

listen

point

read

repeat

write

Pronunciation

CD 1
TR 11

Final consonant /t/

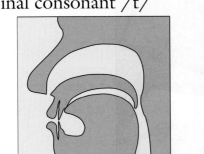

Verbs

Actions = Verbs

D Practice (listen, point, read, write).

EXAMPLE:
Student A: Listen.

Student B:

Presentation 2   7–10 mins. ■■■□

With the books closed, pantomime the five actions shown in Exercise C. Write the five words on the board. When you think students are comfortable with the new vocabulary, pantomime the actions again and have them identify what you are doing.

C Write.

Prepare students for Exercise D by pantomiming the actions for individual students. Do this for *listen, point, read,* and *write.*

Briefly read the grammar box with students. Explain as necessary using examples.

Also, teach students the proper way to pronounce a final /t/.

Pronunciation

Final /t/

Because the imperatives in this unit are often single-word sentences, and since sentences in English often end with the mouth open and relaxed, this is a good time to demonstrate the final /t/.

In many other languages, final consonants, especially at the end of sentences, end with the tongue or the lips touching. This often makes it difficult to hear the final sound completely. In English, on the other hand, the tongue or lips touch and then release. With /t/ the release explodes with air, making it relatively easy to hear the final sound. This release of air most often occurs at the end of a sentence or phrase before a pause.

Practice the pronunciation of the final /t/ sounds of *write, point,* and *repeat* until students begin to mimic your pronunciation.

🎧 Listening Script   CD 1, Track 11

write…write…write…write
point…point…point…point
repeat…repeat…repeat…repeat

Practice 2   5–7 mins. ■■□

D Practice (listen, point, read, write).

Ask students to work in pairs. Another way to do this activity is to have students stand up and talk to five different students.

Teaching Tip

Inside/outside circles

Pair work can take many forms. Changing pairs after each practice is useful because students are more likely to speak clearly with each new partner, tending to concentrate on their language production more with each partner change.

One technique of having students change partners is called "Inside/Outside Circle." In this activity, students form two circles with the same number of students in each. One circle is inside the other. Students face one another and speak to the person they are facing. When indicated by the instructor, one circle shifts one space clockwise so students are lined up with a new partner.

For classrooms with limited space, students can be in two lines across the front of the classroom. The students in one line face the students in the other and form pairs. Then, when indicated, one of the lines shifts. The last person at the end of the line moves to the front of the line.

Evaluation 2   3 mins. ■■□

Observe the activity and ask a few pairs to come to the front and do the activity for the class.

Presentation 3   7–10 mins.

Introduce three new words to the students with their books closed: *pencil*, *pen*, and *paper*. Use items in the classroom to demonstrate this vocabulary. These words are not the target vocabulary, but they are associated with the act of writing. Consequently, they further expand the linguistic context. Ask students what words are associated with reading. Help them, if necessary, to say *book(s)*. Do the same for *point* (finger), *listen* (ear), and *repeat* (mouth).

Tell students that you are going to give them a test. Write the word *test* on the board. Briefly drill students by showing or pointing to the objects previously introduced and asking students to respond with the correct verb.

E Read.

Tell students that you will show them ways to take written tests and that they will take tests like this in the class from time to time. Go over circling and bubbling.

Practice 3   10 mins.

F Listen and circle the answers.

Do the first item with students.

 Listening Script   CD 1, Track 12

1. *listen*
2. *point*
3. *write*
4. *repeat*

G Listen and bubble in the answers.

Explain to students that they should listen for other words associated with the target vocabulary, too. Do the first item with students.

 Listening Script   CD 1, Track 13

1. *People use their ears to listen for important information.*
2. *The teacher is pointing with her finger at the poster in front of the class.*
3. *I need a paper and a pencil so I can write a letter.*
4. *Students, open your mouths and repeat the words clearly.*

Teaching Tip

Listening

Students are often under the misconception that in order to do listening tasks they must understand every word. Actually, a lot of listening, even by native speakers, involves focused listening where the person listening decides on meaning from just a few key words. Exercises such as Exercise G allow students to develop this listening strategy by listening for key words and filtering out words they may not understand.

Evaluation 3   2 mins.

Ask students to compare their answers with a partner.

Refer students to *Stand Out Basic Grammar Challenge*, Pre-Unit, Challenge 3 for more practice with action verbs.

Application   5–7 mins.

H Follow the instructions.

Activity Bank

Lesson 3, Worksheet 1: Classroom Instructions

Instructor's Notes

_____

_____

_____

_____

_____

_____

_____

_____

GOAL ➤ **Follow classroom instructions**

E Read.

Circle.	Bubble in.
1. pencil	3. pencil
a. pen	○ pen
(b.) pencil	● pencil
c. paper	○ paper
2. paper	4. pen
(a.) paper	● pen
b. pen	○ paper
c. pencil	○ pencil

F Listen and circle the answers.

CD 1
TR 12

1.	2.	3.	4.
a. point	(a.) point	a. point	a. point
b. repeat	b. repeat	b. repeat	(b.) repeat
(c.) listen	c. listen	c. listen	c. listen
d. read	d. read	d. read	d. read
e. write	e. write	(e.) write	e. write

G Listen and bubble in the answers.

CD 1
TR 13

1.	2.	3.	4.
○ point	● point	○ point	○ point
○ repeat	○ repeat	○ repeat	● repeat
● listen	○ listen	○ listen	○ listen
○ read	○ read	○ read	○ read
○ write	○ write	● write	○ write

H Follow the instructions.

1. Circle the phone number. 02219   ⟨(212) 555-7763⟩   04/08/09

2. Bubble in the answer.   2 + 2 = _____   ○ 3   ○ 5   ● 4

3. Write the name of your teacher. _____(Answers will vary.)_____

My Dictionary

Make flash cards to improve your vocabulary.

1. Choose four new words from this unit.
2. Write each word on an index card or on a piece of paper.
3. On the back of the card or paper, draw a picture of the word, find and write a sentence from the book with the word, and write the page number.
4. Study the words.

phone

Chinh's phone number is (714) 555-3450
page P6

Learner Log

Write the page number(s).

	Page Number	I can do it. ✓
1. Say: *I'm* (your name).	P2	
2. Say: *hello, hi, goodbye, bye.*	P1	
3. Say and write phone numbers.	P5	
4. Follow instructions.	P7	

Presentation 1 15-20 mins.

My Dictionary

Show students an example of 3-by-5 index cards that have been made into flash cards as described in My Dictionary. For students new to this concept, you will need to walk them through the process. Provide index cards, if necessary.

Practice 1 5-7 mins.

Do My Dictionary.

Evaluation 1 5 mins.

Ask students to share their cards in groups or with the whole class.

Presentation 2 5 mins.

Learner Log

Review the concepts in the Learner Log. Make sure students understand the concepts and how to complete the log.

Teaching Tip

Learner Logs

Learner logs function to help students in many different ways.

1. They serve as part of the review process.
2. They help students to gain confidence and to document what they have learned. Consequently, students see that they are progressing in their learning.
3. They provide students with a tool that they can use repeatedly to check and recheck their understanding of the target language. In this way, students become independent learners.

Practice 2 10-15 mins.

Ask students to do the Learner Log in pairs.

Evaluation 2 2 mins.

Go over the Learner Log with students.

Application 2 5-7 mins.

Ask students to write down their favorite lesson in the unit.

Instructor's Notes

_____
_____
_____
_____
_____
_____
_____
_____
_____
_____
_____
_____
_____
_____

AT-A-GLANCE PREP

Objective: Identify classmates
Grammar: Subject pronouns
Pronunciation: Rhythm
Vocabulary: Subject pronouns, students

RESOURCES

Activity Bank: Lesson 1, Worksheets 1 and 2
Reading and Writing Challenge: Unit 1
Grammar Challenge: Unit 1, Challenge 1

Audio: CD 1, Tracks 14–16
Heinle Picture Dictionary: Wave, Greet, Smile, pages 40–41

 1.5 hour classes   2.5 hour classes   3+ hour classes

Stand Out Basic Assessment CD-ROM with *ExamView*®

 Preassessment *(optional)*

Use the Stand Out Basic Assessment CD-ROM with *ExamView*® to create a pretest for Unit 1.

Warm-up and Review   2-5 mins.

Review greeting one another. Write on the board: *I'm _____ (your name). Nice to meet you.* Review the American style of shaking hands. Ask students to circulate around the room shaking hands with their classmates, giving their names, and saying: *Nice to meet you.*

Introduction   2 mins.

Write the day of the week, the date, and the agenda on the board. Say the date while pointing to it and have students repeat. State the objective: *Today we will learn to identify our classmates.*

Presentation 1   10-15 mins.

Ask a few students, male and female, for their names. Then ask the class for the names of the students who have just responded. Then say: *He is _____ (name). She is _____ (name).*

Write these questions on the board: *What's his name? What's her name? What's your name?* Practice them with the students. Have students practice by doing a question-and-answer chain:

Student A: *What's your name?*
Student B: *(student name).*
Student C: *What's his/her name?*
Student D: *(student name).*

Then Student D starts with a new student.

Ask students to open their books and look at the four pictures.

Ⓐ Listen and point.

After listening to the recording, students will listen to you. Read the sentences in random order. Ask students to point to the appropriate picture. Help them distinguish *he* and *she*.

> 🎧 **Listening Script**   CD 1, Track 14
>
> *Here are three friends of mine from school. He is Amal, she is Chinh, and they are Chinh and Elsa. They are all students in Mrs. Adams's class. Amal is a student, Chinh is a student, and Elsa is a student.*

Create a dialog with the questions on the board.

Student A: *What's your name?*
Student B: *(name). I am a student.*
Student A: *What's his/her name?*
Student B: *(name). He/She is a student.*

Practice 1   7-10 mins.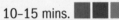

Ⓑ Ask a partner the questions above.

Ask students to walk around the room and talk to ten students. Ask them to write the students' names on a sheet of paper. Encourage students to spell out names and not write the information for their partner.

Evaluation 1   5-7 mins.

Ask for students to demonstrate the dialog.

STANDARDS CORRELATIONS

CASAS: 0.1.1, 0.2.1 (See CASAS Competency List on pages 167-173.)
SCANS: Basic Skills Reading, writing, listening, speaking

EFF: Communication Speak so others can understand

UNIT 1

Personal Information

GOALS

➤ **Identify classmates**
➤ **Express nationalities**
➤ **Express marital status**

➤ **Say and write your address**
➤ **Say and write dates**

LESSON 1

What's your name?

GOAL ➤ Identify classmates

A Listen and point.

CD 1
TR 14

What's his name?

He is a student.

What's her name?

She is a student.

What are their names?

They are students.

What's your name?

I am a student.

 B Ask a partner the questions above.

EXAMPLE: **A:** What's his name?
B: He is Amal. He is a student.

C Listen and repeat.

CD 1
TR 15

I

you

he

she

we

they

D Write.

1. What's his name? _____ He is Amal. _____

2. What's her name? _____ She _____ is Chinh.

3. What are their names? _____ They _____ are Elsa and Chinh.

4. What's your name? _____ (Answers will vary.) _____

Pronunciation

➤ WHAT'S your name?

Presentation 2 10-15 mins.

C Listen and repeat.

Look at the illustrations and the words below them with students.

 Listening Script CD 1, Track 15

I
You
He
She
We
They

I am a student.
You are a student.
He is a student.
She is a student.
We are students.
They are students.

D Write.

Have students write the correct pronouns. This is still the presentation stage so do the exercise as a class.

Model this same pattern with students in the class. For example, walk up to one male student and say to the class: *What's his name?* Use proper stress and rhythm as you do this. Encourage students to respond: *He is _____.* Do the same with a few more students. Have a volunteer ask the question about a different student this time and you give the answer. Then ask for two students to model the exercise using another classmate.

For shorter classes, ask students to do Exercise D for homework.

Rhythm with questions

Help students hear the stress and rhythm patterns of the question *What's your name?* This pattern will be repeated throughout the unit. Start by having students repeat *What's* several times with emphasis. You may want to have the whole class say *What's* while one or two students follow with *your name?* Next, have them clap out the rhythm and then repeat. You may wish to make a song or game out of it as you ask individuals their names in the class. Ask the whole class to clap and repeat:

Teacher: *What's ... your name?*
Student 1: *I am ... Amal.*
Teacher: *What's ... his name?*
All Students: *He is ... Amal.*

Practice 2 5-7 mins.

Have students walk around the room, asking the questions about their classmates. Have them continue practicing until you stop them.

Evaluation 2 3-5 mins.

Ask for volunteers to demonstrate the questions and answers.

Presentation 3   10–15 mins.

E   Listen.

Ask students who the women in the picture are. Ask them if you use *he* or *she* with women and girls. Play the recording. Go over each line with the students. Ask them to repeat after you. Practice the conversation as a class; you read Chinh's lines, half the class reads Satsuki's lines, and the other half reads Elsa's line. Then, ask for three students to demonstrate the conversation in front of the class.

 Listening Script   *CD 1, Track 16*

The listening script matches the conversation in Exercise E.

Practice 3   5–7 mins. ▪

F   **Practice the conversation.**

Divide students into groups of three and have them practice the conversation, switching roles each time they practice.

Evaluation 3   3–5 mins. ▪

Ask groups to present the dialog in front of the class.

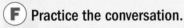 **Refer students to *Stand Out Basic Grammar Challenge*, Unit 1, Challenge 1 for more practice with subject pronouns.**

Application   5–7 mins. ▪▪▪

G   **Work with a partner. Write classmates' names.**

Ask students to work in pairs. Show them how to do this activity by using a student as your partner. Write: *He is a student. She is a student. They are students.* Then have students replace the pronouns *he, she,* and *they* with names and write sentences in their notebooks. For example, instead of writing *He is a student,* they write *Nicolai is a student.*

Have students, in pairs, complete Exercise G, using classmates' names. Then have them practice saying sentences such as: *Brian and Jason are students.*

Teaching Tip

Presenting dialogs

The first levels of *Stand Out* use dialogs. In the *Stand Out* approach, dialogs should be used as opportunities for students to use the language and become familiar with pronunciation and vocabulary.

The following steps demonstrate how to present dialogs effectively:

1. Present the dialog in context in its entirety, allowing students to hear the model either by the instructor or by listening to the recording.
2. Have students repeat each line as a class. Work on rhythm and other pronunciation features.
3. Have students take one role while you take the other role, and then reverse roles.
4. Ask one student to practice the dialog with you. Then reverse roles.
5. Ask two or three students to demonstrate for the class.
6. Add substitutions where appropriate or when called for and repeat the above steps.

Activity Bank

Lesson 1, Worksheet 1: Say *Hello!*
Lesson 1, Worksheet 2: Use Subject Pronouns

Instructor's Notes

_____

_____

_____

_____

_____

_____

_____

GOAL ➤ **Identify classmates**

 E **Listen.**

CD 1
TR 16

Chinh: Hi, Satsuki.
Satsuki: Hello, Chinh.
Chinh: Elsa, this is Satsuki. He is a student.
Elsa: Hello, Satsuki. I am a student, too.
Satsuki: Nice to meet you.

F **Practice the conversation.**

G **Work with a partner. Write classmates' names.** (Answers will vary.)

Pronoun		Name
I	I am a student.	(your name)
you	You are a student.	(your partner's name)
he	He is a student.	
she	She is a student.	
we	We are students.	
they	They are students.	

Where are you from?

GOAL ➤ Express nationality

CD 1
TR 17

A Read and listen.

Fort Lauderdale,
Florida
Adult School

My name is
Concepción.

I'm from Cuba.

B Write.

1. What's her name? _Concepción_

2. Where is she from? _Cuba_

C Ask your classmates.

1. What's your name?

2. Where are you from?

Objective: Express nationality
Grammar: Simple present tense
Academic Strategy: Focused listening
Vocabulary: *from, native country, birthplace*

RESOURCES

Activity Bank: Lesson 2, Worksheet 1
Reading and Writing Challenge: Unit 1
Grammar Challenge: Unit 1, Challenge 2

 1.5 hour classes ■ 2.5 hour classes ■ 3⁺ hour classes

AGENDA
Review asking questions.
Ask: Where are you from?
Listen for countries of origin.
Ask classmates: Where do you live?

Audio: CD 1, Tracks 17–23
Heinle Picture Dictionary: Nationalities, pages 44–45

Stand Out Basic Assessment CD-ROM with Exam*View*®

Warm-up and Review   8-12 mins. ■■■

Write on the board: *What's your name?* Remind students to use correct pronunciation and rhythm. Ask students to walk around the room and ask their classmates these questions. They may record the information on a sheet of paper.

Introduction   2 mins. ■■■

Write the date and agenda on the board. Ask students what day it is. If you have a world map, show them what state or region they live in and where the city is. State the objective: *Today we will identify our nationalities.*

Presentation 1   7-10 mins. ■■■

List countries on the board. Make sure you include the native countries of all the students. Circle your native country and put a check mark next to it. Ask students to come up and do the same for their native countries. Ask students to find their country on a map. If most students are from the same country, have them tell their hometown.

Have students open their books and ask where Concepción is from. Ask for a volunteer to find Cuba on a world map. Ask students to repeat the sentences in the speech bubbles.

 **A** Read and listen.

Play the recording and ask students to listen. Then play it again and ask them to point to the speech bubble when they hear each statement.

Listening Script   CD 1, Track 17

Mr. Jackson: *Hello, I'm Mr. Jackson. What's your name?*
Concepción: *My name is Concepción. I'm new in the class.*
Mr. Jackson: *Nice to meet you. Won't you have a seat?*
Concepción: *Thank you.*
Mr. Jackson: *Where are you from, Concepción?*
Concepción: *I'm from Cuba.*
Mr. Jackson: *That's great! Welcome to the class.*

 B Write.

Ask students to write information about Concepción. Walk around the room and check their work. One-word answers are expected at this level, not complete sentences.

Practice 1   5-7 mins. ■■■

 C Ask your classmates.

Ask students to walk around the room and ask several classmates what their names are and where they are from.

Evaluation 1   7-10 mins. ■■■

Ask one student where another student is from. Ask that student about a different student. Every time you hear a new country, point to it on the list.

STANDARDS CORRELATIONS

CASAS: 0.1.2, 0.2.1, 1.1.3, 4.8.7 (See CASAS Competency List on pages 167-173.)
SCANS: **Basic Skills** Reading, writing, listening, speaking
Information Acquire and evaluate information, organize and maintain information, interpret and communicate information

Interpersonal Work with cultural diversity
EFF: Communication Speak so others can understand, listen actively
Interpersonal Cooperate with others

Presentation 2

12–15 mins.

D Predict.

Prepare students for listening by asking them simple questions about the picture. Help them to predict where the teacher and students are from. All answers are acceptable at this stage. Make a list on the board.

Discuss focused listening with students.

> ### Teaching Tip
>
> #### Focused listening
>
> There are several different ways that people listen. One important way is to focus on essential information while filtering out what is not important. Students learning another language are often under the misconception that they must understand every word. It is important to teach students how to listen for important information even when they understand very little of the extraneous vocabulary used. They will develop the skill to make educated guesses about the additional information. Future tasks in this book will rely more and more on the students' ability to develop and incorporate this skill.

Go over the vocabulary box. Students need to understand *birthplace* in order to complete application forms and other forms. Review briefly the possessive pronouns *his* and *her*, which students have already practiced in Lesson 1 of this unit.

Practice 2

10–15 mins.

E Listen and write.

Play the recording. Ask students to listen and identify the students being described. Students will need to practice focused listening because several sentences are not related to nationality. You may need to play the recording two or three times.

Listening Script CD 1, Tracks 18–22

Conversation 1
Mrs. Adams: *Hello, I'm Mrs. Adams. What's your name?*
Concepción: *My name is Concepción. I'm new in the class.*
Mrs. Adams: *Nice to meet you. Won't you have a seat?*
Concepción: *Thank you.*
Mrs. Adams: *Where are you from, Concepción?*
Concepción: *I'm from Cuba.*

Conversation 2
Mrs. Adams: *Are you the new student from Lebanon?*
Amal: *Yes, my name is Amal.*
Mrs. Adams: *I hope you enjoy our class.*
Amal: *I will, thank you.*

Conversation 3
Mrs. Adams: *Hello, Chinh.*
Chinh: *Hi, Mrs. Adams.*
Mrs. Adams: *Chinh, where are you from?*
Chinh: *I'm from Vietnam.*

Conversation 4
Mrs. Adams: *Hello, Elsa. It is so good to see you today.*
Elsa: *Yes, I was sick yesterday, but I feel better today.*
Mrs. Adams: *That's good. I thought you might have gone back to Russia.*

Conversation 5
Mrs. Adams: *Hello. Welcome to the class. What's your name?*
Shiro: *I'm Shiro. I came to the United States last week.*
Mrs. Adams: *Where are you from, Shiro?*
Shiro: *I'm from Japan.*

F Practice.

Have students practice with a partner. Make sure they substitute information for all the students in the conversations on the CD.

Evaluation 2

5 mins.

Ask students the same questions in Exercise F about themselves. Check for understanding.

GOAL ➤ **Express nationality**

D **Predict.** (Answers will vary.)

1. Where is Shiro from? _____

2. Where is Amal from? _____

3. Where is Chinh from? _____

4. Where is Elsa from? _____

  E **Listen and write.**

CD 1
TR 18-22

1. She is from Cuba. _____ Concepción _____

2. He is from Lebanon. _____ Amal _____

3. She is from Vietnam. _____ Chinh _____

4. She is from Russia. _____ Elsa _____

5. He is from Japan. _____ Shiro _____

> **Birthplace**
>
> Where is he from?
>   He is from Japan.
>
> What's *his* birthplace?
> Japan.
>
> What's *her* birthplace?
> Cuba.

 F **Practice.**

EXAMPLE: *A:* Where is <u>Concepción</u> from?   *A:* What's her birthplace?
             B: She is from <u>Cuba</u>.   *B:* <u>Cuba</u>.

GOAL ➤ Express nationality

G Read.

Simple Present		
I	live	in Los Angeles.
He	lives	in Fort Lauderdale.
She		in Chicago.

H Complete the sentences.

1. Concepción ____is from Cuba____. She ____lives____ in Fort Lauderdale.

2. Shiro ____is from Japan____. He ____lives____ in Fort Lauderdale.

3. Amal ____is from Lebanon____. He ____lives____ in Fort Lauderdale.

4. Elsa ____is from Russia____. She ____lives____ in Fort Lauderdale.

5. Chinh ____is from Vietnam____. She ____lives____ in Fort Lauderdale.

6. I am from ____(Answers will vary.)____. I _____.

I Listen and practice using <u>Shiro</u>, <u>Amal</u>, <u>Elsa</u>, and <u>Chinh</u>.

CD 1
TR 23

Mrs. Adams: Hi, <u>Concepción</u>. Where are you from?
Concepción: I'm from <u>Cuba</u>.
Mrs. Adams: Where do you live?
Concepción: I live in <u>Fort Lauderdale, Florida</u>.

J Practice and write. Ask your classmates. (Answers will vary.)

You: Hi, _____. Where are you from?
Classmate: I'm from _____.
You: Where do you live?
Classmate: I live in _____.

Name (What's your name?)	Birthplace (Where are you from?)	Current City (Where do you live?)
1.		
2.		
3.		
4.		

Presentation 3   15-20 mins. ■■■□

G Read.

Go over the chart with students. At this stage, students are not ready for a lot of grammatical information. For now, it is appropriate to only focus on the first- and third-person singular forms of present-tense verbs. Emphasize that an *s* is only added to the end of a present-tense verb when the subject is in the third person.

Teaching Tip

Grammar charts

For students who are used to them, grammar charts are simple and easy to read. But an instructor should never assume students can read a chart. Some students may have very limited education. Walk students through charts carefully. When they can read them without assistance, they will be closer to being independent learners.

Drill the students by saying *he, she,* or *I* and asking them to respond with the correct form of *live*. Ask individual students where they live. Then have the rest of the class respond: *He (She) lives in _____.*

Work on pronunciation. Students will sometimes "swallow" the final *s*. Make sure students blend the *i* in *in* with the *s* in *lives* so that together they make a /z/ sound.

Teaching Tip

Drills

Drills can be a good way to help students become familiar with vocabulary and pronunciation. They also help students gain confidence, especially when performing together with their classmates. However, drills should not be the sole practice or method used to help students learn English. There are several ways to drill (choral repetition, substitution, build-up, backward build-up, etc.) If particular drills are overused, there is a risk of losing meaning for structure.

H Complete the sentences.

Complete the sentences as a class to confirm that students understand the grammar point.

I Listen and practice using <u>Shiro</u>, <u>Amal</u>, <u>Elsa</u>, and <u>Chinh</u>.

Play the recording. Help the students repeat the dialog with proper intonation.

 Listening Script   CD 1, Track 23

The listening script matches the conversation in Exercise I.

Show students how to replace *Concepción* with *Shiro, Amal, Elsa,* and *Chinh.*

Practice 3   5-7 mins. ■

Ask students to practice the dialog with a partner, substituting the other names.

Evaluation 3   2 mins. ■

Ask students to demonstrate in front of the classroom.

Refer students to *Stand Out Basic Grammar Challenge*, Unit 1, Challenge 2 for more practice with first- and third-person singular and the simple present.

Application   5-7 mins. ■■□

J Practice and write. Ask your classmates.

Demonstrate this activity with a volunteer.

Activity Bank

Lesson 2, Worksheet 1: Write about Countries and Cities

AT-A-GLANCE PREP

Objective: Express marital status
Grammar: *be* verb and contractions with *be*
Pronunciation: Rhythm and prominence
Academic Strategies: Focused listening, team work
Vocabulary: *married, divorced, single, marital status*

RESOURCES

Activity Bank: Lesson 3, Worksheets 1 and 2
Reading and Writing Challenge: Unit 1
Grammar Challenge: Unit 1, Challenge 3

Audio: CD 1, Tracks 24–25
Heinle Picture Dictionary: Family, pages 26–27

■ 1.5 hour classes ■ 2.5 hour classes ■ 3⁺ hour classes

Stand Out Basic Assessment CD-ROM with Exam*View*®

AGENDA

Learn about marital status.
Study the verb be.
Practice the verb be.

Warm-up and Review 10-12 mins. ■■■

Ask students to walk around the room and ask six other students where they are from. Ask students to keep a list. Then ask them to form groups and report to their group.

Teaching Tip

Reporting to a group

Reporting in groups gives students more opportunity to speak. Monitoring is easier if students are encouraged to stand up to report.

Introduction 2 mins. ■■■

Write the day of the week, the date, and the agenda on the board. Say the date while pointing to it and have students repeat it. State the objective: *Today we will learn to speak about marital status.*

Presentation 1 7-10 mins. ■■■

Post signs that say *single* and *married.* Ask students to go to the sign that describes them. Some students will not know the words, but encourage them to ask their classmates.

Teaching Tip

"Corners"

Students go to corners or places in the room based on facts or beliefs. Once they get there, they may answer questions or perform a dialog.

While students are standing, write *Marital Status* on the board. Say *I'm _____* (*single* or *married*). Ask students to say *I'm married,* or *I'm single.* Ask students to be seated.

(A) Listen and write.

Present *divorced* to students. Go over the pictures and do the listening as a class. Prepare students to do Exercise B.

🎧 Listening Script   CD 1, Track 24

Amal is a student at Fort Lauderdale Adult School. He is single. His birth date is August 3, 1988. He is from Lebanon. Chinh is from Vietnam. Jeff is from the United States. They are married. They got married two years ago. Mirna and Paul are from Russia. Mirna is a student and wants to speak English better. Mirna and Paul are divorced. They have three children.

Practice 1 3 mins. ■■■

(B) With a partner, point at the pictures in Exercise A and say: *He is single, They are married,* or *They are divorced.*

Allow students to practice. Then ask them to cover the sentences and keep practicing.

Evaluation 1 2 mins. ■■■

Ask students to demonstrate in front of the class.

STANDARDS CORRELATIONS

CASAS: 0.1.2, 0.2.1 (See CASAS Competency List on 167-173.)
SCANS: Basic Skills Reading, listening, speaking
Interpersonal Participate as a member of a team

EFF: Communication Speak so others can understand, listen actively
Interpersonal Cooperate with others

Are you married?

GOAL ➤ Express marital status

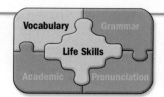

  A Listen and write.

CD 1
TR 24

| single | married | divorced |

He is _____single_____.

They are _____married_____.

They are _____divorced_____.

 B With a partner, point at the pictures in Exercise A and say: *He is single, They are married,* or *They are divorced.*

GOAL ➤ Express marital status

C Read.

Be Verb			
Pronoun	***Be* verb**	**Marital status**	**Example sentence**
I	am	married	I am married.
he	is	single	He is single. (Amal is single.)
she		divorced	She is divorced. (Mirna is divorced.)
we	are	divorced	We are divorced.
you		married	You are married.
they		single	They are single.

  D Listen, circle *Yes* or *No*, and write.

CD 1
TR 25

1.

Is she married? (Yes)   No

She _____is married_____.

2.

Is he married?   Yes   (No)

He _____is single_____.

3.

Are they married? (Yes)   No

They _____are married_____.

E Write *am*, *are*, or *is*.

1. Mr. and Mrs. Johnson ___are___ married.

2. Orlando ___is___ divorced.

3. Omar, Natalie, and Doug ___are___ single.

4. We ___are___ divorced.

5. They ___are___ single.

6. She ___is___ married.

7. We ___are___ single.

8. You ___are___ married.

Presentation 2

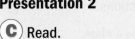 10–15 mins.

C Read.

Present the information in the table to students by writing the example sentences on the board and underlining the *be* verb. Explain to students how each pronoun uses a different form of the verb.

Provide practice for students by calling out a pronoun and having them respond with the correct form of the *be* verb.

Teaching Tip

Recycling

At all levels, but especially at the lower levels, recycling is very important. *Recycling* means reintroducing concepts previously taught in different contexts. Don't expect students to learn every concept and always remember it at this level. They will forget some things as they learn new concepts, so it becomes essential to teach them past concepts again.

D Listen, circle *Yes* or *No*, and write.

Since the vocabulary needed to describe marital status and the verb *be* is still being presented, this exercise can be done as a class. Refer to the chart in Exercise C after answering each question.

 Listening Script CD 1, Track 25

Hans: *Maria, are you single?*
Maria: *No, I'm married. Hans, are you married?*
Hans: *No, I'm single. Are Mr. and Mrs. Johnson married?*
Maria: *Yes, I think so.*

For shorter classes, ask students to do Exercises E, F, and G for homework.

Practice 2

5–7 mins.

E Write *am, are,* or *is.*

Help students as necessary.

Evaluation 2

3 mins.

Check students' work in their books.

Presentation 3 10-15 mins.

Introduce the concept of contractions by reminding students of the contraction for *I am* that they learned in the Pre-Unit. Write it on the board.

Contractions are important because native speakers use them a lot. They affect the rhythm of the language and, therefore, students sound more like a native speaker when they use them. Some students will resist using contractions; however, it is imperative to encourage them to use contractions.

Pronunciation

Rhythm and prominence

English sentence rhythm is not a consistent pattern. Various aspects of the language affect it. English has a series of stops and starts based on prominent words and the pauses that sometimes follow. For example, one could pronounce *I am married* in various ways, depending on the information the speaker would like to stress.

If a speaker is saying emphatically that he or she is married, it might be: *I AM (slight pause) married*. If the speaker wants to differentiate between being married and single, he or she might say *I am MARried* in which case the first two words might be rushed through quickly. (*MAR* in this case is more prominent than the final example in this box.)

More often, however, and for this lesson, the statement is a statement of fact. In this case, it would be *I am married* with little or no word prominence. This pronunciation is not very common and comes across a bit stilted.

Changing the phrase to a contraction allows for more dimension and is much more common in everyday speech. The key word is *married* so it receives prominence.
I'm MARried.

F Read and write contractions.

This exercise can be done as a class.

For shorter classes, ask students to do Exercise G for homework.

Practice 3 5-7 mins.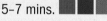

G Write.

Ask students to do the activity alone and then, go over as a class.

Evaluation 3 2 mins. ▪

Check students' work in their books.

Refer students to *Stand Out Basic Grammar Challenge*, Unit 1, Challenge 3 for more practice with contractions and the verb *be*.

Application 5-7 mins.

H Read.

Drill the students briefly on the exchanges. With a few students, model the question: *Are you married?* Ask two students to model the question and appropriate response.

I Speak to five classmates.

Show students how to complete the table and then ask them to talk to five students about their marital status. In this case, and others where personal information is requested, give students the option to respond with the phrase *That's personal*. Write the phrase on the board.

Activity Bank

Lesson 3, Worksheet 1: Marital Status
Lesson 3, Worksheet 2: *Be* Verb

GOAL ➤ Express marital status

F **Read and write contractions.**

I + am = I'm
You + are = You're
He + is = He's
She + is = She's
We + are = We're
They + are = They're

1. _____I'm_____ married.
2. _____You're_____ divorced.
3. _____He's_____ single.
4. _____She's_____ divorced.
5. _____We're_____ married.
6. _____They're_____ single.

G **Write.**

1. We _____are_____ married.   We're married.
2. They _____are_____ divorced.   They're divorced.
3. I _____am_____ single.   I'm single.
4. He _____is_____ divorced.   He's divorced.
5. You _____are_____ married.   You're married.
6. She _____is_____ single.   She's single.

H **Read.**

A: Hans, are you single? | *A:* Lin, are you single? | *A:* Pam, are you married?
B: Yes, I'm single. | *B:* No, I'm married. | *B:* No, I'm divorced.

I **Speak to five classmates.** (Answers will vary.)

Name	Marital status (Are you married?)
Hans	single
1.	
2.	
3.	
4.	
5.	

What's your address?

GOAL ➤ Say and write your address

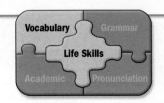

A Read.

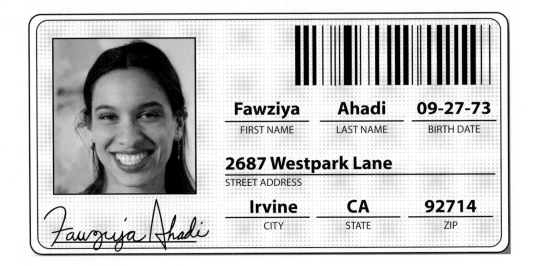

Fawziya	Ahadi	09-27-73
FIRST NAME	LAST NAME	BIRTH DATE

2687 Westpark Lane
STREET ADDRESS

Irvine	CA	92714
CITY	STATE	ZIP

 B Listen and point to the addresses.

CD 1
TR 26

3259 Lincoln Street

51 Apple Avenue

12367 Elm Road

C Write.

First Name: Fawziya

Last Name: Ahadi

Street Address: 2687 Westpark Lane

City: Irvine

State: CA

Zip Code: 92714

AT-A-GLANCE PREP

Objective: Say and write your address
Grammar: Review: *he/she/it is*
Academic Strategy: Focused listening
Vocabulary: *street, address, city, state, zip*

RESOURCES

Activity Bank: Lesson 4, Worksheets 1 and 2
Reading and Writing Challenge: Unit 1
Grammar Challenge: Unit 1, Challenge 4

■ 1.5 hour classes ■ 2.5 hour classes ■ 3⁺ hour classes

Audio: CD 1, Tracks 26–27
Heinle Picture Dictionary: Post Office, pages 52–53

Stand Out Basic Assessment CD-ROM with Exam*View*®

Warm-up and Review   2-5 mins.

Write the following chart on the board and ask students to copy it.

What's your name?	Are you married?	Where do you live?	Where are you from?
1.			

Ask students to talk to five students and report to a group.

Introduction   2 mins.

Write the day of the week, the date, and the agenda on the board. Say the date while pointing to it and have students repeat it. State the objective: *Today you will learn to say and write your address.*

Presentation 1   10-12 mins.

Ask students if they have ID cards. Show students your driver's license if you have one and encourage students to do the same.

 Read.

Read the ID card with students and ask them questions such as: *Where does Fawziya live? What's the city, state,* and *zip code?* Use the proper stress and rhythm. Review numbers 1–10.

 Listen and point to the addresses.

Confirm that students are following along with the recording. If time allows, you may produce more examples to give students more practice.

> 🎧 **Listening Script**   CD 1, Track 26
>
> 1. *Write down the following address so you can find the location easily. It is 51 Apple Avenue.*
> 2. *I need to talk to the resident at 12367 Elm Road. Do you know her?*
> 3. *Amal's address is not 51 Apple Avenue. It is different.*
> 4. *Let's go to the new adult school. I think the address is 3259 Lincoln Street.*

Practice 1   3 mins.

Ⓒ Write.

Do this as an information-gap activity. Write these questions on the board: *What's the street address? What's the city? What's the state?* Have students work in pairs. Student A covers Fawziya's ID card and asks for Fawziya's information from Student B who reads from the ID card. Have students reverse roles.

Evaluation 1   3 mins.

Observe students as they work.

STANDARDS CORRELATIONS

CASAS: 0.1.2, 0.2.1, 1.1.3, 4.8.7 (See CASAS Competency List on pages 167-173.)
***SCANS:* Basic Skills** Reading, writing, listening, speaking

Information Acquire and evaluate information, organize and maintain information, interpret and communicate information
***EFF:* Communication** Speak so others can understand, listen actively

---

Presentation 2   7–10 mins. ▪▪▫

D Listen to your teacher. Write the numbers.

Review numbers with students once again. Dictate a few numbers to them that might be street numbers such as: *2034, 129, 23651,* and *689.* Ask students to compare answers and then, as a class, go over each one.

Write your school's address on the board. Help students see what words are capitalized and where commas go. Ask students to copy the address and then have partners peer-edit for accuracy.

Practice 2   7–10 mins. ▪▪

Have students look at the pictures and ask them who these people are. Then ask them what information is missing from the address.

E Listen and write.

Play the recording a few times until most of the students have gotten the answers. You may wish to have students compare answers with others in a group between listening sessions.

 Listening Script   CD 1, Track 27

    Amal is a student at Fort Lauderdale Adult School. His address is 8237 Augustin Street, Fort Lauderdale, Florida 33310. Chinh is also a student at Fort Lauderdale Adult School. She lives at 23905 Fin Road, Fort Lauderdale, Florida 33310. Elsa is from Russia. She is a good student. Her address is 23 San Andrew Street, Fort Lauderdale, Florida 33310.

F Write.

Call out the names of the students in Exercise E and encourage students to respond with the correct address. Then have students complete the exercise by writing the addresses next to the names.

Evaluation 2   7–10 mins. ▪▫

Check students' work. Help students use commas and capital letters correctly.

  D Listen to your teacher. Write the numbers. (Answers will vary.)

1. _____   2. _____   3. _____   4. _____

 E Listen and write.

CD 1
TR 27

Address:

_____8237_____ Augustin Street

Fort Lauderdale, FL 33310

Address:

_____23905_____ Fin Road

Fort Lauderdale, FL 33310

Address:

_____23_____ San Andrew Street

Fort Lauderdale, FL 33310

F Write.

Name	Address
Amal	8237 Augustin Street, Fort Lauderdale, FL 33310
Chinh	23905 Fin Road, Fort Lauderdale, FL 33310
Elsa	23 San Andrew Street, Fort Lauderdale, FL 33310

GOAL ➤ **Say and write your address**

 Read.

Chinh: Hi, Amal. What's your address?
Amal: Hello, Chinh. My address is 8237 Augustin Street, Fort Lauderdale, Florida 33310.
Chinh: Thanks.

Be verb	
He	
She	
It	*is*
The address	

H **Write.**

Pair practice. Student A, look at page 12. Student B, look at page 11.

Student A: Hi, Chinh. What's your address?
Student B: Hello, Amal. My address is <u>23905 Fin Road, Fort Lauderdale, FL 33310</u>.
Student A: Thanks.

Student A: Hi, Elsa. What's your address?
Student B: Hello, Amal. My address is <u>23 San Andrew Street, Fort Lauderdale, FL 33310</u>
Student A: Thanks.

Student A: Hi, Amal. What's your address?
Student B: Hello, Elsa. My address is <u>8237 Augustin Street, Fort Lauderdale, FL 33310</u>
Student A: Thanks.

I **Write.** (Answers will vary.)

My name	Address
My partner	**Address**

Presentation 3

Write a sentence on the board with the school address already there. Write: *The school address is _____.* Remind students once again about capital letters and commas. Show them that on an ID card, the state is usually abbreviated but when speaking, the whole word is uttered.

Explain to students that *is* is a form of *be* that they have already learned. Refer them to the grammar box at the top of the page to help them visualize it. You may decide to go back to page 8 and look at the chart at the top of the page. It might help here to have students add *it* to the chart and give them a brief explanation. Write on the board:

> *address = it*
> *dog = it*
> *book = it*

G Read.

Read the dialog with students and teach them about proper rhythm. Here you may wish to stress that usually a native speaker will ask *WHAT'S* (slight pause) *your address?*

Practice the dialog with students. You are preparing them for the information-gap activity that they will do in Exercise H. Prepare students for this activity by modeling it with various students.

Teaching Tip

Information gaps

In an information-gap activity, two students work together. Each student has different pieces of information needed to complete the task. The two students have to ask each other questions in order to get the information they need. In most cases, one student is looking at one page, while the other student is looking at a different page.

Practice 3

H Write.

Have students complete the information gap. Student A looks at page 12 while Student B looks at page 11. Then they switch.

Evaluation 3

Ask students to demonstrate the dialogs they used to obtain the information in front of the class.

Refer students to *Stand Out Basic Grammar Challenge*, Unit 1, Challenge 4 for more practice with the verb *be*.

Application

I Write.

Write these two questions on the board: *What's your name? What's your address?* Show students how to complete this exercise by doing it with a few students on the board.

Teach the students the question *How do you spell that?* They may need to ask this question in order to spell the street and city names correctly.

Activity Bank

Lesson 4, Worksheet 1: Write Addresses
Lesson 4, Worksheet 2: Personal Information

Objective: Say and write dates
Grammar: Review contractions
Pronunciation: Final /t/
Academic Strategy: Focused listening
Vocabulary: *birthday, birth date, today, tomorrow,* numbers 1–30, months and days

RESOURCES

Activity Bank: Lesson 5, Worksheets 1 and 2
Reading and Writing Challenge: Unit 1
Grammar Challenge: Unit 1, Challenge 5

■ *1.5 hour classes* ■ *2.5 hour classes* ■ *3+ hour classes*

Audio: CD 1, Tracks 28–29
Heinle Picture Dictionary: Calendar, pages 6–7

Stand Out Basic Assessment CD-ROM Exam*View*®

AGENDA

Learn months and days.
Practice new vocabulary.
Complete a calendar.

Warm-up and Review   7-10 mins.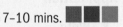

Write on the board: *How do you spell that?* Ask students to practice asking for and writing classmates' names.

Introduction   2 mins.

Write the day of the week, the date, and the agenda on the board. Say the date while pointing to it and have students repeat it. State the objective: *Today we will say and write dates.*

Presentation 1   20-30 mins.

Ask students for the date: month, day, and year. Write the first letter of each month on the board. See if students can identify each month. After they have practiced, complete the names of the months.

(A) Circle this year.

Ask students to circle the current year. Write *2000* on the board and help with the pronunciation. Read each of the years in Exercise A and ask students to repeat.

(B) Listen to your teacher and point.

Review numbers 1–30. (Ordinal numbers are not covered in this lesson. Students may say the cardinal numbers, but the audio uses ordinal

numbers.) Practice days of the week if you feel your students are ready.

(C) Number the months.

Show students how to number the months. Then show how to point to each month as you say it.

Practice 1   3 mins.

(D) Listen to the months and say the number. Listen again and write the months on a sheet of paper.

The months are read three times. The first time students should listen. The second time they should say the number. Then give them time to write the names of the months. Play the recording again so they can confirm their answers.

> ### Listening Script   CD 1, Track 28
>
> | | | | |
> |---|---|---|---|
> | *May* | *February* | *August* | *June* |
> | *March* | *November* | *July* | *September* |
> | *January* | *December* | *April* | *October* |

Evaluation 1   3 mins.

Observe students and check their work.

STANDARDS CORRELATIONS

CASAS: 0.1.2, 0.2.1, 2.3.2 (See CASAS Competency List on pages 167-173.)
SCANS: **Basic Skills** Writing, listening, speaking
Information Acquire and evaluate information, organize and maintain information

Thinking Skill See things in the mind's eye
EFF: **Communication** Read with understanding, speak so others can understand, listen actively
Interpersonal Cooperate with others

What's your birth date?

GOAL ➤ **Say and write dates**

A Circle this year.   2007   2008   2009   2010   2011
(Answers will vary.)

B Listen to your teacher and point.

09-17-2009

SEPTEMBER 2009						
Sunday	Monday	Tuesday	Wednesday	Thursday	Friday	Saturday
		1	**2**	**3**	**4**	**5**
6	**7**	**8**	**9**	**10**	**11**	**12**
13	**14**	**15**	**16**	**17**	**18**	**19**
20	**21**	**22**	**23**	**24**	**25**	**26**
27	**28**	**29**	**30**			

C Number the months.

January	February	March	April
01	02	03	04

May	June	July	August
05	06	07	08

September	October	November	December
09	10	11	12

CD 1
TR 28

D Listen to the months and say the number. Listen again and write the months on a sheet of paper.

(Instructor: Months read in the following order:)
May   February   August   June   March   November
July   September   January   December   April   October

GOAL ➤ Say and write dates

birthday   birth date

today   tomorrow

E **Read.**

September 17, 2009   May 7, 2007   August 26, 1974
(month day, year)   (month day, year)   (month day, year)

F **Read.**

September 17, 2009   May 7, 2007   August 26, 1974
09 / 17 / 2009   05 / 07 / 2007   08 / 26 / 1974
(mm / dd / yyyy)   (mm / dd / yyyy)   (mm / dd / yyyy)

G **Write the dates with words and numbers (September 17, 2009).** (Answers will vary.)

1. The date today: _____

2. Your birth date: _____

3. The date tomorrow: _____

4. Your friend's birth date: _____

H **Write the dates with numbers only (09/17/2009).** (Answers will vary.)

1. The date today: _____

2. Your birth date: _____

3. The date tomorrow: _____

4. Your friend's birth date: _____

Presentation 2   15–20 mins.

Draw a birthday cake on the board. Sing a happy birthday song to help students identify with the new vocabulary.

Ask students what month their birthdays fall in.

Make a distinction between *birthday* and *birth date*. This can be done by covering the year with your hand and saying *birthday*. Then ask students what month their birthdays are in. Ask volunteers to write their birthdays or birth dates on the board. Then write your birth date on the board. Under the dates mark the words and numbers as in Exercise E.

Help students make a distinction between the two terms and their pronunciation by releasing the /t/ in *birth date* clearly so the /t/ explodes with air as the tongue releases.

Pronunciation Practice

Final /t/

Write *birth date* in the top right-hand corner of the board and *birthday* in the top left-hand corner. Demonstrate to students how they should point to the word when they hear it.

1. Say the two words in isolation several times in no particular order, repeating one or the other often.
2. Say the words in the context of sentences.
3. Say the words in the context of a paragraph.

Ask a student to do the first item above with the class.

Ask students what the date is today once again. Write this date on the board with the same notation under it. Write tomorrow's date on the board and say: *Tomorrow is* _____ (tomorrow's date). Make the same notations under that date. Write *17* somewhere arbitrary on the board. Write *September* and *2009* also in the same fashion. Ask a student to come to the board and put the three items together.

Ask students to open their books and review the vocabulary box.

E Read.

Go over the examples and match them with what you did on the board earlier.

F Read.

Go over the examples. Add the numbering system to what you did on the board.

For shorter classes, ask students to do Exercises G, and H for homework.

Teaching Tip

Eliciting information

In the *Stand Out* approach, we suggest that instead of merely giving students information, you elicit from them what they may already know in the presentation stage.

This rather lengthy presentation could have been much shorter if students first opened their books and looked at the examples and the vocabulary. However, we recommend the longer approach where students are involved in the presentation and give information themselves because they will remember more of the experience, therefore allowing for better learning.

Practice 2   5–7 mins.

G Write the dates with words and numbers (September 17, 2009).

Help students as necessary.

H Write the dates with numbers only (09/17/2009).

Help students as necessary.

Evaluation 2   5 mins.

Check students' work. Look for commas and proper spelling.

Presentation 3   10–15 mins.

Ⓘ Listen and write the dates.

Have students listen as a class and write the answers in the chart. Students will hear contractions used again. Go over the contractions and make sure students understand how to form them.

To further expand, ask students to turn to the appendices of their books and find the listening script or write the script on the board. Read it with them, pointing out the contractions as well as the other information.

 Listening Script   CD 1, Track 28

1. *My name is Amal. Today is a great day. It's June 25, 2008. I study at school. Next week, July 3 is my birthday. My birth date is July 3, 1988.*

2. *Elsa is my friend. I see her every day at school. Her birth date is January 12, 1990. That means that she's 19 years old because it's January 12, 2009, today.*

3. **Chinh:** *What's the date today?*
   Orlando: *It's March 2, 2008.*
   Chinh: *Thanks. It's almost my birthday.*
   Orlando: *When is your birthday?*
   Chinh: *March 14!*
   Orlando: *What year?*
   Chinh: *1988.*

Prepare students to do Exercise J by going over the conversations. Show students how to substitute new dates for the underlined dates.

Practice 3   10–15 mins. ■

Ⓙ Read and practice with a partner using the dates from Exercise I.

Evaluation 3   5–7 mins. ■

Ask volunteers to demonstrate their dialogs in front of the class.

📖 **Refer students to *Stand Out Basic Grammar Challenge*, Unit 1, Challenge 5 for more practice with contractions.**

Application   5–7 mins. ■■■

Ⓚ Complete the calendar for this month and circle today.

Help students as necessary.

Ⓛ Write the date today.

_____ ____, _____

or ___ / ___ / ___

Make sure students see that they need to write the date in two ways.

Activity Bank 💿

Lesson 5, Worksheet 1: Calendars and Dates
Lesson 5, Worksheet 2: Ordinal Numbers

Instructor's Notes

_____

_____

_____

_____

_____

_____

_____

_____

_____

_____

_____

_____

_____

_____

GOAL ➤ **Say and write dates**

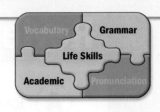

I Listen and write the dates.

Today	Birth date
1. June 25, 2008	July 3, 1988
2. January 12, 2009	January 12, 1990
3. March 2, 2008	March 14, 1988

Contractions

What is = *What's*

It is = *It's*

J Read and practice with a partner using the dates from Exercise I.

Student A: What's the date today?
Student B: It's <u>June 25, 2008</u>.
Student A: Thanks.

Student A: What's your birth date?
Student B: It's <u>July 3, 1988</u>.
Student A: Thanks.

K Complete the calendar for this month and circle today. (Answers will vary.)

Calendar						
_____ (this month)						
Sunday	Monday	Tuesday	Wednesday	Thursday	Friday	Saturday

L Write the date today. _____ _____, _____ or ____ / ____ / ____
(Answers will vary.)

Review

A Read. (Lessons 1–5)

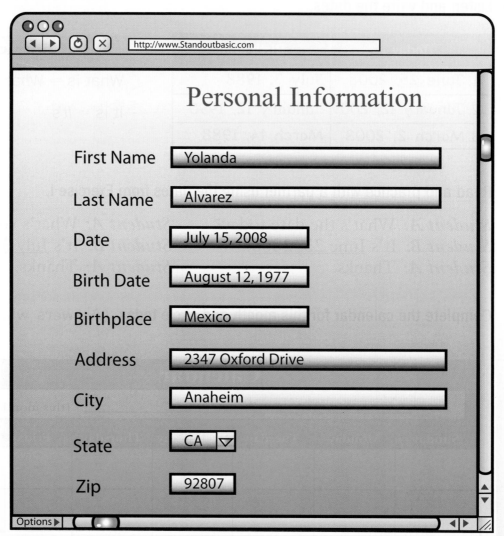

B Write. (Lessons 1–5)

1. What's her first name? __Yolanda__

2. What's her last name? __Alvarez__

3. What's her address? __2347 Oxford Drive, Anaheim, CA 92807__

4. What's her birth date? __August 12, 1977__

5. What's her birthplace? __Mexico__

Objective: All unit objectives
Grammar: All unit grammar
Academic Strategies: Focused listening,
   reviewing, evaluating, developing study skills
Vocabulary: All unit vocabulary

AGENDA
Discuss unit objectives.
Complete the review.
Do My Dictionary.
Evaluate and reflect on progress.

 1.5 hour classes 2.5 hour classes ■ 3⁺ hour classes

Stand Out Basic Assessment CD-ROM with Exam*View*®

Warm-up and Review   10–15 mins.

**Ask students to write their address and phone
number on a 3-by-5 card.** Collect the cards
and pass them out again to different people. Ask
the students to find the author of their cards
by asking questions. Write the questions on the
board and show them how to do this activity by
practicing with a few students.

Introduction   2 mins. ■■■

**Write all the objectives on the board from
Unit 1.** Show the students the first page of the
unit and mention the five objectives. Explain
that today is review and that they will review
the whole unit.

Note: Depending on the length of the term,
you may decide to have students do Presentation
and Practice 1 for homework and then review
students' work as either the warm-up or another
class activity.

Presentation 1   10–15 mins. ■■■

This presentation will cover the first three pages
of the review. Quickly go to the first page of
each lesson. Discuss the objective of each one.
Ask simple questions to remind students of what
they have learned.

Practice 1   15–20 mins. ■■■

Ⓐ Read. (Lessons 1–5)

Ⓑ Write. (Lessons 1–5)

Teaching Tip

Recycling/Review

The review process and the project that follows
are part of the recycling/review process.
Students at this level need to be reintroduced
to concepts to solidify what they have learned.
Many concepts are learned and then forgotten
while learning other new concepts. This is
because students learn but are not necessarily
ready to acquire language concepts.

Therefore, it becomes very important to review
and to show students how to review on their
own. It is also important to recycle the new
concepts in different contexts.

STANDARDS CORRELATIONS

CASAS: 0.1.1, 0.2.1, 7.4.1, 7.4.2, 7.4.3 (See CASAS Competency List
on pages 167–173.)
SCANS: **Basic Skills** Reading, writing, listening, speaking
Information Acquire and evaluate information, organize and maintain
information, interpret and communicate information

Thinking Skill See things in the mind's eye
EFF: **Communication** Speak so others can understand
Lifelong Learning Take responsibility for learning, reflect and evaluate

Practice 1 (continued)

C Speak to a partner. Write. (Lessons 1–4)

Monitor students' conversations.

D Match. (Lesson 3)

Go over the answers as a class.

C Speak to a partner. Write. (Lessons 1–4) (Answers will vary.)

You ask: What's your first name? What's your last name?
          What's your address? What's your phone number?

Adult School Application

Last Name	First Name

Birth Date / / /	Birthplace

Street Address

City	State	Zip Code

Phone Number

D Match. (Lesson 3)

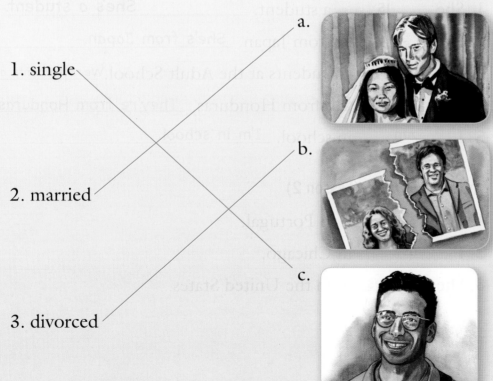

1. single

2. married

3. divorced

a.

b.

c.

Review

E Circle. (Lessons 1 and 2)

1.

(She) / He / They
is from Germany.

3.

She /(He)/ They
is Ron Carter.

2.

She / He /(They)
are in school.

4.

She / He /(We)
live in Fort Lauderdale.

F Write the *be* verb. Then, write the sentence with a contraction. (Lesson 3)

1. She _____is_____ a student. _____She's a student._____

2. She _____is_____ from Japan. _She's from Japan._

3. We _____are_____ students at the Adult School. _We're students at the Adult School._

4. They _____are_____ from Honduras. _They're from Honduras._

5. I _____am_____ in school. _I'm in school._

G Write *live* or *lives*. (Lesson 2)

1. He _____lives_____ in Portugal.

2. I _____live_____ in Chicago.

3. She _____lives_____ in the United States.

Practice 1 (continued)

(E) Circle. (Lessons 1 and 2)

Help as necessary.

(F) Write the *be* verb. Then, write the sentence with a contraction. (Lesson 3)

Help as necessary.

(G) Write *live* or *lives*. (Lesson 2)

Help as necessary.

Evaluation 1   5 mins. ■■■

Go around the room and check on student progress. If you see consistent errors among several students, interrupt the class and give a mini lesson or review to help students feel comfortable with the concept.

Presentation 2 — 15–20 mins.

My Dictionary

Show students an example of a set of 3-by-5 index cards that have been made into flash cards as described in My Dictionary. For students who are new to this concept, you will need to walk them through it. You may choose to do some of the four words with them.

Practice 2 — 5–7 mins.

Do My Dictionary.

Evaluation 2 — 5 mins.

Ask students to share their cards.

Presentation 3 — 5 mins.

Learner Log

Review the concepts in the Learner Log. Make sure students understand the concepts and how to do the log, including the check marks.

Teaching Tip

Learner Logs

Learner logs function to help students in many different ways.

1. They serve as part of the review process.
2. They help students to gain confidence and document what they have learned. In this way, students see that they are progressing and want to move forward in learning.
3. They provide students with a tool that they can use over and over to check and recheck their understanding. In this way, students become independent learners.

Practice 3 — 10–15 mins.

Ask students to do the Learner Log in pairs.

Evaluation 3 — 2 mins.

Go over the Learner Log with students.

Application — 5–7 mins.

Ask students to write down the page number of their favorite lesson in the unit.

My Dictionary

Make flash cards to improve your vocabulary.

1. Choose four new words from this unit.
2. Write each word on an index card or on a piece of paper.
3. On the back of the card or paper, draw a picture of the word, find and write a sentence from the book with the word, and write the page number.
4. Study the words.

You are married.
page 8

Learner Log

Write the page number(s).

	Page Number	I can do it. ✓
1. *I / You / He / She / We / They*	2	
2. Birthplace	5	
3. *am / are / is*	8	
4. *divorced / married / single*	7	
5. Address	10	
6. The date today	14	
7. Birth date	14	

My favorite page in this unit is <u>(Answers will vary.)</u>

Team Project

Make a class book.

I am Yolanda Alvarez. My address is ...

1. Form a team with four or five students. In your team, you need:

POSITION	JOB	STUDENT NAME
Student 1: Team Leader	See that everyone speaks English. See that everyone participates.	
Student 2: Writer	Write information.	
Student 3: Artist	Draw pictures.	
Students 4/5: Spokespeople	Organize presentation.	

2. Write the information for the members of your team.

   What's your first name?

   What's your last name?

   What's your address?

   What's your phone number?

   What's your birth date?

   What's your marital status? (Are you married?)

3. Draw a picture or add a photo of each member.

4. Make a team book.

5. Do a presentation about your team.

6. Make a class book with the other teams.

Introduction

5 mins. ■■□□

In this project, students will work in teams to create a book. First, they will make a mini book in teams of four or five. Then you can bring the mini books together to create a class book. These books can be about real class members, but due to the personal nature of the information to be published, you may opt to have the students create fictitious characters. The teams can complete the project, including a presentation on a second day if necessary.

Stage 1

10–15 mins. ■■■□

Form a team with four or five students.

 Refer to the Activity Bank CD-ROM for a profile template (AB Unit 1, Project 1).

Complete two or three example profiles with students as a class. Write the position responsibilities on the board as identified on the project page. Simulate a group activity by arbitrarily assigning positions. Help students understand the process.

Next, help students form groups and assign positions within their groups. On the spot, students will have to choose who will be the leader of their group. Review the responsibility of the leader and ask students to write the name of their leader in the books.

Do the same with the remaining positions: writer, artist, and spokesperson. If there are five people in the group, double up on the position of spokesperson. Every member of a group should have a responsibility.

Stage 2

20–30 mins.

Write the information for all the members of your team on a separate sheet of paper.

Ask students to complete the worksheet as a team.

Stage 3

10–15 mins.

Draw a picture or add a photo of each member.

Stage 4

10–15 mins.

Make a team book.

Ask teams to decorate the five pages and combine them to make a book.

Stage 5

10–30 mins.

Do a presentation about your team's members.

Ask teams to prepare a presentation. Each student on the team will talk about one page. The presentation can be merely students introducing themselves and reading the information while showing the picture. The activity can be more effective if you videotape the presentations for student review.

Stage 6

20–30 mins.

Make a class book with the other teams.

Collect all the pages and create a class book. As a class, you might suggest putting the pages in alphabetical order by students' last names and creating a table of contents and cover page. (Show examples of this from actual books.) Be sure to display the students' work.

STANDARDS CORRELATIONS

CASAS: 0.1.1, 0.2.1, 4.8.1 (See CASAS Competency List on pages 167–173.)
SCANS: Basic Skills Reading, writing, listening, speaking
Resources Allocate time, allocate money, allocate materials and facility resources, allocate human resources
Information Acquire and evaluate information, organize and maintain information, interpret and communicate information, use computers to process information
Interpersonal: Participate as a member of a team, teach others, serve clients and customers, exercise leadership, negotiate to arrive at a decision, work with cultural diversity

Systems Understand systems, monitor and correct performance, improve and design systems
Thinking Skills Think creatively, make decisions, solve problems, see things in the mind's eye
Personal Qualities Responsibility, sociability, self management
EFF: Communication Read with understanding, convey ideas in writing, speak so others can understand, listen actively, observe critically
Decision Making Solve problems and make decisions, plan
Interpersonal Cooperate with others, advocate and influence, resolve conflict and negotiate, guide others
Lifelong Learning Take responsibility for learning, reflect and evaluate

Objective: Introduce your classmates
Grammar: Possessive pronouns
Pronunciation: Question intonation
Academic Strategy: Focused listening
Vocabulary: *introduce, lives, address, phone number, this is, meet*

RESOURCES

Activity Bank: Lesson 1, Worksheets 1 and 2
Reading and Writing Challenge: Unit 2
Grammar Challenge: Unit 2, Challenge 1

■ 1.5 hour classes ■ 2.5 hour classes ■ 3+ hour classes

Audio: CD 1, Tracks 30–31
Heinle Picture Dictionary: Wave, Greet, Smile, pages 40–41

Stand Out Basic Assessment CD-ROM with Exam*View*®

AGENDA

Line up in alphabetical order by first name.
Learn and practice possessive adjectives.
Learn different forms of introduction.
Ask questions.

 Preassessment *(optional)*

Use the Stand Out Basic Assessment CD-ROM with Exam*View*® to create a pretest for Unit 2.

Warm-up and Review 10-12 mins.

Write the alphabet across the board. Review each letter by pointing to it and asking students to call out the name of the letter. Then write a student's name on the board under the letter that corresponds to the student's first name. Show the students, for example, that *Juan* goes under *J.* Next, show students how to form a line in alphabetical order by first name.

Introduction 2 mins.

Write the day of the week, the date, and the agenda on the board. Say the date while pointing to it and have students repeat it. Introduce yourself to the class. State the objective: *Today we will introduce classmates.*

Presentation 1 12-15 mins.

Invite three volunteers to the front of the classroom. Ask them: *What's your name? What's your address? What's your phone number?* Teach students that if they don't want to give out this information, they may say, *That's personal.* Write the phrase on the board.

A **Look at the picture. Predict. Where are they from?**

Ask students to open their books and briefly discuss the picture. Ask students where they think Edgar and Julie are from. Some students may read ahead to the information in Exercise B. This is expected.

B **Listen and practice.**

Play the recording. Ask students to follow along as they listen.

> **Listening Script** CD 1, Track 30
>
> The listening script matches the paragraphs in Exercise B.

Practice 1 5-7 mins.

Ask students in groups of three to write a conversation, using the student names as well as the teacher's name, Mr. Jackson, in Exercise B. Ask them to switch roles until all students have played the role of Mr. Jackson.

Evaluation 1 3-5 mins.

Ask volunteers to perform their conversation in front of the class.

STANDARDS CORRELATIONS

CASAS: 0.1.4 (See CASAS Competency List on pages 167-173.)
SCANS: Basic Skills Reading, writing, listening, speaking

EFF: Communication Convey ideas in writing, speak so others can understand, listen actively

Our Class

GOALS

➤ Introduce your classmates
➤ Describe your classroom
➤ Identify classroom activities

➤ Tell time
➤ Describe weather

LESSON 1

Meet my friend.

GOAL ➤ Introduce your classmates

A Look at the picture. Predict. Where are they from?

  B Listen and practice.

CD 1
TR 30

    I want to introduce two new students today. This is Edgar. He is from Senegal. He lives in Sacramento. His phone number is (916) 555-3765.
    Meet Julie. She is also a new student. She is from Canada. She lives in Folsom. Her number is (916) 555-4565.

C Read the chart.

		Possessive Adjectives
Subject	**Possessive adjective**	**Example sentence**
I	my	**My** phone number is 555-3456.
you	your	**Your** address is 2359 Maple Drive.
he	his	**His** name is Edgar.
she	her	**Her** name is Julie.
we	our	**Our** last name is Perez.
they	their	**Their** teacher is Mr. Jackson.

D Look at the pictures and complete the sentences.

This is Mr. Jackson.

____His____ phone number is

555-2813. ____His____ address

is 3317 Maple Drive.

Irma and Edgar are married.

____Their____ phone number is

555-2350. ____Their____ address

is 1700 Burns Avenue.

E Complete the sentences.

1. John is single. ____His____ address is 3215 Park Street.

2. You are a student here. ____Your____ phone number is 555-2121, right?

3. We are from Russia. ____Our____ address is 1652 Main Street.

4. I am a new student. ____My____ name is Julie.

Presentation 2   7–10 mins. ■■■

Write on the board: *My name is* ____ (your name). Ask students to introduce themselves using the phrase. After each student says his or her name in a sentence, ask the class a question: *What's his/her name?* Write the answers on the board. For example, if a student's name is John, write: *His name is John.* Circle *His* or *Her* in each sentence you write on the board. Check for understanding by pointing to the people on the previous page and asking: *What's his name? What's her name?*

C) Read the chart.

Ask students to look at the chart at the top of the page. Point out to them the relationship between the pronouns and the possessive adjectives. Drill students by pointing to a male student in the class and asking them to say: *His name is* _____ (student's name). Then point to a female student, prompting them to say: *Her name is* _____ (student's name). Do this with groups of students to show all forms. Be careful to always include *name* so students don't confuse *he* and *she* with the possessive adjective.

Teaching Tip

Metalanguage

Metalanguage in teaching English refers to the labels we give grammatical structures. In this case, we are introducing the possessive adjective.

Students don't need metalanguage to speak English well or to understand grammar. Some English speakers may never know what the *third-person singular* is. However, sometimes when working with adults, some identification of grammar structures can help them to identify things they have learned earlier and to apply them to new structures.

For shorter classes, ask students to do Exercises D and E for homework.

Practice 2   5–7 mins. ■■

D) Look at the pictures and complete the sentences.

Give the students minimal instructions (if any) to do this activity. Allow them time to figure out what to do. Have them work together, if necessary. The instructions don't say to use the possessive adjectives, but students should be able to relate the practice to the presentation.

E) Complete the sentences.

Help as necessary.

Evaluation 2   7–10 mins. ■■

Check students' book work.

Presentation 3   12-15 mins.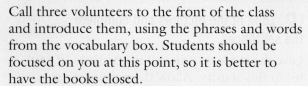

Call three volunteers to the front of the class and introduce them, using the phrases and words from the vocabulary box. Students should be focused on you at this point, so it is better to have the books closed.

F **Learn the introductions.**

Students may resist using *this* because the form isn't common in some other languages. However, it is important that they learn it in preparation for future projects they will do in *Stand Out Basic*.

Show them how *this* is only used when introducing one person and is not used in the plural.

At this point if you feel your students are ready, you may add other ways to make introductions.

Write the three phrases across the board. Say each one in random order and ask students to point to the one you say. This activity will prepare them for the listening practice that will follow.

Practice 3   5 mins.

G **Listen and circle.**

 Listening Script   CD 1, Track 31

1. **Mr. Jackson:** *Hi, Edgar. I want to introduce you to Susan. She is a friend of mine from class.*
   Edgar: *Hello, Susan. Nice to meet you.*
   Susan: *Nice to meet you, too.*
2. **Mr. Jackson:** *Class, it is my pleasure to tell you about a new student. Please meet Jonathan. He is from Canada. His address and phone number are available if you want to contact him.*
3. **Susan:** *My name is Susan and this is my good friend, Emanuel. Emanuel is from Israel. We live in Sacramento. Our class is next door.*
   John: *Nice to meet you. What's your teacher's name?*
   Susan: *It's Mr. Jackson.*

Evaluation 3   3 mins.

Check students' answers. Play the recording more than once if necessary.

 Refer students to *Stand Out Basic Grammar Challenge*, Unit 2, Challenge 1 for more practice with possessive adjectives.

Application   5-7 mins.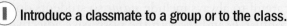

Review the pronunciation box with students. Show them that the emphasis is placed on the first word in this type of question. You may drill students by having them stand when saying the emphasized word and sitting afterwards.

H **Talk to four classmates.**

Have students complete the chart with the information they gather from four classmates.

I **Introduce a classmate to a group or to the class.**

Have students present the information about one of the classmates they talked to in Exercise H.

GOAL ➤ Introduce your classmates

F Learn the introductions.

This is …

Meet …

I want to introduce …

This is

This is Oscar.

This is Julie.

G Listen and circle.

CD 1
TR 31

1. This is   Meet   (I want to introduce)

2. This is   (Meet)   I want to introduce

3. (This is)   Meet   I want to introduce

Pronunciation

Emphasis

➤ WHAT'S your name?

➤ WHAT'S your address?

➤ WHAT'S your phone number?

H Talk to four classmates. (Answers will vary.)

Name (What's your name?)	Phone number (What's your phone number?)	Address (What's your address?)
1.		
2.		
3.		
4.		

I Introduce a classmate to a group or to the class.

LESSON **2** # Where's the pencil sharpener?

GOAL ➤ Describe your classroom

 A Listen and repeat. Point to the picture.

CD 1
TR 32

> | trash can   file cabinets   board   bookcase   plant   door |

B Write in the picture: *desk, tables, computers, chairs,* and *books.*

  C Listen and point.

CD 1
TR 33

Pronunciation

Emphasis

➤ WHERE'S the door?

➤ WHERE'S the trash can?

➤ WHERE'S the pencil sharpener?

 D Ask questions and point. *Where's the <u>desk</u>? (trash can, board, bookcase, plant, door, pencil sharpener, computer)*

Objective: Describe your classroom
Grammar: Prepositions of location
Pronunciation: Question intonation
Academic Strategy: Focused listening
Vocabulary: Classroom objects, prepositions

RESOURCES

Activity Bank: Lesson 2, Worksheet 1
Reading and Writing Challenge: Unit 2
Grammar Challenge: Unit 2, Challenge 2

Audio: CD 1, Tracks 32–33
Heinle Picture Dictionary: Classroom, pages 18–19: In, On, Under, pages 12–13

■ 1.5 hour classes   ■ 2.5 hour classes   ■ 3⁺ hour classes

AGENDA

Learn classroom vocabulary.
Learn prepositions of location.
Draw your classroom.
Write about your classroom.

Warm-up and Review   10-15 mins. ■■■

Ask students to get in groups of three and introduce each member to another group.

Introduction   5 mins. ■■■

Write the day, the date, and the agenda on the board. Say the date and have students repeat it. Ask students to point to objects in the classroom, for example: *Point to the teacher's desk.* Help them understand by modeling. Next, express where the item is by using a preposition of location. State the objective: *Today we will describe our classroom.*

Presentation 1   15-20 mins. ■■■

Go over the new vocabulary in the picture.

 Listen and repeat. Point to the picture.

 Listening Script   CD 1, Track 32

Listening script matches the word list in Exercise A.

 Write in the picture: *desk, tables, computers, chairs,* and *books.*

To prepare for the next activity, use the new vocabulary in sentences and ask students to point.

 Listen and point.

Briefly go over the pronunciation box.

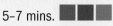 **Listening Script**   CD 1, Track 33

May I have your attention, please? Class, I want to give you a quick tour of the classroom and talk about some class rules. Look around and see if you can find the items I will describe to you. Of course, the board is in the front of the class. Here, I write important information. If you need a pencil sharpener, please use the electric one during group work, and not when I am talking. We can move tables in the classroom when it is necessary to do group work. If you need to borrow a book, go to the bookcase. Please don't leave trash around the room. Use the trash can whenever possible. Finally, we will use the computers in the back of the room twice a week. I hope you know that I don't want you sitting in your chairs all the time. You will have many opportunities to get up and walk around. Also, we will keep the door closed during class, so you can concentrate on your work in the class. Any questions?

Practice 1   5-7 mins. ■■■

 Ask questions and point. *Where's the **desk**?* *(trash can, board, bookcase, plant, door, pencil sharpener, computer)*

Ask students to work in pairs.

Evaluation 1   5-7 mins. ■■■

Observe students doing the activity.

STANDARDS CORRELATIONS

CASAS: 0.1.5 (See CASAS Competency List on pages 167–173.)
SCANS: **Basic Skills** Listening, speaking
Information Acquire and evaluate information, organize and maintain information, interpret and communicate information

Interpersonal Teach others
EFF: **Communication** Speak so others can understand, listen actively

Presentation 2

12-15 mins.

With books closed, ask students where something is in the classroom. Try to elicit information from the students instead of merely giving them prepositions. The conversation with students might go something like this:

Teacher: *Where's the file cabinet?*
[Students point.]
Teacher: *Where?*
Students point again. One or two students say: *There.*
Teacher: *Where is it?*
One or two students might say *next to the desk* or something similar. If they don't, the teacher can cue them.
Teacher: *Next to . . .* Pause for student responses.

Teaching Tip

Eliciting information

The *Stand Out* approach suggests that— as much as possible—instructors elicit information from students, first, before giving them the information. This is an important principle in Student-Centered Instruction (SCI). By first eliciting information, the teacher is able to better determine what students already know.

E Read.

Guide students through the information.

F Read.

Drill the students on the new prepositions by looking back at the previous page and asking them where various items are. This might also be a good place to use or create hand signals to identify certain or all the prepositions.

Briefly show the students how Exercises E and F are different. The point of this lesson is not to show students how to make singular and plural questions using *where;* however, students need to be aware that there is a difference.

Show students how to do Practice 2. Take plenty of time to set this up for them. Model it with several students until you are confident that they will have success when they do it in pairs.

Practice 2

10-12 mins.

G Ask *where is the* teacher, plant, and trash can. Ask *where are the* file cabinets, students, and books.

Student A asks the questions from Exercises E and F. Student B answers while Student A checks to see that Student B is correct. Student B should only look at page 24. After completing the activity, students should reverse roles.

Evaluation 2

5 mins.

Ask volunteers to perform their conversations.

E Read.

Prepositions of Location	
	Where is the desk? It is **next to** the door.
	Where is the plant? It is **on** the desk.
	Where is the trash can? It is **between** the desk and the bookcase.

F Read.

Prepositions of Location	
	Where are the file cabinets? They are **in back of** the computers.
	Where are the students? They are **in front of** the board.
	Where are the books? They are **in** the bookcase.

G Ask *where is the* teacher, plant, and trash can. Ask *where are the* file cabinets, students, and books.

EXAMPLE: *A:* Where is the teacher?
　　　　　B: He is next to the door.

LESSON **2**

GOAL ➤ **Describe your classroom**

H In groups, draw your classroom. (Answers will vary.)

[blank drawing box]

I Write. (Answers will vary.)

1. Where is the teacher's desk? _____

2. Where is the trash can? _____

3. Where is the board? _____

4. Where are the books? _____

5. Where are the file cabinets? _____

Presentation 3 — 15-20 mins. ■■■

Ask students again where things in the classroom are. When you are confident that students understand that they are to draw the classroom showing where objects are in relation to each other, divide them into groups.

For shorter classes, ask students to do Exercise H for homework.

Practice 3 — 15-20 mins. ■

(H) In groups, draw your classroom.

Encourage students to use prepositions of location in their groups. Walk around during this activity and ask students questions using the prepositions.

Teaching Tip

Random grouping

Sometimes grouping students randomly without consideration for native language or proficiency is appropriate. A few techniques for random grouping include the following:

Counting off: You want four students in each group. You have 32 students in the class. Have students count off from one to eight. All ones work together, all twos work together, etc.

Birthday months: Students whose birthdays are in the same month work together. The benefit is that students get to know one another better and they recycle learning about months. This method, however, takes a lot of instructor assistance because it is difficult to get even groups. Try having students stand for each month of the year and forming groups from those who are standing.

Playing cards: If you have 28 students in your class, you would use all the playing cards from aces to sevens. Shuffle and pass out the cards to all students. The students with aces work together as do the students with twos, etc.

Evaluation 3 — 15-20 mins. ■

Observe students' work.

 Refer students to *Stand Out Basic Grammar Challenge*, Unit 2, Challenge 2 for more practice with prepositions of location.

Application — 5-7 mins. ■■■

(I) Write.

Have students complete the exercise in groups or in pairs.

Activity Bank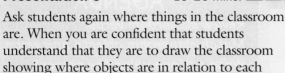

Lesson 2, Worksheet 1: Prepositions of Location

Instructor's Notes

_____
_____
_____
_____
_____
_____
_____
_____
_____
_____
_____
_____
_____
_____
_____
_____
_____
_____
_____
_____
_____
_____

Objective: Identify classroom activities
Grammar: Present continuous
Academic Strategy: Focused listening
Vocabulary: Classroom verbs; *pen, pencil, book, notebook, CD, magazine*

RESOURCES

Activity Bank: Lesson 3, Worksheet 1
Reading and Writing Challenge: Unit 2
Grammar Challenge: Unit 2, Challenge 3

Audio: CD 1, Track 34
Heinle Picture Dictionary: Listen, Read, Write, pages 20–21

■ 1.5 hour classes ■ 2.5 hour classes ■ 3· hour classes

AGENDA

Review classroom verbs.
Match classroom objects and verbs.
Write actions using the present continuous.

Warm-up and Review 12–15 mins.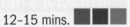

Write these words on the board: *pencil sharpener, board, teacher's desk, trash can, bookcase, door, file cabinet.* Write a sentence describing the location of the trash can, for example: *It's next to the teacher's desk.* Ask students to name the item. Ask students to write sentences about each item using *It's* and quiz a partner. Have a few students report to the class.

Introduction 2 mins.

Write the day of the week and the date on the board. Say the date and have students repeat. Pantomime *reading, talking, listening, sitting, standing,* and *writing.* State the objective: *Today we will identify classroom activities.*

Note: In this lesson, students will be introduced to the present continuous. Students are not expected to fully grasp the structure at this time.

Presentation 1 7–10 mins.

Ask students to open their books. Look at the picture with them. Ask them to point to any activities they recognize. Pantomime the actions again and write the words in Exercise B on the board. Ask students to find these actions in the picture. Help students to prepare for the listening task by using the words in sentences and asking them to point to each action.

(A) Listen and point.

🎧 **Listening Script** CD 1, Track 34

> All the students work hard in Mr. Jackson's English class. Two students are talking in the back of the room about their homework. One student is writing at his desk. Shiro is at his desk, too. He is listening to a tape. Julie is reading. She is a good student.

Practice 1 3 mins.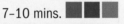

(B) Write the names of the students.

Do the first item as a class. After students complete this exercise, have them work in pairs. Student A reads a word and Student B points to the picture. Then they reverse roles. Then ask them to invert the activity. Student A points to an action and Student B says the word.

Evaluation 1 3 mins.

Observe students as they perform the task.

Teaching Tip

Step-by-step

At this level, it is important that you only ask students to do one at a time. Carefully model the target behavior. Let students know how much time they have to complete each task, but monitor them to make sure they don't lose interest sooner.

STANDARDS CORRELATIONS

CASAS: 0.1.5 (See CASAS Competency List on pages 167-173.)
SCANS: Basic Skills Listening, speaking
Information Acquire and evaluate information, organize and maintain information, interpret and communicate information

Interpersonal Teach others
EFF: Communication Speak so others can understand, listen actively

 **LESSON 3**

What are you doing?

GOAL ➤ Identify classroom activities

  A Listen and point.

CD 1
TR 34

Shiro • Julie • Concepción • Edgar

B Write the names of the students.

1. listen _____Shiro_____
2. read _____Julie_____
3. write _____Edgar_____
4. talk _____Concepción_____

GOAL ➤ **Identify classroom activities**

Vocabulary   Grammar
Life Skills
Academic   Pronunciation

| pen | pencil | book | notebook | CD | magazine | teacher |

C **Write and match.**

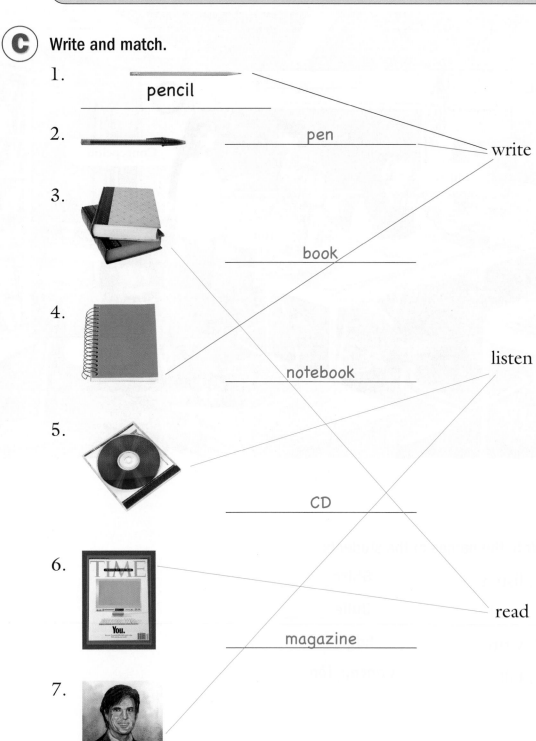

1. pencil

2. pen

3. book

4. notebook

5. CD

6. magazine

7. teacher

write

listen

read

Presentation 2   10-12 mins. ▪▪□

Put examples of the items listed in the vocabulary box on a table in front of the room. Go over the vocabulary and help students with correct pronunciation.

Do a Total Physical Response (TPR) activity. In this activity, students learn the vocabulary by standing up and going through simple motions. Demonstrate the activity and then ask students to do it. Ask different students to stand up, come to the front of class, pick up, and put down a designated item.

Write the four verbs on the board again: *listen, write, read,* and *talk.*

Ask students to do another TPR activity slightly different from the one you have just done. Have a student come to the board and circle one of the four verbs that can best be associated with the item you give them. For example, if you give the student a pencil, he or she should circle the verb *write.*

Teaching Tip

Total Physical Response

Total Physical Response, or TPR, was developed by Dr. James J. Asher. The basic idea is that when students engage physically, learning improves. Also, TPR permits students to react to the language without speaking immediately.

For shorter classes, ask students to do Exercises C, D, and E for homework.

Practice 2   5-7 mins. ▪□

 Write and match.

Ask students to complete this activity either in pairs or on their own. Note: that the verb *write* has three matches: *pencil, pen,* and *notebook.*

Evaluation 2   5-7 mins. ▪▪□

Drill students by saying one of the nouns and asking students to respond with the corresponding verb. You can check students' understanding better if you assign each verb a number. Instead of responding with the verb, ask students to show the number of fingers that corresponds to the verbs you have numbered.

Presentation 3   7-10 mins. ▪▪▪

Play the recording from page 27 (CD 1, Track 34) again. Ask students to listen carefully to the verbs. Write on the board: *Julie is reading.* Play the recording one more time and ask students to listen for this sentence.

(D) Read.

Read the chart with students. This is their first exposure to the present continuous. It is not separated into morphemes and students are not expected at this point to transfer the information to other verbs. Spelling is also a consideration, but since this structure is only presented for awareness purposes, spelling rules are not introduced. Students will be asked to copy the sentences in the next activity. Point out the spelling issues but avoid offering rules at this point.

Practice 3   7-10 mins. ▪

(E) Write.

Ask students to write the information in the lines provided. Point out that a period is necessary at the end of each sentence they produce.

Evaluation 3   5-7 mins. ▪

Ask students to write their sentences on the board.

 Refer students to *Stand Out Basic Grammar Challenge*, Unit 2, Challenge 3 for more practice with the present continuous.

Application   5-7 mins. ▪▪▪

(F) Write four sentences about your classmates.

Help as necessary.

 Read.

Present Continuous	
He is reading.	She is reading.
He is writing.	She is writing.
He is listening.	She is listening.
He is talking.	She is talking.
He is sitting.	She is sitting.
He is standing.	She is standing.

She is standing.

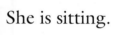

She is sitting.

E **Write.**

1. She is reading.
2. She is listening.

3. He is standing.
4. He is talking.

5. She is sitting.
6. She is writing.

F Write four sentences about your classmates. (Answers will vary.)

EXAMPLE: Juan is sitting.

1. _____
2. _____
3. _____
4. _____

When is English class?

GOAL ➤ Tell time

 A Read and listen.

CD 1
TR 35

Shiro's Schedule
MONDAY

9:00 a.m.	English Class
12:00 p.m.	Lunch
1:00 p.m.	Pronunciation Class
4:00 p.m.	Work

Pronunciation

Emphasis

➤ WHEN'S English class?

➤ WHEN'S lunch?

➤ WHEN'S pronunciation class?

B Look at Shiro's schedule. Write.

1. When's English class? _____ It's at 9:00 A.M.

2. When's lunch? _____ It's at 12:00 P.M.

3. When's pronunciation class? _____ It's at 1:00 P.M.

4. When's work? _____ It's at 4:00 P.M.

AT-A-GLANCE PREP

Objective: Tell time
Pronunciation: Question intonation
Academic Strategies: Focused listening, scheduling
Vocabulary: *schedule, lunch, work, pronunciation, bed*

RESOURCES

Activity Bank: Lesson 4, Worksheets 1, 2, and 3
Reading and Writing Challenge: Unit 2
Grammar Challenge: Unit 2, Challenge 4

Audio: CD 1, Tracks 35–37
Heinle Picture Dictionary: Time, pages 4–5

 1.5 hour classes   2.5 hour classes   ▨ 3⁺ hour classes

AGENDA
Review classroom actions.
Study a schedule.
Read clocks.
Practice talking about time.

Warm-up and Review   2-5 mins. ▰▰▱

Write on the board: *write.* Have students repeat the word a few times. Pantomime *listen, read, talk, sit,* and *stand.* Ask students in groups to choose one person to pantomime the verbs while the rest of the group responds with the action word.

Introduction   10-12 mins. ▰▰▰

Write the day of the week and the date on the board. Say the date while pointing to it. Write your daily schedule on the board using the format on page 30. Review your schedule by giving the time for each activity. State the objective: *Today we will learn to tell time.*

Presentation 1   12-15 mins. ▰▰▱

(A) Read and listen.

Go over the schedule in the book with students and ask them the time of each activity. Be sure to teach *A.M.* and *P.M.*, and practice the pronunciation of *o'clock.* Play the recording.

 Listening Script   CD 1, Track 35

Shiro has a busy schedule. He has English class at 9 A.M. At 12:00 he eats lunch. He goes to class again at 1:00 in the afternoon. He has pronunciation class. He goes to work at 4 P.M.

Review the pronunciation box. Make sure students understand on which word to place the emphasis.

Practice 1   3 mins. ▰▰▰

(B) Look at Shiro's schedule. Write.

Ask students to complete the exercise on their own. Then ask students to practice questions and answers in pairs. Help them use the correct pronunciation. The student asking the questions looks at Exercise B. The student answering looks only at Shiro's schedule in Exercise A. After a few minutes, ask students to reverse roles.

Evaluation 1   3 mins. ▰▰▰

Ask students to demonstrate for the class.

STANDARDS CORRELATIONS

CASAS: 0.2.1, 0.2.4, 2.3.1 (See CASAS Competency List on pages 167–173.)
SCANS: **Basic Skills** Writing, listening, speaking
Resources Allocate time

Information Acquire and evaluate information, organize and maintain information, interpret and communicate information
Systems Understand systems, monitor and correct performance
EFF: **Communication** Speak so others can understand, listen actively

Presentation 2   10–15 mins. ■■□

C What time is it now? Write.

D What time is it now? Bubble in and write.

Go over each of the clocks in Exercises C and D. These exercises should be done as a class. Help students to understand that they should only say *o'clock* on the hour.

If you have a clock that you can remove from the wall, write times on the board and have students come up and change the clock to the time given. Ask students when they eat lunch. Change the clock to read this time.

If students are ready, you might also teach them *quarter past* and *quarter to* the hour as well as other ways of giving the time.

Teaching Tip

Extending vocabulary

No textbook will give students every vocabulary word they will need. On the other hand, students at times may be overburdened by too many words. If you use a picture dictionary or add more vocabulary to a lesson, make sure students know what vocabulary items are a priority. Students with little formal education may get frustrated when given too much vocabulary. These students may only be able to handle six to ten new words a day.

Be aware of student needs. You may choose to use a vocabulary list that students maintain to help them know which words they are responsible for. One possible list is in the appendices of their books. To further remind them of what they absolutely need to learn and to add some accountability, consider giving a weekly spelling test on the words from their lists.

Practice 2   8–12 mins. ■■□

E Point and practice.

Ask students to work in pairs.

Teaching Tip

Group work

At this level, it is important to model group activities. A variety of grouping strategies are suggested depending on the task.

1. Allow students to self-select groups. Students sometimes perform well with people they feel comfortable with.
2. Arrange groups according to skill level. Proficient students can excel, while less proficient students don't feel intimidated.
3. Arrange diverse-ability groups. More proficient students often enjoy helping, and you'll have several mentors in the class instead of just one teacher.
4. Avoid homogeneous language groups to encourage the use of English.

Evaluation 2   7–10 mins. ■□

Observe students as they work together.

GOAL ➤ Tell time

C What time is it now? Write.

1.
It's ___3:00___.

2.
It's ___5:00___.

3.
It's ___7:00___.

4.
It's ___10:00___.

D What time is it now? Bubble in and write.

1.
● 3:30
○ 4:30
It's ___3:30___.

2.
○ 5:00
● 5:30
It's ___5:30___.

3.
○ 5:00
● 7:30
It's ___7:30___.

4.
● 10:30
○ 10:00
It's ___10:30___.

E Point and practice.

EXAMPLE: *A:* (Point to Number 3 in Exercise D.) What time is it?
　　　　　B: It's 7:30.

CD 1
TR 36

F **Listen and write.**

Julie's Schedule MONDAY		
__9:00__	**English Class**	
11:00	**Work**	
1:30	**Lunch**	
10:30	**Bedtime**	

CD 1
TR 37

G **Listen and read.**

Julie: When's English class?
Mr. Jackson: It's at 9:00.
Julie: What time is it now?
Mr. Jackson: It's 7:30.

Pronunciation

➤ WHEN'S English class?
It's *at* 9:00.

➤ What TIME is it now?
It's *at* 7:30.

H **Practice.** (Answers will vary.)

A: When's _____?

B: It's _____.

A: What time is it now?

B: It's _____.

I **Write your schedule on another piece of paper.** (Answers will vary.)

Presentation 3   15–20 mins.

(F) Listen and write.

Do this listening activity as a class, starting and stopping the CD several times.

 Listening Script   CD 1, Track 36

Cameron: *Hi, Julie. How are you?*
Julie: *Fine, thanks.*
Cameron: *What is your schedule today?*
Julie: *I have English class at 9:00, work at 11:00, lunch at 1:30, and finally I go to bed at 10:30 tonight.*
Cameron: *I see you are very busy. Maybe we could have lunch at 1:30.*
Julie: *That would be great!*

(G) Listen and read.

Practice the conversation with students. Ask them to practice briefly in pairs. Prepare students for Exercise H by going over the dialog and reviewing the pronunciation, as well as when and when not to use *at*.

 Listening Script   CD 1, Track 37

The listening script matches the conversation in Exercise G.

Practice 3   5 mins.

(H) Practice.

Ask students to take on the role of Julie or Mr. Jackson and ask questions about the schedule in Exercise F.

Evaluation 3   3 mins. ▪

Ask students to demonstrate the conversation in front of the class.

Teaching Tip

Demonstrations

Student demonstrations often help you to evaluate what students have learned. They also provide a model for the other students. Sometimes it becomes necessary to correct students in this circumstance to ensure that no faulty learning is occurring. Be careful to only correct where the error directly relates to the lesson objective. If a lot of correction is necessary, this indicates that more practice is needed.

 Refer students to *Stand Out Basic Grammar Challenge*, Unit 2, Challenge 4 for more practice with when and when not to use *at*.

Application   5–7 mins. ▪▪▪

(I) Write your schedule on another piece of paper.

Ask students to write their schedules on another piece of paper or use the template available on the Activity Bank CD-ROM.

Activity Bank

Lesson 4, Worksheet 1: Telling Time
Lesson 4, Worksheet 2: Schedules and Times
Lesson 4, Worksheet 3: Daily Planner

Instructor's Notes

Objective: Describe the weather

Grammar: Simple present with *need*

Pronunciation: Question intonation

Academic Strategy: Focused listening

Vocabulary: *windy, cloudy, foggy, sunny, rainy, snowy, cold, hot, weather*

RESOURCES

Activity Bank: Lesson 5, Worksheet 1

Reading and Writing Challenge: Unit 2

Grammar Challenge: Unit 2, Challenge 5

 1.5 hour classes   2.5 hour classes   3⁺ hour classes

AGENDA

Review schedules.

Listen about weather.

Talk about weather.

Talk about weather and clothes.

Predict the weather.

Audio: CD 1, Tracks 38–40

Heinle Picture Dictionary: Weather, pages 166–167

Warm-up and Review   10-12 mins.

Ask students to work in pairs, ask for their partner's schedule for the day, and write it down. Then ask them to report to another pair.

Introduction   2 mins.

Write the day of the week and the date on the board. Say the date while pointing to it and have students repeat it. Look outside and ask students if it is cold or hot today. State the objective: *Today we will learn to describe the weather.*

Presentation 1   5 mins.

Draw the sun on the board and label it. If you have a world or U.S. map, ask students where it might be sunny. You might want to cut out a sun and a picture of rain and have students tape the pictures on the map. Draw weather symbols for your city and say: *It's sunny (cloudy, rainy, etc.) in _____ (your city) today.* Ask students to repeat several times. Make gestures like fanning your face to indicate *It's hot!*

A Listen and repeat.

Discuss the meaning of each word and repeat the activity of finding places on the map that might have that particular weather. Do this for each new word.

Listening Script   CD 1, Track 38

The listening script matches the word list in Exercise A.

Prepare the students for Exercise B by saying the words and asking them to point to them. If you think the students are ready, try a short dictation of the words in the list.

Practice 1   3 mins.

B Listen and write.

Students often stop listening when they begin writing. Show them how to write the first letter of the word so that they can go back and complete it after the listening. You might need to play the recording several times.

Listening Script   CD 1, Track 39

This is Express Weather from Miami, Florida. We are happy to bring you the latest weather throughout the world. Let's start with Havana, Cuba. It's hot today in Havana with a temperature of 98 degrees. In Tokyo, Japan, it is cloudy and unusually cold for this time of year. In Patagonia, Chile, be careful when driving. It's very windy today. Moving along to the north of us in Montreal, Canada, the bitter cold is keeping everyone indoors. Yes, it's very cold. In Lisbon, Portugal, it's foggy at the docks and shipping is hampered. In Mombasa, Kenya, it's rainy and the rain will continue for several days.

STANDARDS CORRELATIONS

CASAS: 0.1.2, 0.2.1, 1.1.3, 2.3.3 (See CASAS Competency List on pages 167-173.)

SCANS: Basic Skills Reading, writing, listening, speaking

Information Acquire and evaluate information, organize and maintain information, interpret and communicate information

Interpersonal Participate as a member of a team, teach others

EFF: Communication Convey ideas in writing, speak so others can understand, listen actively

Interpersonal Cooperative with others

It's cold today.

GOAL ➤ Describe weather

  A Listen and repeat.

CD 1
TR 38

| windy | cloudy | foggy | rainy | snowy | cold | hot | sunny |

  B Listen and write.

CD 1
TR 39

hot

Havana, Cuba

cold

Montreal, Canada

cloudy

Tokyo, Japan

foggy

Lisbon, Portugal

windy

Patagonia, Chile

rainy

Mombasa, Kenya

GOAL ➤ Describe weather

C Review the weather.

Havana, Cuba

London, England

Capetown, South Africa

Moscow, Russia

Vancouver, Canada

Ensenada, Mexico

Pronunciation

CD 1
TR 40

Emphasis

➤ HOW'S the weather in Havana?

D Read and practice.

A: How's the weather in Havana, Cuba today?
B: It's hot and sunny.

Evaluation 1 2 mins.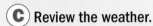

Go over the answers with the students.

Presentation 2 12-15 mins.

C Review the weather.

Ask students how the weather is in Havana, Cuba. Go on to ask them how it is in the other places listed. If you are using a world map, you can show them on the map, or cut out the symbols from the Activity Bank CD-ROM and place them on the map. You can also make flash cards with the symbols that you print from the Activity Bank CD-ROM and ask students to briefly quiz each other.

Say: *How's the weather?* Place the stress on *How's*.

Pronunciation

Information questions

To help students understand where to place the stress on the correct part of the question, you may try several different techniques.

1. Ask most of the students to say *How's* and ask only a few to finish the sentence with *the weather*.
2. Ask students to stand up on emphasized words and to sit on the others.
3. Ask students to repeat the phrase and add an exaggerated pause after *How's*.
4. Ask students to clap every time they say *How's*.
5. Create a song like the one below with emphasis on *How*, where *How* is spoken for a longer duration than other words.

 Listening Script *CD 1, Track 40*

How's the weather? How is the weather?
How's the weather in Havana today?
How's the weather? How is the weather?
How's the weather? It's hot today.

Practice 2 7-10 mins.

D Read and practice.

Show students how to substitute information about each location as they complete the conversation.

Evaluation 2 5 mins.

Ask for volunteers to demonstrate the questions and answers for different locations in front of the class.

Teaching Tip

Realia

Using realia is always effective in the ESL classroom. For example, in this lesson, if you were to bring in an umbrella, a heavy coat, mittens, or a ski mask, students would be able to associate the weather with the objects.

Presentation 3

12-15 mins. ■■■□

The following activities are in preparation for Exercise G. In exercise G, students will describe their needs when planning to come to class. To do this, they will need some additional vocabulary and possibly the simple present tense. Help students to prepare by going over the new vocabulary and doing Exercises E and F with them.

Use realia when possible with the vocabulary. Act out being very cold and ask students what you can do about it. A few students might know to use the word *coat, sweater,* or *jacket.* Write the words on the board and refer to the vocabulary.

(E) **Write the clothes above with the weather.**

(F) **Read.**

This grammar is still being introduced. Help students see that they need an *s* on the third-person singular. There is still no need to transfer this information to other verbs, but students can refer back to other pages in their books where the final *s* has been introduced. Specifically, see page 6.

Practice 3

7-10 mins. ■

(G) **Practice with *I, you, he, she, we,* and *they.***

Show students how to substitute information.

Evaluation 3

2 mins. ■

Ask volunteers to demonstrate Exercise G in front of the class.

📖 **Refer students to *Stand Out Basic Grammar Challenge*, Unit 2, Challenge 5 for more practice with the simple present.**

Application

5-7 mins. ■■□

(H) **In a group, predict the weather for the week. Write *sunny, windy, cloudy,* etc.**

After groups do this activity, ask them to report to the class and to compare what other groups wrote.

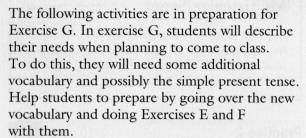 **(I)** **Active Task. Go to the Internet or look in the newspaper. How is the weather in your home country today?**

Instructor's Notes

_____

_____

_____

_____

_____

_____

_____

_____

_____

_____

_____

_____

_____

_____

_____

_____

_____

GOAL ➤ **Describe weather**

sandals

boots

a t-shirt

an umbrella

E Write the clothes above with the weather.

rainy

boots

an umbrella

sunny

sandals

a t-shirt

F Read.

Simple Present		
I, you, we, they	need	I **need** an umbrella.
he, she	needs	She **needs** an umbrella.

G Practice with *I, you, he, she, we,* and *they*.

A: How's the weather today?
B: It's rainy.
A: He needs an umbrella.

A: How's the weather today?
B: It's sunny.
A: I need a t-shirt.

H In a group, predict the weather for the week. Write *sunny, windy, cloudy,* etc. (Answers will vary.)

Monday	Tuesday	Wednesday	Thursday	Friday	Saturday	Sunday

  I **Active Task.** Go to the Internet or look in the newspaper. How is the weather in your home country today?

A Read. (Lesson 1)

1.

Application

Name
Choi Soon Young

Country of Origin
South Korea

Address
2237 Oakhave St.

City
Sacramento

State
CA

Zip Code
94203

Phone Number
916-555-7562

2.

Application

Names
Binh and Anh Duong

Country of Origin
Vietnam

Address
4471 Broadway

City
Sacramento

State
CA

Zip Code
94203

Phone Number
916-555-3765

B Complete. (Lesson 1)

1. This is Choi Soon. He is from South Korea. _____His_____ address is
2237 Oakhave St., Sacramento, CA 94203. _____His_____ phone number
is _____(916) 555-7562_____.

2. I want to introduce _____Binh_____ and _____Anh Duong_____. They are from
_____Vietnam_____. _____Their_____ address is 4471 Broadway, Sacramento, CA 04203.
_____Their_____ phone number is _____(914) 555-3765_____.

C Ask a classmate for information. Introduce your classmate to another student. (Lesson 1)

AT-A-GLANCE PREP

Objective: All unit objectives
Grammar: All unit grammar
Academic Strategies: Focused listening,
  reviewing, evaluating, developing study skills
Vocabulary: All unit vocabulary

AGENDA

Discuss unit objectives.
Complete the review.
Do My Dictionary.
Evaluate and reflect on progress.

■ 1.5 hour classes ■ 2.5 hour classes ■ 3⁺ hour classes

Warm-up and Review   5–7 mins.

Ask students to go through the unit and find
their favorite activity. Ask for volunteers to speak
up about what they liked about it.

Introduction   2 mins.

**Write all the objectives on the board from
Unit 2.** Show students the first page of the unit
and mention the five objectives. Explain that
today is review and that they will review the
whole unit.

Note: Depending on the length of the term, you
may decide to have students do Exercises A–H
for homework and then review student work as
the warm-up for another class meeting.

Presentation 1   10–15 mins.

This presentation will cover the first three pages
of the review. Quickly go to the first page of
each lesson. Discuss the objective of each. Ask
simple questions to remind students what they
have learned.

Practice 1   15–20 mins.

Ⓐ Read. (Lesson 1)

Ask students to read the application forms silently.

Ⓑ Complete. (Lesson 1)

Ask students to complete the personal
information using the application forms from
Exercise A.

Ⓒ Ask a classmate for information. Introduce
your classmate to another student. (Lesson 1)

Teaching Tip

Recycling/Review

The review process and the project that
follows are part of the recycling/review
process. Students at this level often need to be
reintroduced to concepts to solidify what they
have learned. Many concepts are learned and
forgotten while learning other new concepts.
This is because students learn but are not
necessarily ready to acquire language concepts.

Therefore, it becomes very important to review
and to show students how to review on their
own. It is also important to recycle the new
concepts in different contexts.

STANDARDS CORRELATIONS

CASAS: 0.1.5, 2.3.1, 2.3.2, 2.3.3, 7.4.1, 7.4.2, 7.4.3 (See CASAS
Competency List on pages 167–173.)
SCANS: **Basic Skills** Reading, writing, listening, speaking
Information Acquire and evaluate information, organize and maintain
information, interpret and communicate information

Thinking Skills See things in the mind's eye
***EFF:* Communication** Speak so others can understand, listen actively
Lifelong Learning Take resposibility for learning, reflect and evalute

Practice 1 *(continued)*

D Read. (Lessons 4 and 5)

Ask students to read the information in the exercise silently.

E Write. (Lessons 4 and 5)

Have students work by themselves to complete the activity using the information from Exercise D.

Seoul, Korea

Guadalajara, Mexico

Roanne, France

Lao Cai, Vietnam

E Write. (Lessons 4 and 5)

1. How's the weather in Korea? _It's rainy in Korea._
   What time is it? _It's 8:00._

2. How's the weather in France? _It's windy in France._
   What time is it? _It's 1:00._

3. How's the weather in Mexico? _It's sunny in Mexico._
   What time is it? _It's 6:00._

4. How's the weather in Vietnam? _It's cloudy in Vietnam._
   What time is it? _It's 6:00._

Review

F Write. (Lesson 4)

It's 3:30.   It's 6:30.   It's 12:00.   It's 7:00.

G Match. Draw a line. (Lesson 3)

1.

       a. He is listening.

2.

       b. He is writing.

3.

       c. She is talking.

4.

       d. He is reading.

H Write. (Lesson 2)

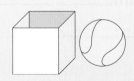  

in   next to   between   on

Practice 1 (continued)

F Write. (Lesson 4)

Have students work independently to write the correct times.

G Match. Draw a line. (Lesson 3)

Have students work independently to match the pictures with the classroom activity.

H Write. (Lesson 2)

Have students work independently to write the correct prepositions.

Evaluation 1   15 mins. ■■■■

Go around the room and check on students' progress. Help individuals when needed. If you see consistent errors among several students, interrupt the class and give a mini lesson or review to help students feel comfortable with the concept.

Presentation 2   15–20 mins. ■■■

My Dictionary

Show students an example of a set of 3-by-5 index cards that have been made into flash cards as described in My Dictionary. For the students new to this concept, you will need to walk them through it. You may choose to do some of the four words with them.

Practice 2   5–7 mins. ■■

Do My Dictionary.

Evaluation 2   5 mins. ■■

Ask students to share their cards.

Presentation 3   5 mins. ■■■

Learner Log

Review the concepts in the Learner Log. Make sure students understand the concepts and how to do the log including the check marks.

Teaching Tip

Learner Logs

Learner logs function to help students in many different ways.

1. They serve as part of the review process.
2. They help students to gain confidence and document what they have learned. In this way, students see that they are progressing and want to move forward in learning.
3. They provide students with a tool that they can use over and over to check and recheck their understanding. In this way, students become independent learners.

Practice 3   10–15 mins.

Ask students in pairs to do the Learner Log.

Evaluation 3   2 mins. ■

Go over the Learner Log with students.

Application   5–7 mins. ■■■

Ask students to write down the page number of their favorite lesson in this unit.

My Dictionary

Make flash cards to improve your vocabulary.

1. Choose four new words from this unit.
2. Write each word on an index card or on a piece of paper.
3. On the back of the card or paper, draw a picture, find and write a sentence from the book with the word, and write the page number.
4. Study the words.

It's hot and sunny.
page 34

Learner Log

Write the page number(s).

	Page Number	I can do it. ✓
1. Introduce my classmates.	21	
2. Describe my classroom.	24	
3. Identify classroom activities.	27	
4. Tell time.	30	
5. Talk about the weather.	33	

My favorite page in this unit is (Answers will vary.)

Team Project

Make a display.

1. Form a team with four or five students. In your team, you need:

POSITION	JOB	STUDENT NAME
Student 1: Team Leader	See that everyone speaks English. See that everyone participates.	
Student 2: Writer	Help team members write.	
Student 3: Artist	Arrange a display with help from the team.	
Students 4/5: Spokespeople	Prepare a presentation.	

2. Draw information about you on the team sheet of paper.

   Draw a picture of yourself.

   Draw a map of your country.

   Draw a clock with the time in your country.

   Draw the weather in your country.

3. Present each student's work in your group to the class.

Introduction
5 mins.

In this project, students will work in teams to create a collage showing the diversity of their group. They will section off a large sheet of paper, allowing room in each section for a picture of a group member, a map of the group member's country, and a depiction of the weather that is most common there.

Note: You may decide to bring a map to help students see the outline of your state, province, or region.

Stage 1
10–15 mins.

Form a team with four or five students.

 Refer to the Activity Bank CD-ROM for a profile template.

Help students form groups and assign positions in their groups. On the spot, students will have to choose who will be the leader of their group. Review the responsibility of the leader and ask students to write the name of their leader in the books.

Do the same with the remaining positions: *writer, artist,* and *spokesperson*. If there are five people in the group, double up on the position of spokesperson. Every member of each group should have a responsibility.

Stage 2
40–50 mins.

Draw a information about you on the team sheet of paper.

Stage 3
10–30 mins.

Present each student's work in your group to the class.

Ask teams to prepare a presentation. Each student on the team will talk about one of the other students introducing that student to the class. The activity can be more effective if you videotape the presentations for student review.

STANDARDS CORRELATIONS

CASAS: 0.1.5, 2.3.1, 2.3.2, 2.3.3, 4.8.1 (See CASAS Competency List on pages 171–177.)
SCANS: **Basic Skills** Reading, writing, listening, speaking
Resources Allocate time, allocate money, allocate materials and facility resources, allocate human resources
Information Acquire and evaluate information, organize and maintain information, interpret and communicate information, use computers to process information
Interpersonal Participate as a member of a team, teach others, serve clients and customers, exercise leadership, negotiate to arrive at a decision, work with cultural diversity

Systems Understand systems, monitor and correct performance, improve and design systems
Thinking Skills Think creatively, make decisions, solve problems, see things in the mind's eye
Personal Qualities Responsibility, sociability, self management
EFF: **Communication** Read with understanding, convey ideas in writing, speak so others can understand, listen actively, observe critically
Decision Making Solve problems and make decisions, plan
Interpersonal Cooperate with others, advocate and influence, resolve conflict and negotiate, guide others
Lifelong Learning Take responsibility for learning, reflect and evaluate

Objective: Identify common foods
Grammar: Prepositions of location
Academic Strategy: Working in a group
Vocabulary: Common foods, *breakfast*, *lunch*, and *dinner*

RESOURCES

Activity Bank: Lesson 1, Worksheet 1
Reading and Writing Challenge: Unit 3
Grammar Challenge: Unit 3, Challenge 1
Audio: CD 1, Tracks 41–42

■ 1.5 hour classes   ■ 2.5 hour classes   ■ 3⁺ hour classes

AGENDA

Ask information about a picture.
Talk about foods in a refrigerator.
Review prepositions of location.
Practice prepositions of location.
Discuss breakfast, lunch, and dinner.

Heinle Picture Dictionary: Inside the Refrigerator, pages 88–89; Fruits and Nuts, pages 82–83; Meat, Poultry, and Seafood, pages 86–87; Vegetables, pages 84–85

Stand Out Basic Assessment CD-ROM with Exam*View*®

 Preassessment *(optional)*
Use the Stand Out Basic Assessment CD-ROM with Exam*View*® to create a pretest for Unit 3.

Warm-up and Review   10–15 mins.

Ask students to look at the picture. Ask them to guess where the two students are from. There is no one correct answer. Next, ask where they think the students are now. Finally, ask what foods they like to eat. Make a list on the board.

Listen.

Ask students to listen to the conversation. Ask what Silvina is eating.

> **Listening Script**   CD 1, Track 41
>
> The listening script matches the conversation in Exercise B.

Introduction   10 mins. ■■■

Write the agenda on the board. Ask a volunteer to write the day of the week and the date above the agenda. Ask students if they like American food. Ask individuals to name one food item from their country. Ask students which of the four sandwiches listed in the picture they like best. Help students

with the new vocabulary. State the objective: *Today we will identify common foods.*

Presentation 1   30–45 mins. ■■■

B Listen again and read. Practice with a *chicken sandwich*, a *tuna fish sandwich*, and a *ham sandwich.*

Play the recording again and ask students to read the dialog. Ask students what ingredients you need to make a turkey sandwich. At this level, they may not completely understand. Lead them through different parts of a turkey sandwich, including *bread*, *mayonnaise*, *cheese*, *lettuce*, etc.

Show students how to substitute different sandwiches in the conversation.

Practice 1   7–10 mins.

Ask students to practice substituting different sandwiches. Then ask students to reverse roles.

You might want to expand this activity so students ask each other which sandwich they prefer. Ask students to write five student responses and the students' names.

Evaluation 1   3–5 mins.

Ask for volunteers to demonstrate the dialog in front of the class.

STANDARDS CORRELATIONS

CASAS: 1.3.8 (See CASAS Competency List on pages 167–173.)
SCANS: **Basic Skills** Reading, writing, listening, speaking
Resources Allocate human resources

Information Acquire and evaluate information, organize and maintain information, interpret and communicate information
EFF: **Communication** Speak so others can understand, listen actively
Interpersonal Cooperate with others

Food

GOALS

➤ Identify common foods
➤ Express hunger
➤ Express quantity

➤ Make a shopping list
➤ Express preferences

LESSON 1

Let's eat!

GOAL ➤ Identify common foods

A Listen.

CD 1
TR 41

What's the name of the school?
Where are they?

B Listen again and read. Practice with a *chicken sandwich*, a *tuna fish sandwich*, and a *ham sandwich*.

CD 1
TR 41

Andre: The food looks good!
Silvina: Yes, it does.
Andre: What are you eating?
Silvina: A <u>turkey sandwich</u>.

GOAL ➤ **Identify common foods**

Vocabulary · Grammar
Life Skills
Academic · Pronunciation

CD 1
TR 42

 C Listen and point.

apples	butter	eggs	milk	tomatoes
bananas	cheese	lettuce	oranges	turkey
bread	chicken	mayonnaise	potatoes	water

 D Write.

a. _____milk_____ f. _____bread_____ k. _____apples_____

b. _____water_____ g. _____cheese_____ l. _____oranges_____

c. _____eggs_____ h. _____turkey_____ m. _____potatoes_____

d. _____chicken_____ i. _____tomatoes_____ n. _____mayonnaise_____

e. _____bananas_____ j. _____lettuce_____ o. _____butter_____

Presentation 2

10–15 mins. ◼◼◻

C Listen and point.

Go over each vocabulary word with students. It is important that students don't work on Exercise D while you are doing Presentation 2. To prevent this from happening, ask students to cover Exercise D with a sheet of paper. There are considerably more words in this lesson than in most other lessons. These are very high frequency words that your students have undoubtedly heard, so elicit the vocabulary before merely giving them the information. You might do this by asking students questions about the picture such as: *What is your favorite food in the picture? What do you eat for breakfast? What do you have in YOUR refrigerator?*

For shorter classes, ask students to do Exercise D for homework.

 Listening Script   CD 1, Track 42

a.	*milk*	i.	*tomatoes*
b.	*water*	j.	*lettuce*
c.	*eggs*	k.	*apples*
d.	*chicken*	l.	*oranges*
e.	*bananas*	m.	*potatoes*
f.	*bread*	n.	*mayonnaise*
g.	*cheese*	o.	*butter*
h.	*turkey*		

Practice 2

10–15 mins. ◼◼

D Write.

Ask students to complete the exercise in pairs.

Evaluation 2

3 mins. ◼◼

Ask students to write the information on the board. Check for accuracy in spelling.

Teaching Tip

Keeping student attention

At times, it is appropriate and advisable that higher-level students are given opportunities to work faster or ahead of the rest of the class. Most classes are multilevel in nature and some students may naturally complete an assignment some time before others. The best way to manage these situations is to be prepared to give students who finish an assignment before everyone else additional challenging work as an extension to the practice.

Having said this, it is nevertheless important to keep students from starting the practice before you give the assignment. In the presentation stage of a lesson, you need the support, attention, and involvement of all students. Often, students will attempt to do an exercise in the book before you assign it. Some students might be ready, but in order to ensure that all students are doing the correct assignment and doing it appropriately, it is important that you keep their attention throughout the presentation. You also want to be sure that all students have the opportunity to get all the information you provide in the presentation. Finally, if students do the exercises early, they become bored because they often finish before the rest of the students start.

Some strategies for keeping student attention include the following:

1. Asking students to stop writing and tell them that they will have plenty of time to do the assignment
2. Asking all the students to cover the practice part of the page so they are not tempted to do the work
3. Getting students who are writing in the book when it isn't time involved in the presentation by asking them questions.

Presentation 3

10-15 mins.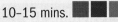

E Read.

Review prepositions of location with students. You may also wish to go back to page 25. In this lesson, students will be introduced to a new preposition of location: *over*.

Another idea is to teach them the prepositions as if for the first time. Use the picture on the previous page to identify all the objects. Ask: *What is next to the butter?*

Prepare students to do the exercise by modeling it with several students and asking a few pairs to model it for the class. Show students how to substitute important information.

F Read the sentences and write the prepositions *(in, on, over, next to, between).*

Do this together as a class as part of the review of prepositions of location.

Teaching Tip

Recycling

At all levels, but especially at the lower levels, recycling is very important. Recycling means introducing concepts already taught again in different contexts. Don't expect students to learn every concept and always remember it at this level. They will forget some things as they learn new concepts, so it becomes essential to teach them past concepts again. Also, students who may have missed a previous lesson will benefit from the review.

Practice 3

10-15 mins.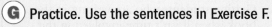

G Practice. Use the sentences in Exercise F.

Ask students to practice this activity in pairs. Make sure they understand that they will be describing the location of all the labeled foods in the picture on page 42. Monitor students closely to make sure they are using the correct prepositions.

Evaluation 3

5-7 mins.

Ask for volunteers to demonstrate.

Activity Bank

Lesson 1, Worksheet 1: Food

Application

10-15 mins.

H What do you eat? Write.

Ask students to use vocabulary they have learned from this lesson, foods they know, foods they find in a bilingual dictionary, and foods that are from their country to complete the chart. Then ask them to share their chart with other students.

Teaching Tip

Vocabulary categorizing

Find different ways to allow students to classify vocabulary so that you meet the needs of different learning styles. Also, students at this level should be introduced to ways to think critically when they are ready and have enough information and resources to do so.

 Refer students to *Stand Out Basic Grammar Challenge*, Unit 3, Challenge 1 for more practice with prepositions of location.

E **Read.**

The potatoes are **in** the box.

The tomatoes are **on** the counter.

The oranges and apples are **over** the counter.

F **Read the sentences and write the prepositions** *(in, on, over, next to, between).*

1. The water is ___next to___ the milk.

2. The bananas are ___over___ the counter.

3. The turkey is ___between___ the bread and the cheese.

4. The milk is ___in___ the refrigerator.

5. The lettuce is ___on___ the counter.

G **Practice. Use the sentences in Exercise F.**

EXAMPLE: **A:** Where's the <u>milk?</u>
             B: It's <u>in the refrigerator</u>.

H **What do you eat? Write.** (Answers will vary.)

Breakfast	Lunch	Dinner

LESSON 2

I'm hungry!

GOAL ➤ Express hunger

A Look at the picture.

Saul and Chen are studying English. What's for dinner?

B Listen and read.

CD 1
TR 43

Saul: I'm hungry.
Chen: Me, too.
Saul: What's for dinner?
Chen: chicken and vegetables

C Practice Exercise B.

What's for dinner?

a chicken sandwich and fruit

a hamburger and fries

a taco and chips

rice and vegetables

Objective: Express hunger
Grammar: *Be* verb + adjective
Academic Strategy: Focused listening
Vocabulary: Common foods, *hungry, thirsty, snack*

AGENDA

Review fruits and vegetables.
Learn to express feelings of hunger and thirst.
Review and practice be.
Discuss snacks.

RESOURCES

Activity Bank: Lesson 2, Worksheet 1
Reading and Writing Challenge: Unit 3
Grammar Challenge: Unit 3, Challenge 2
Audio: CD 1, Tracks 43–48

Heinle Picture Dictionary: Inside the Refrigerator, pages 88–89; Fruits and Nuts, pages 82–83; Meat, Poultry, and Seafood, pages 86–87; Vegetables, pages 84–85; Feelings, pages 38–39

■ 1.5 hour classes   ■ 2.5 hour classes   ■ 3⁺ hour classes

Warm-up and Review   10-15 mins. ■■■

Ask students in groups to make lists of all the fruits and vegetables they know. They can include words in their own languages. Ask them to make a table or use a two-column chart template from the Activity Bank CD-ROM.

Fruits	Vegetables
apples	*lettuce*

Introduction   2 mins. ■■■

Write the day, the date, and the agenda on the board. Say the date and have students repeat. Rub your stomach and say: *I'm hungry! Is there anything to eat?* State the objective: *Today we will learn how to express hunger.*

Presentation 1   30-40 mins. ■■■

Ask students what they eat for dinner. They may want to look back to page 42.

 **Look at the picture.**

Ask questions about the picture to see how much students understand. You may introduce the word *homework* and other words that they may need. Ask students to read the clock. Ask: *What time is it?* Ask if it is night or morning.

 Listen and read.

Play the recording once and ask students to read along. Next, ask students to practice the exchange a few times with a partner.

> 🎧 **Listening Script**   *CD 1, Track 43*
>
> The listening script matches the conversation in Exercise B.

Ask students to do a Corners activity. In this activity, students go to a different corner of the room, depending on their preferences. The four preferences in this case are the foods listed in Exercise C. Once in the corners, prepare students to do Practice 1.

Practice 1   15-20 mins. ■■■

 Practice Exercise B.

Ask students to practice the conversation in Exercise B in their corner. They will then leave their corners and go to the other corners and practice with at least one person. Continue this activity until all students have practiced the conversation.

Evaluation 1   15-20 mins. ■■■

Observe as students practice the conversation.

Presentation 2   10-15 mins.

Review the verb *be* with students. You may want to do this first with the books closed to see how much students remember from Unit 1, Lesson 3, page 8. Recreate the chart from this page on the board, only leave out the forms of *be*. Ask for volunteers to complete the chart with their books closed.

D Read.

Present *hungry* and *thirsty* to students by showing them the pictures and pantomiming. This will be the first time students have been exposed to the negative form of *be*. Demonstrate many times so that they clearly understand.

Present the grammar table to students and have students repeat the sentences after you. You may want to give them actions to demonstrate what they are saying, such as rubbing their tummy for hungry and shaking their head for negative statements.

For shorter classes, ask students to do Exercise E for homework.

Practice 2   8-10 mins.

E Write. Follow the example sentences in the chart.

Do the example as a class. Show students how the second sentence is negative.

Evaluation 2   9-12 mins.

Review students' book work. Ask for volunteers to write the sentences on the board.

GOAL ➤ **Express hunger**

D Read.

Saul is hungry. He is not thirsty.

Chen is thirsty. He is not hungry.

Be Verb			
Subject	**Be**		**Example sentence**
I	am (not)		I **am** hungry. I**'m** hungry.
he	is (not)	hungry very hungry thirsty	He **is** hungry. He**'s** hungry.
she			She **is** hungry. She**'s** hungry.
we	are (not)		We **are** hungry. We**'re** hungry.
you			You **are** hungry. You**'re** hungry.
they			They **are** hungry. They**'re** hungry.

E Write. Follow the example sentences in the chart.

EXAMPLE: Edgar ___is___ hungry.
He's not thirsty.

1. Roselia and Thanh ___are___ thirsty.
They're not hungry.

2. We ___are___ hungry.
We're not thirsty.

3. She ___is___ not hungry.
She's thirsty.

4. I ___am___ thirsty.
I'm not hungry.

5. You ___are___ not hungry.
You're thirsty.

GOAL ➤ **Express hunger**

  F **Read and listen.**

CD 1
TR 44

carrots   oranges   apples   chips

cookies   milk   water

  G **Listen and write the snack.**

CD 1
TR 45–48

1. __carrots__
2. __water__
3. __apples__
4. __bananas__

H **Practice.**

A: I'm hungry.
B: What's good?
A: How about <u>carrots</u>?
B: Great!

I Ask your classmates about their favorite snacks. Write what they say. (Answers will vary.)

Name	Food

Presentation 3   10–15 mins. ■■■ ■

Introduce the word *snack* to students. You may choose to do this by drawing three clocks on the board with no hands. Write *breakfast, lunch,* or *dinner* under each clock. Ask students what time to put for each meal and complete the clocks. Now, make a clock with a time between the ones given and ask students what the meal would be. Explain that this is *a snack*. Ask students what they eat for snacks. Get as much information from them as you can before they open their books.

F **Read and listen.**

Practice the pronunciation of each word in the picture with students. Then have them point to objects and repeat them as you say them.

Listening Script			CD 1, Track 44
carrots	*oranges*	*apples*	*chips*
cookies	*milk*	*water*	

Practice 3   10–15 mins. ■

G **Listen and write the snack.**

Ask students to listen to the four conversations and write the snack they hear.

Listening Script   CD 1, Tracks 45–48

1. **A:** *I'm hungry.*
   B: *Me, too. I really need something healthy.*
   A: *Carrots are always good and healthy, too.*

2. **A:** *I'm thirsty.*
   B: *Can I get you anything?*
   A: *Maybe some water would help.*
   B: *I'll get it right away.*

3. **A:** *Do you have anything to eat?*
   B: *Sure, but what do you want?*
   A: *I don't know. I'm very hungry.*
   B: *How about an apple?*
   A: *Thanks.*

4. **A:** *My sister is very hungry. She needs to eat.*
   B: *What can I get her?*
   A: *Do you have any bananas?*
   B: *I'll get her one.*

Evaluation 3   3 mins. ■

Check students' book work.

Activity Bank

Lesson 2, Worksheet 1: I'm Hungry!

Application   10–15 mins. ■ ■ ■

H **Practice.**

Review the dialog with a volunteer. Then practice a few more times with different students asking them to insert their own preferences for snacks.

I **Ask your classmates about their favorite snacks. Write what they say.**

Have students list the snacks they like. Then have them practice the conversation in Exercise H again with a few partners, this time inserting the snacks they like.

📖 **Refer students to *Stand Out Basic Grammar Challenge*, Unit 3, Challenge 2 for more practice with using the *be* verb in the affirmative and the negative.**

Objective: Express quantity
Grammar: Singular and plural nouns
Pronunciation: Final consonant /s/
Academic Strategies: Focused listening, skimming
Vocabulary: Common foods and ingredients, packaging

RESOURCES

Activity Bank: Lesson 3, Worksheet 1
Reading and Writing Challenge: Unit 3
Grammar Challenge: Unit 3, Challenge 3
Audio: CD 1, Tracks 49–53

■ 1.5 hour classes ■ 2.5 hour classes ■ 3⁺ hour classes

AGENDA

Review breakfast, lunch, and dinner.
Read a recipe.
Learn about containers and measurements.
Practice plurals.
Write a recipe.

Heinle Picture Dictionary: Inside the Refrigerator, pages 88–89; Fruits and Nuts, pages 82–83; Meat, Poultry, and Seafood, pages 86–87; Vegetables, pages 84–85; Measurements and Containers, pages 96–97; Cooking, pages 92–93

Warm-up and Review 10-15 mins.

Write this dialog and chart on the board.

A: *What do you eat for <u>dinner</u>?*
B: _____

Name	Breakfast	Lunch	Dinner

Ask students to ask five other students what they eat for breakfast, lunch, and dinner and write the answers in the chart. Then ask individuals to share what they wrote.

Introduction 5-7 mins.

Write the agenda on the board. Ask a volunteer to write the day and the date above the agenda. Then point to some objects that students have learned. Ask students what they are. Write the words on the board. Choose some plural items and stress the final *s* when you say and write the word. Make a chart on the board with columns for singular and plural. Ask students to help you

put the words in the correct column. State the objective: *Today we will express quantity.*

Presentation 1 30-40 mins.

Write *spaghetti* on the board. Ask students if they like spaghetti.

(A) Read the ingredients.

Go over the new vocabulary with students. Make sure students understand *jar*, *pound*, and *package*.

(B) Write.

Ask students to answer the questions. Prepare students for the practice by asking them to point at particular packaging as you say it in isolation and in a sentence.

Practice 1 5-7 mins.

(C) Listen and circle.

(See next page for the listening script.)

Evaluation 1 5-7 mins.

Go over students' answers.

Let's have spaghetti.

GOAL ➤ Express quantity

A Read the ingredients.

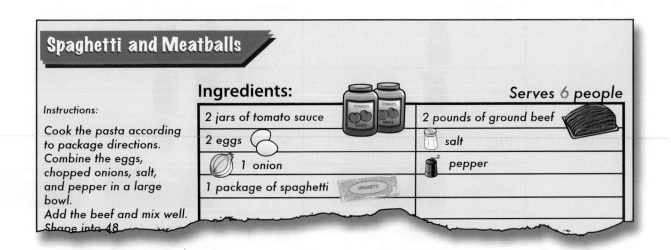

Spaghetti and Meatballs

Instructions:

Cook the pasta according to package directions. Combine the eggs, chopped onions, salt, and pepper in a large bowl. Add the beef and mix well. Shape into 48

Ingredients: Serves 6 people

2 jars of tomato sauce   2 pounds of ground beef

2 eggs   salt

1 onion   pepper

1 package of spaghetti

B Write.

1. How many jars of tomato sauce do you need? _____ 2 jars _____

2. How many eggs do you need? _____ 2 eggs _____

3. How many onions do you need? _____ 1 onion _____

4. How many packages of spaghetti do you need? _____ 1 package _____

5. How many pounds of ground beef do you need? _____ 2 pounds _____

  C Listen and circle.

CD 1
TR 49–52

1. jar   (package)   pound

2. jar   package   (pound)

3. jar   (package)   pound

4. (jar)   package   pound

GOAL ➤ Express quantity

 D Read the chart. Listen. Repeat.

CD 1
TR 53

| Singular and Plural Nouns ||
Singular	**Plural**
jar	jars
can	cans
bag	bags
package	packages
pound	pounds
Exceptions: Singular	**Plural**
potato	potato**es**
tomato	tomato**es**
sandwich	sandwich**es**

E Write and say the plural forms to a partner.

EXAMPLE: *A:* What do you need?
   B: I need <u>apples</u>.

Pronunciation

Plurals

/s/	/z/	/iz/
chips	jars	packag**es**
carrots	cans	orang**es**

Fruit		Vegetables	
apple	/z/ apples	carrot	/s/ carrots
orange	/iz/ oranges	tomato	/z/ tomatoes
banana	/z/ bananas	potato	/z/ potatoes
pear	/z/ pears	pepper	/z/ peppers

Listening Script CD 1, Tracks 49–52

1. **Omar:** *There is so much we need at the store.*
   Maria: *What do you mean? What do we need?*
   Omar: *We need a package of spaghetti, for one thing.*
   Maria: *OK, I'll write it on the list. What else?*

2. **Omar:** *Well, let's see . . . We need at least one pound of chicken for dinner tonight.*
   Maria: *Are you sure one pound is enough?*
   Omar: *Yes. We have a pound in the refrigerator.*
   Maria: *I'm adding it to the list. What else?*

3. **Omar:** *We need a package of cheese for sandwiches.*
   Maria: *No, we don't. I have three packages in the refrigerator.*
   Omar: *Oh, I didn't see them.*
   Maria: *What else?*

4. **Omar:** *We need a jar of mayonnaise for the sandwiches.*
   Maria: *I don't like mayonnaise, but I will put it on the list for you.*
   Omar: *Thanks!*

Presentation 2   10-15 mins. ◾◾◾

Pantomime making a cake. Crack a few eggs into a bowl and stir them up. Add flour and milk. Say what you are doing throughout: *I'm cracking three eggs and mixing them with flour and milk.* Stop and do it again. Repeat this three times. Then ask: *How many eggs?* Some students will understand this expression and answer. Write on the board: *How many?*

Ⓓ Read the chart. Listen. Repeat.

Show students how the plurals of regular nouns are formed. Use some additional examples that are not in the book. This is not a lesson on count and noncount nouns so students don't need to understand that some words are not plural at this point, but if you feel they are ready, you can introduce the concept here.

Also, introduce the various pronunciations of the final *s* here. Sometimes the final *s* is problematic for students because they may not fully pronounce final consonants.

 Listening Script CD 1, Track 53

jar	jars
can	cans
bag	bags
package	packages
pound	pounds

Pronunciation

Final consonant s

In many languages, the final consonant of words is deemphasized and often not completely pronounced. When English is spoken in a natural way, the final consonants blend into the next word; however, at the end of phrases, it becomes important to pronounce the sound and release it. Therefore, it is essential to help students not only say the *s* sound at the end of the word but to release it so the sound resonates.

To further complicate the pronunciation of the final *s* sound, some languages don't mark nouns plural or singular. In other words, they don't distinguish between the plural and singular forms. Make sure that students understand that the *s* is essential to being understood.

Overemphasizing a sound is OK for demonstration as long as you also demonstrate the sound in context with appropriate emphasis.

Practice 2   7-10 mins. ◾◾

Ⓔ Write and say the plural forms to a partner.

Show students how to practice this activity with a partner.

Evaluation 2   7-10 mins. ◾◾

Observe students as they practice.

Presentation 3   10–15 mins.

Dictate the words in the list below to students. Then ask for volunteers to write the words on the board. Now ask students to write the plural form on their paper. Again, ask for volunteers to write the plural forms on the board.

1. apple
2. chip
3. cookie
4. carrot
5. orange

(F) Write the words and the quantity.

Do this activity together as part of the presentation. Repeat the words as many times as necessary.

Prepare students to do the conversation in Exercise G. Practice the short conversation a few times so students are comfortable with it. Demonstrate with a few students.

Practice 3   20–30 mins. ■

(G) Practice the conversation. Use the pictures.

Evaluation 3   2–3 mins. ■

Observe students as they practice the conversation.

Activity Bank

Lesson 3, Worksheet 1: Singular and Plural

Application   10–15 mins. ■■■

(H) Make a fruit salad. What do you need?

Go over the recipe card with students. Help them to see that this salad will serve six people. Ask students in groups to complete the list of ingredients by adding names of fruit and quantities.

 Refer students to *Stand Out Basic Grammar Challenge*, Unit 3, Challenge 3 for more practice with forming plurals.

GOAL ➤ **Express quantity**

F Write the words and the quantity.

five eggs

one tomato

one apple

three carrots

one cookie

four oranges

one sandwich

one banana

G Practice the conversation. Use the pictures.

1.    2.    3.    4.

A: What are the ingredients?
B: two eggs and one onion

H Make a fruit salad. What do you need? (Answers will vary.)

	Fruit Salad	Serves 6 people
Ingredients	1 banana ___ _____ 2 apples ___ _____ ___ pear ___ _____ ___ orange ___ _____	

What's for dinner?

GOAL ➤ Make a shopping list

  A Listen and point.

CD 1
TR 54

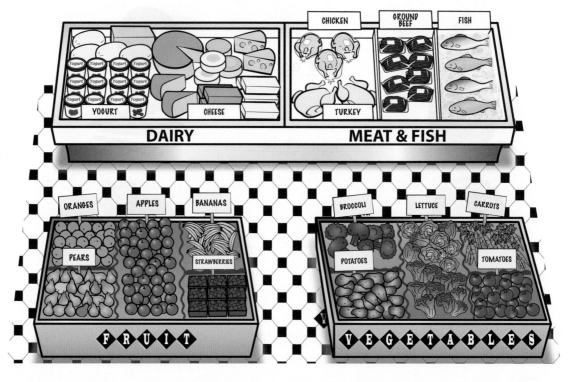

B Write the words on the correct shopping lists. (Unnumbered answers will vary.)

Shopping List	Shopping List	Shopping List	Shopping List
Meat and Fish	Vegetables	Fruit	Dairy
1. chicken	1. broccoli	1. oranges	1. yogurt
2. ground beef	2. lettuce	2. apples	2. cheese
3. fish	3. carrots	3. bananas	
4. turkey	4. potatoes	4. pears	
	5. tomatoes	5. strawberries	

C Do you know more food words? Add them to the shopping lists.

AT-A-GLANCE PREP

Objective: Make a shopping list
Grammar: Simple present with *want*
Academic Strategies: Focused listening, teamwork skills, categorizing and organizing information
Vocabulary: Sections in a supermarket and their associated foods

RESOURCES

Activity Bank: Lesson 4, Worksheet 1
Reading and Writing Challenge: Unit 3
Grammar Challenge: Unit 3, Challenge 4
Audio: CD 1, Tracks 54–55

■ 1.5 hour classes   ■ 2.5 hour classes   ■ 3⁺ hour classes

AGENDA

Review and categorize food.
Read a shopping list.
Express things you want.
Complete a Venn diagram.
Make a shopping list.

Heinle Picture Dictionary: Inside the Refrigerator, pages 88–89; Fruits and Nuts, pages 82–83; Meat, Poultry, and Seafood, pages 86–87; Vegetables, pages 84–85; Supermarket, pages 98–99

Warm-up and Review   15-20 mins.

On the board, list all the vocabulary used in this unit thus far. Make a four-column chart with the following headers: *fruit*, *vegetables*, *meat*, and *drinks*. Ask students to work in groups to put all the items in the correct columns. Provide one chart per group.

Ask representatives from groups to put the information on the chart on the board. Erase the board and have a dictation with a few words.

Introduction   5 mins. ■■■

Write the agenda on the board. Ask a volunteer to write the day and the date. Ask students if they take a shopping list to the store. State the objective: *Today we will make a shopping list.*

Presentation 1   10-15 mins. ■■■

Have students look at the picture.

(A) Listen and point.

Have students point at each food item as they hear it. Then turn the recording off and call out items in a different order. Ask students to point.

Listening Script   CD 1, Track 54

oranges	apples	pears	bananas
strawberries	carrots	tomatoes	potatoes
broccoli	lettuce	chicken	ground beef
turkey	fish	cheese	yogurt

Practice 1   10-15 mins.

(B) Write the words on the correct shopping lists.

Write the column headings on the board and have students help you write a few items. Then let them finish their lists by themselves.

(C) Do you know more food words? Add them to the shopping lists.

Ask groups to add more words to the lists.

Evaluation 1   7-10 mins.

Ask pairs to share their answers. Then complete the columns on the board.

STANDARDS CORRELATIONS

CASAS: 1.3.8 (See CASAS Competency List on pages 167-173.)
SCANS: Basic Skills Reading, writing, listening, speaking
Resources Allocate human resources
Information Acquire and evaluate information, organize and maintain information, interpret and communicate information

Interpersonal Participate as a member of a team, teach others
Thinking Skills See things in the mind's eye
EFF: Communication Speak so others can understand, listen actively
Interpersonal Cooperate with others

Presentation 2   10–15 mins.

 D **Read Amadeo's shopping list.**

Ask for a volunteer to read the list out loud. Then go back to page 50 and ask students to decide in which column each word would go. Ask students to look back at page 42, where the vocabulary was first introduced.

Teaching Tip

Text as a tool

Students become independent learners when they realize that they can do their own review. The learner logs at the end of each unit will help them learn this concept.

You will also see in the *Stand Out* approach many opportunities for students to go back to pages they completed days and weeks before. This is an important part of effective review. Doing this makes the book as much a tool for learning English as a day-to-day textbook.

E **What does Amadeo want? Circle the items.**

Have students circle each of the items on Amadeo's list.

This simple activity introduces students to the skill of scanning for information. Students will get more practice with this important skill throughout the text.

Go over the new vocabulary in Exercise E and prepare students for listening in Exercise F.

For shorter classes, ask students to do Exercises F and H for homework.

Practice 2   7–10 mins.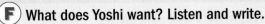

F **What does Yoshi want? Listen and write.**

Prepare students for the listening by talking briefly about the things you personally need to get at the grocery store. Do this until they realize that they only have to listen for the food words. Ask students to tell you what food words they heard.

Play the recording and have students write the words they hear. You may need to play this listening several times. Have students work in groups between sessions to share answers with one another.

 Listening Script   CD 1, Track 55

Amadeo: *Yoshi, I'm going to the supermarket. What do you want?*
Yoshi: *Um, I want some oranges, apples, and strawberries.*
Amadeo: *Is that all?*
Yoshi: *No. I think I want some yogurt, cheese, and eggs, too.*
Amadeo: *OK, is that it?*
Yoshi: *No. Get me some potatoes, fish, and water.*
Amadeo: *Anything else?*
Yoshi: *No, that's it.*
Amadeo: *OK, let me read it back to you. You want oranges, apples, strawberries, yogurt, cheese, eggs, potatoes, fish, and water.*
Yoshi: *Yep, that's all!*

Evaluation 2   5–10 mins.

Ask students to share their list with a partner and then ask for two or three volunteers to write Yoshi's list on the board.

GOAL ➤ **Make a shopping list**

D Read Amadeo's shopping list.

Shopping List	
apples	tomatoes
water	chicken
milk	eggs
carrots	chips
cheese	

E What does Amadeo want? Circle the items.

oranges   potatoes

apples   cheese

eggs   broccoli

F What does Yoshi want? Listen and write.

CD 1
TR 55

Shopping List	
oranges	eggs
apples	potatoes
strawberries	fish
yogurt	water
cheese	

GOAL > **Make a shopping list**

G Read.

Simple Present		
Subject	**Verb**	**Example sentence**
I, you, we, they	want	They **want** apples.
he, she	wants	She **wants** apples.
		He **wants** apples.

H Write and report. He wants ... She wants ... They want ...

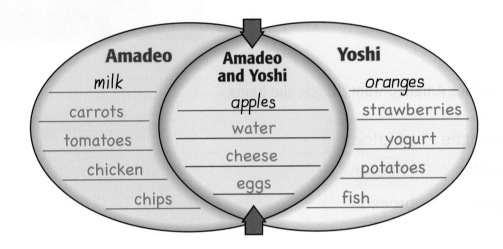

Amadeo
milk
carrots
tomatoes
chicken
chips

Amadeo and Yoshi
apples
water
cheese
eggs

Yoshi
oranges
strawberries
yogurt
potatoes
fish

I What do you want? Make a list.
(Answers will vary.)

Shopping List

J What does your partner want? Ask your partner. Write your partner's list.
(Answers will vary.)

Shopping List

Presentation 3   15–20 mins. ■■□

G Read.

Go over the grammar box with students. Show them that the rule for the third-person singular is the same in other places in the book. Ask them to find those places or guide them to pages 6 and 35. In the next lesson, the regular simple present will be completely introduced.

Prepare students to do the Venn diagram by drawing two interlocking circles on the board and asking them to give you one food that both Yoshi and Amadeo want. Write the food item in the space where the circles overlap. Then ask them to give you one food that only Amadeo wants and one food that only Yoshi wants. Write these items in the appropriate spaces. Make sure they understand the placement of the items before they go on to the practice. Use *he/she wants,* and *they want* while preparing students.

Teaching Tip

Graphic organizers

Graphic organizers are a productive way to allow students to think critically; for example, to understand similarities and differences in the vocabulary being studied. Venn diagrams are also an effective means to comprehend and visually categorize vocabulary at all levels of English study.

Practice 3   15–20 mins. ■

H Write and report. He wants . . . She wants . . . They want . . .

Help as necessary.

Activity Bank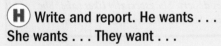

Lesson 4, Worksheet 1: Simple Present: *Want*

Application   20–30 mins. ■■□

I What do you want? Make a list.

Ask students to write their own shopping lists.

J What does your partner want? Ask your partner. Write your partner's list.

Pair students up and have them ask each other: *What do you want?* Have them write their partner's list in their books.

 Refer students to *Stand Out Basic Grammar Challenge,* **Unit 3, Challenge 4 for more practice with the simple present.**

Instructor's Notes

_____
_____
_____
_____
_____
_____
_____
_____
_____
_____
_____
_____
_____
_____
_____
_____
_____
_____
_____
_____
_____
_____
_____
_____
_____

AT-A-GLANCE PREP

Objective: Express preferences
Grammar: Simple present
Pronunciation: Final /s/
Academic Strategies: Focused listening, organizing information
Vocabulary: Dessert foods

RESOURCES

Activity Bank: Lesson 5, Worksheet 1
Reading and Writing Challenge: Unit 3
Grammar Challenge: Unit 3, Challenge 5

Audio: CD 1, Tracks 56–60
Heinle Picture Dictionary: Restaurant, pages 100–101

■ 1.5 hour classes ■ 2.5 hour classes ■ 3⁺ hour classes

AGENDA

Review foods you like.
Listen for foods.
Write sentences.
Complete a Venn diagram.

Warm-up and Review   5–7 mins. ■■■

Make a list of foods included thus far in the unit. Read the list to students. Ask students to stand up when they hear a food item they like and to sit back down when they hear a food they don't like.

Introduction   5–7 mins. ■■■

Write the agenda on the board. Ask a student and write the day and the date above the agenda. State the objective: *Today we express our preferences.*

Presentation 1   15–20 mins. ■■■

(A) Circle the desserts you like to eat. Then, listen and repeat.

Do a quick listening practice where students point to the item you say.

 Listening Script   *CD 1, Track 56*

cake	*pie*	*ice cream*	*yogurt*
cookies	*bar of chocolate*	*bag of candy*	

Practice 1   10–15 mins. ■■■

(B) Listen and point to the desserts in Exercise A.

 Listening Script   *CD 1, Tracks 57–59*

1. **Man:** *What dessert would you like?*
   Woman: *Well, I really like chocolate, but the apple pie looks good, too.*

2. **Woman:** *Just wait until you see what's for dessert.*
   Man: *What is it?*
   Woman: *I have cake and cookies. We also have some candy for later.*

3. **Man:** *Let me take you out and buy you a special dessert.*
   Woman: *That sounds great. What dessert?*
   Man: *I don't know. What do you want?*
   Woman: *How about ice cream or pie?*
   Man: *OK. We could also have cookies if you want.*

(C) Listen. Write what Maria likes.

After you play the recording, as a class write the words in the spaces provided.

Evaluation 1   10–15 mins. ■■■

Observe students doing this activity

 Listening Script   *CD 1, Track 60*

Maria likes dessert. She especially likes cake. She also likes cookies. She eats dessert after every meal.

STANDARDS CORRELATIONS

CASAS: 1.3.8 (See CASAS Competency List on pages 167–173.)
SCANS: Basic Skills Reading, writing, listening, speaking
Resources Allocate human resources
Information Acquire and evaluate information, organize and maintain information, interpret and communicate information
Interpersonal Participate as a member of a team, teach others
Thinking Skills See things in the mind's eye
EFF: Communication Speak so others can understand, listen actively
Interpersonal Cooperate with others

What do you like?

GOAL ➤ **Express preferences**

CD 1
TR 56

(A) Circle the desserts you like to eat. Then listen and repeat.
(Answers will vary.)

cake

pie

ice cream

yogurt

cookies

bar of chocolate

bag of candy

CD 1
TR 57–59

(B) Listen and point to the desserts in Exercise A.

CD 1
TR 60

(C) Listen. Write what Maria likes.

1. Maria likes __dessert_____.

2. She likes __cake_____.

3. She likes __cookies_____.

GOAL ➤ Express preferences

D Read the chart.

Simple Present		
Subject	**Verb**	**Example sentence**
I, you, we, they	like	I **like** ice cream.
	eat	We **eat** ice cream.
	want	They **want** ice cream.
he, she	likes	She **likes** chocolate.
	eats	He **eats** chocolate.
	wants	She **wants** chocolate.

E Write about the pictures.

1. <u>He wants cookies.</u>

2. <u>He eats pie.</u>

3. <u>He likes ice cream.</u>

F Write the verb.

1. Maria ____<u>likes</u>____ (like) ice cream.

2. I ____<u>want</u>____ (want) apple pie.

3. You ____<u>eat</u>____ (eat) pie.

4. They ____<u>eat</u>____ (eat) cookies.

5. We ____<u>like</u>____ (like) fruit.

6. Saul ____<u>likes</u>____ (like) candy.

7. We ____<u>want</u>____ (want) yogurt.

8. He ____<u>wants</u>____ (want) cake.

9. We ____<u>eat</u>____ (eat) chocolate.

10. They ____<u>eat</u>____ (eat) candy.

11. Rhonda and Sue ____<u>eat</u>____ (eat) pie.

12. I ____<u>like</u>____ (like) <u>(Answers will vary.)</u>.

Presentation 2   10-15 mins. ■■■

Read the chart.

Go over the chart with students and drill them with substitution drills where you change the pronoun or the subject and students say the correct form of the verb. This is the first time students are given various verbs in the simple present to work with. Help them to see the rule for the use of the final *s* with the third person. Don't forget, however, that this is still only exposure to the simple present. Although they can learn it here, students will need to be taught the form many more times before they acquire it.

Pronunciation

Emphasize again the final *s* sound in the third-person singular.

Ask a student what he or she likes and then write a sentence about it on the board. For example: Cristina, what do you like? When Cristina says yogurt, write on the board: Cristina likes yogurt. Do a few more examples.

Write about the pictures.

For shorter classes, ask students to do Exercise F for homework.

Practice 2   10-15 mins. ■■

Write the verb.

Ask students to complete the sentences. Go over the answers as a class.

Evaluation 2   7-10 mins. ■■

Check students' book work and ask volunteers to write their answers on the board.

Presentation 3

G Read.

Make sure students are ready to do the practice in Exercise H. Show students how to substitute information.

Draw the chart on the board.

Name	Likes

Practice 3

10-15 mins.

H Practice the conversation in Exercise G. Use all the words in Exercise A.

Ask students to perform the dialog and complete the chart on the board.

Teaching Tip

Dialog cards

The use of dialog cards is another way to do pair work when substitution is involved.

1. Pass out 3-by-5 index cards to each student.
2. List the vocabulary on the board.
3. Divide the number of words by the number of students. In other words, if there are thirty-two students and eight vocabulary words, the answer would be four.
4. Instruct every four students to write a designated vocabulary word. In other words, when you are finished, you will have four cards for each word.
5. Collect the cards and randomly distribute them.
6. Now students are to find other students with the same word on their card. They discover who has the same word by doing the conversation. The student recites the information on his or her card.
7. When students find a match, they write the classmate's name on the card. They continue until they find all matches.

Evaluation 3

5-7 mins.

Ask students to report what desserts students they interviewed like. You may want to write an example: *Maria likes chocolate.*

Activity Bank

Lesson 5, Worksheet 1: Simple Present: *Like*

Application

10-15 mins.

I Complete the diagram.

Students will need to interview their partner to complete the diagram. They should be familiar with the diagram from the previous lesson, but you may need to review it with them.

Refer students to *Stand Out Basic Grammar Challenge*, Unit 3, Challenge 5 for more practice with the simple present.

GOAL ➤ **Express preferences**

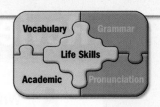

G Read.

Student A: Do you like <u>ice cream</u> for dessert?
Student B: No, I like <u>pie</u>.

H Practice the conversation in Exercise G. Use all the words in Exercise A.

I Complete the diagram.
(Answers will vary.)

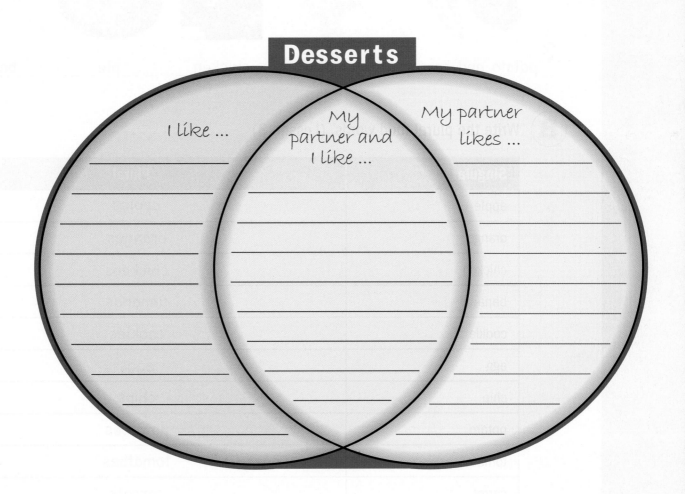

Desserts

I like ...

My partner and I like ...

My partner likes ...

Review

A Write the food words. (Lessons 1–5)

apple · eggs · chocolate · oranges · fish

potato and carrots · chips · chicken · pie · banana

B Write the plural food words. (Lesson 3)

Singular	Plural
apple	apples
orange	oranges
chicken	chickens
banana	bananas
cookie	cookies
egg	eggs
chip	chips
potato	potatoes
tomato	tomatoes
carrot	carrots

Objective: All unit objectives

Grammar: All unit grammar

Academic Strategies: Focused listening, reviewing, evaluating, developing study skills

Vocabulary: All unit vocabulary

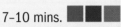 1.5 hour classes 2.5 hour classes 3⁺ hour classes

AGENDA

Discuss unit objectives.
Complete the review.
Do My Dictionary.
Evaluate and reflect on progress.

Warm-up and Review   7-10 mins.

Ask individuals what they like to eat. Make a list on the board of all the vocabulary students can come up with from the unit.

Introduction   5 mins.

Write all the objectives on the board from Unit 3. Show students the first page of every lesson so they understand that today will be review. Complete the agenda.

Note: Depending on the length of the term, you may decide to have students do Presentation 1 and Practice 1 for homework and then review student work as the warm-up for another class meeting.

Presentation 1   10-15 mins.

This presentation will cover the first three pages of the review. Quickly go to the first page of each lesson. Discuss the objective of each. Ask simple questions to remind students what they have learned.

Practice 1   15-20 mins.

Ⓐ Write the food words. (Lessons 1-5)

Ⓑ Write the plural food words. (Lesson 3)

Teaching Tip

Recycling/Review

The review process and the project that follows are part of the recycling/review process. Students at this level often need to be reintroduced to concepts to solidify what they have learned. Many concepts are learned and forgotten while learning other new concepts. This is because students learn but are not necessarily ready to acquire language concepts.

Therefore, it becomes very important to review and to show students how to review on their own. It is also important to recycle the new concepts in different contexts.

STANDARDS CORRELATIONS

CASAS: 1.3.8, 7.4.1, 7.4.2, 7.4.3 (See CASAS Competency List on pages 167-173.)

SCANS: Basic Skills Basic Skills Reading, writing, listening, speaking

Information Acquire and evaluate information, organize and maintain information, interpret and communicate information

Thinking Skills See things in the mind's eye

EFF: Communication Speak so others can understand, listen actively

Lifelong Learning Take responsibility for learning, reflect and evaluate

Practice 1 (continued)

C Write *am*, *is*, or *are*. (Lesson 2)

D Write sentences. (Lesson 2)

E Write the simple present. (Lessons 4–5)

C Write *am*, *is*, or *are*. (Lesson 2)

1. Maria _____is_____ thirsty.

2. Kim and David _____are_____ not hungry.

3. Lan and Mai _____are_____ hungry.

4. Rafael _____is_____ not thirsty.

5. Colby _____is_____ hungry.

6. I am (Answers will vary.) _____.

D Write sentences. (Lesson 2)

EXAMPLE: Eric is hungry. _____He's not thirsty._____

1. Maria is thirsty. _____She's not hungry._____

2. Saul and Chen are hungry. _____They're not thirsty._____

3. I am thirsty. _____I'm not hungry._____

E Write the simple present. (Lessons 4–5)

1. Chrissy _____likes_____ (like) hamburgers.

2. You _____eat_____ (eat) tacos.

3. Laura _____wants_____ (want) vegetables.

4. Rosie and Amadeo _____like_____ (like) rice.

5. We _____eat_____ (eat) fish and chicken.

6. I (Answers will vary.) _____.

Review

F Talk to two classmates. Ask: *What do you want?* (Lesson 4) (Answers will vary.)

Partner 1		Partner 2	
Shopping List		**Shopping List**	

G Read the lists in Exercise F. Write. (Lesson 3) (Answers will vary.)

Singular Foods	Plural Foods

Practice 1 (continued)

F Talk to two classmates. Ask: *What do you want?* (Lesson 4)

G Read the lists in Exercise F. Write. (Lesson 3)

Evaluation 1   5 mins. ■■■

Go around the room and check on students' progress. Help individuals when needed. If you see consistent errors among several students, interrupt the class and give a mini lesson or review to help students feel comfortable with the concept.

Presentation 2

5-7 mins. ■■■

My Dictionary

Review with students what My Dictionary is and help them see the value of it.

Practice 2

7-10 mins. ■■■

Ask students to complete My Dictionary.

Evaluation 2

5 mins. ■■

Ask students to share their cards.

Presentation 3

5 mins. ■■

Learner Log

Review the concepts of the Learner Log. Make sure students understand the concepts and how to do the log including the check marks.

Teaching Tip

Learner Log

Learner logs function to help students in many different ways.

1. They serve as part of the review process.
2. They help students to gain confidence and document what they have learned. In this way, students see that they are progressing and want to move forward in learning.
3. They provide students with a tool that they can use over and over to check and recheck their understanding. In this way, students become independent learners.

Practice 3

10-15 mins. ■■■

Ask students to complete the Learner Log.

Evaluation 3

2 mins. ■■■

Go over the log with students.

Application

5-7 mins. ■■■

Ask students to share their favorite lesson or page in the unit.

Instructor's Notes

My Dictionary

Make flash cards to improve your vocabulary.

1. Choose four new words from this unit.
2. Write each word on an index card or on a piece of paper.
3. On the back of the index card or paper, draw a picture, find and write a sentence from the book with the word, and write the page number.
4. Study the words.

The water is next to the milk.

page 43

Learner Log

Write the page number(s).

	Page Number	I can do it. ✓
1. Identify common foods.	41	
2. Express hunger.	44	
3. Express quantity.	47	
4. Make a shopping list.	50	
5. Express preferences.	53	

My favorite page in this unit is _(Answers will vary.)_

Team Project

Shopping List
apples
oranges
strawberries
chicken
fish
eggs
cheese
carrots
broccoli
tomatoes
bread

Make a shopping list.

1. Form a team with four or five students.
   In your team, you need:

POSITION	JOB	STUDENT NAME
Student 1: Team Leader	See that everyone speaks English. See that everyone participates.	
Student 2: Writer	Write food names.	
Student 3: Artist	Draw pictures for the shopping list with help from the team.	
Students 4/5: Spokespeople	Prepare a presentation.	

2. You are a family. What is your last name?

3. Make a shopping list with food from this unit.

4. Draw pictures of the food on your list.

5. Present your list to the class.

Introduction
5 mins.

In this project, students will work in teams to create a shopping list for their family, incorporating the vocabulary from this unit. They may choose to use Worksheet 8 from the Activity Bank CD-ROM as a template or you may create a larger template on sheets larger than 8 1/2"-by-11".

Stage 1
15-20 mins.

Form a team with four or five members.

Show students examples of the project if you have one. Use Worksheet 8 from the Activity Bank CD-ROM as a simple example if you don't have samples.

Help students to assign positions by asking all the team leaders to stand. On the spot, students will have to choose who will be the leader of their group. Review the responsibility of a leader and ask students to write the name of their leader in their books. Do the same with all positions.

Stage 2
10-15 mins.

You are a family. What is your last name?

Ask students to form a family and choose a name for themselves. Try to encourage them to be original and not to use a name of someone in their group.

Stage 3
40-50 mins.

Make a shopping list with food from this unit.

The team together creates a shopping list using the vocabulary from the unit. Encourage students to choose items that they like and want so they will use the new vocabulary.

Stage 4
10-30 mins.

Draw pictures of the food on your list.

Ask students to dress up the list with pictures from magazines or sketches they make themselves.

Stage 5
10-30 mins.

Present your list to the class.

Ask groups to present their projects. This can be particularly effective if you videotape the presentations.

STANDARDS CORRELATIONS

CASAS: 1.8.8, 4.8.1 (See CASAS Competency List on pages 167-173.)
SCANS: **Basic Skills** Reading, writing, listening, speaking
Resources Allocate time, allocate money, allocate materials and facility resources, allocate human resources
Information Acquire and evaluate information, organize and maintain information, interpret and communicate information, use computers to process information
Interpersonal Participate as a member of a team, teach others, serve clients and customers, exercise leadership, negotiate to arrive at a decision, work with cultural diversity

Systems Understand systems, monitor and correct performance, improve and design systems
Thinking Skills See things in the mind's eye
Personal Qualities Responsibility, sociability, self management
EFF: **Communication** Speak so others can understand, listen actively
Decision Making Solve problems and make decisions, plan
Interpersonal Cooperate with others, advocate and influence, resolve conflict and negotiate, guide others
Lifelong Learning Take responsibility for learning, reflect and evaluate

Objective: Identify types of clothing
Grammar: *a*, simple present with *have*
Academic Strategy: Focused listening
Vocabulary: Basic clothing vocabulary, *closet*

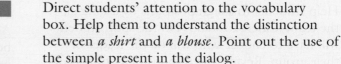

AGENDA
Identify types of clothing.
Talk about a clothing store.
Describe what people are wearing.
Write the items of clothing
in your closet.

RESOURCES

Activity Bank: Lesson 1, Worksheet 1
Reading and Writing Challenge: Unit 4
Grammar Challenge: Unit 4, Challenge 1

Audio: CD 1, Tracks 61–62
Heinle Picture Dictionary: Clothes, pages 104–105

■ 1.5 hour classes   ■ 2.5 hour classes   ■ 3⁺ hour classes

Stand Out Basic Assessment CD-ROM with Exam*View*®

 Preassessment *(optional)* ■■■

Use the Stand Out Basic, Assessment CD-ROM Exam*View*® to create a pretest for Unit 4.

Warm-up and Review   10-15 mins. ■■■

Pantomime putting on a shirt. Put on shoes. If students call out items of clothing, write them on the board. Pantomime being cold. Bring a coat or sweater into class and see if a student will suggest that you put it on. Write *coat* or *sweater* on the board. Then write on the board: *I want a coat. Where can I buy one?* Suggest a few stores.

Introduction   5 mins. ■■■

Pantomime other items of clothing. State the objective: *Today we will identify types of clothing.*

Presentation 1   30-45 mins. ■■■

With their books closed, ask students to listen to the audio (CD 1, Track 61). Ask what clothing words they hear. Play the recording a few times.

 Listen.

Play the recording again and ask students to read the dialog. Ask students what clothing is on the counter and the name of the store. Go over the dialog and allow them to practice it in pairs.

Direct students' attention to the vocabulary box. Help them to understand the distinction between *a shirt* and *a blouse*. Point out the use of the simple present in the dialog.

Ask students which words are plural and which are singular. They may be confused about *pants*. Point out that it ends in *s* and that it refers to an article of clothing that has two legs. Help students recognize that singular nouns need an article before them. Make sure they pronounce the indefinite article *a/uh/*.

 Listening Script   *CD 1, Track 61*

The listening script matches the conversation in Exercise A.

Practice 1   5-7 mins. ■■■

 Write three more sentences.

If students finish early, encourage them to write other sentences or to use *I*.

Evaluation 1   3 mins. ■■■

Ask students to write their sentences on the board. Make sure they use capital letters, periods, and an indefinite article for singular nouns.

STANDARDS CORRELATIONS

CASAS: 1.2.1, 1.3.9 (See CASAS Competency List on pages 167–173.)
SCANS: **Basic Skills** Reading, writing, listening, speaking
Resources Allocate human resources
Information Acquire and evaluate information, organize and maintain information, interpret and communicate information

Interpersonal Participate as a member of a team, teach others
EFF: **Communication** Speak so others can understand, listen actively
Interpersonal Cooperate with others

Clothing

GOALS

➤ **Identify types of clothing**
➤ **Identify and find sections in a store**
➤ **Identify colors and describe clothing**

➤ **Make purchases and count money**
➤ **Read advertisements**

What's on sale?

GOAL ➤ **Identify types of clothing**

What's the name of the store?
What does Maria want?

a blouse

a shirt

pants

shoes

socks

  A Listen.

CD 1
TR 61

Salesperson: May I help you?
Maria: Yes, I want a shirt, pants, a sweater, and shoes.

B Write three more sentences.

1. She wants a shirt.

2. She wants pants.

3. She wants a sweater.

4. She wants shoes.

GOAL ➤ **Identify types of clothing**

C What's in the ad?

D Listen and write the number of the conversation.

CD 1
TR 62

| 3 | shirt |

| 4 | pants |

| 2 | socks |

| 8 | dress |

| 1 | **blouse** |

| 7 | shorts |

| 6 | sweater |

| 5 | coat |

E Write the types of clothing in each picture in Exercise D.

Presentation 2 · 10–15 mins.

C What's in the ad?

Go over the advertisement with students. Go over the meaning of the word *sale*. Say items in Exercise D in random order and ask students to point to the items. Say the words in sentences and ask them to point again. Finally, use the different words to talk about the pictures and ask students to identify which pictures you are talking about.

For shorter classes, ask students to do Exercise E for homework.

Practice 2 · 15–20 mins.

D Listen and write the number of the conversation.

This listening consists of eight short conversations. The object here is not that students understand every word, but that they begin to recognize words they learn in class.

Ask students to listen carefully for each item as it is spoken about. Do the first item as a class.

Unlike previous recordings, the conversations are all in one track with only a short pause between each one. Students are asked to listen and record their answers rapidly. You may play the whole recording more than once, but we suggest that you don't stop in the middle of the recording.

Briefly remind students of the strategy of focused listening.

 Listening Script   CD 1, Track 62

Conversation 1
Saleswoman: *Excuse me. Can I help you?*
Customer: *Yes, I need a few things, but I don't see anything here that will fit.*
Saleswoman: *I think this blouse would be perfect for you. The colors go great with your eyes.*
Customer: *Do you really think so? Maybe you're right.*

Conversation 2
Son: *Mom, can you buy some socks when you are out? I need them for basketball practice.*
Mother: *Sure, son, I will buy you three pairs.*

Conversation 3
Man 1: *This shirt is way too big for me. I really need to be more careful when I go shopping.*
Man 2: *That's why I ask my wife to buy shirts for me. She is a much better shopper than me.*

Conversation 4
Wife: *I have three pairs of pants in my closet, but I don't want to wear any of them.*
Husband: *Why don't you wear the blue pair? They look great on you.*

Conversation 5
Woman 1: *It is so cold out. I wish I brought my coat.*
Woman 2: *You're right. Let's get inside as soon as possible.*

Conversation 6
Daughter: *Mom, can I go to the park for a while with Becky?*
Mother: *Yes, dear, but it is getting cold. Please put on a sweater. Then I won't worry.*

Conversation 7
Son: *Dad, will you play basketball with me? I think I need some help.*
Father: *OK, let me get changed. I need to find my shorts.*

Conversation 8
Husband: *Is this a formal dinner we are going to?*
Wife: *I think so. I'm wearing a dress so you should wear something nice.*

Evaluation 2 · 5–7 mins.

Check students' book work by going over the answers as a class.

E Write the types of clothing in the picture in Exercise D.

Ask students to write the words under each picture as reinforcement and additional practice. See how many can do it without referring to the words in print.

Teaching Tip

Native language in the classroom

In general, avoid speaking the students' first language. Students need to learn to guess at meaning and take risks. In a diverse classroom, students may also perceive you as favoring students who share one native language.

Presentation 3   15–20 mins.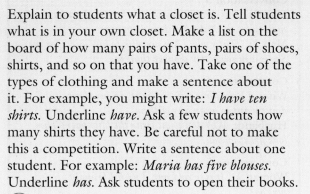

Explain to students what a closet is. Tell students what is in your own closet. Make a list on the board of how many pairs of pants, pairs of shoes, shirts, and so on that you have. Take one of the types of clothing and make a sentence about it. For example, you might write: *I have ten shirts.* Underline *have*. Ask a few students how many shirts they have. Be careful not to make this a competition. Write a sentence about one student. For example: *Maria has five blouses.* Underline *has*. Ask students to open their books.

(F) Read.

Go over the chart with students. Make sure they understand how to read it. Also, if you haven't already, introduce students to the phrase *a pair of*. Explain to students that this phrase can be used with *shoes, socks, pants,* and *shorts*.

(G) Write.

Do this activity as a class. Make sure that students use the simple present form of *have* correctly.

(H) What's in Maria's closet? Write.

Do this activity as a class as well, or ask students to work in pairs and check the answers as a class.

On the board, write: *What does she have in her closet?* Practice the question several times by asking students to respond. Have students ask each other what Maria has in her closet. Make sure their answers include the correct form of *have*. Also, make sure students are doing the activity with appropriate intonation.

For shorter classes, ask students to do Exercise H for homework.

Practice 3   5–7 mins. ▪

Ask students to practice the question and answers with a partner.

Evaluation 3   5–7 mins. ▪

Observe the activity.

Application   10–15 mins. ▪▪▪

(I) What's in your closet? Write.

Ask students to write the items of clothing in their own closets and then to report to a group.

 **Refer students to *Stand Out Basic Grammar Challenge*, Unit 4, Challenge 1 for more practice with have and the simple present.**

Teaching Tip

Inside/Outside circle

At this level, students are asked to do short dialogs often in order to provide fluency practice. Repetition is necessary because students don't have an extensive vocabulary to discuss things yet. It is a good idea to provide different ways to approach pair practice. One approach is called *inside/outside circle*. Here students stand in two circles, one inside the other. There is the same number of students in both circles. Students in the outer circle face students in the inner one. They do the dialog once. Then you ask one of the circles to rotate so each student repeats the activity with another student. This continues until you feel students have had enough practice.

Activity Bank

Lesson 1, Worksheet 1: Clothing

Instructor's Notes

_____

_____

_____

_____

_____

_____

_____

_____

_____

_____

_____

_____

_____

GOAL ➤ **Identify types of clothing**

F **Read.**

Simple Present: *Have*		
Subject	***Have***	**Example sentence**
I, you, we, they	have	I **have** two shirts.
he, she	has	She **has** a dress.

G **Write.**

EXAMPLE: (blouse) She ___has a blouse___.
(shoes) He ___has shoes___. **or** He ___has a pair of shoes___.

1. (dress) She _has a dress_____.

2. (coats) They _have coats_____.

3. (socks) I _have socks (or) have a pair of socks_____.

4. (sweaters) We _have sweaters_____.

5. (pants) You _have pants (or) have a pair of pants_____.

6. (shirt) He _has a shirt_____.

H **What's in Maria's closet? Write.**

Maria's Closet

3 _dresses_____

1 **pair of** _shoes_____

1 _blouse_____

I **What's in your closet? Write.** (Answers will vary.)

My Closet

_____

_____

Where's the fitting room?

GOAL > Identify and find sections in a store

 A Listen and point.

CD 1
TR 63

B Write the clothes you see in Exercise A.

Men's	Women's	Children's	Teen Boys'	Teen Girls'
socks	shoes	hats	shirts	dresses
hats	blouses	socks	sweaters	skirts
shirts	dresses	shirts	pants	
jackets		pants		
		dresses		

AT-A-GLANCE PREP

Objective: Identify and find sections in a store
Grammar: Review prepositions of location
Pronunciation: Minimal pairs, *in/on*
Academic Strategy: Focused listening
Vocabulary: Sections in a clothing store

RESOURCES

Activity Bank: Lesson 2, Worksheets 1 and 2
Reading and Writing Challenge: Unit 4
Grammar Challenge: Unit 4, Challenge 2

Audio: CD 1, Tracks 63–66
Heinle Picture Dictionary: Buying, Wearing, and Caring for Clothes, pages 114–115; Clothes, pages 104–105

■ 1.5 hour classes ■ 2.5 hour classes ■ 3⁺ hour classes

> ## AGENDA
> *Review clothes in your closet.*
> *Talk about clothing stores.*
> *Describe clothing stores.*

Warm-up and Review   10-12 mins.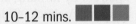

Remind students how to do a Venn diagram. Refer them to page 55 if necessary. Students can create their own diagram or you can supply them one with the template from the Activity Bank CD-ROM. Ask students to recall what they have in their closets. They recorded this information in Exercise I in Lesson 1.

Ask students in pairs to do a Venn diagram about what items they have in their closets.

Introduction   7-10 mins.

Point to the back of the classroom. Without saying anything, walk to the back of the room. Then point to a corner of the room. Again, without saying anything, walk to that corner. Do this for all parts of the classroom. Next, put a coat or another article of clothing in a corner. Walk away, point to that corner, and ask: *What is in the corner of the room?* State the objective: *Today we will identify and find sections in a store.*

Presentation 1   5 mins.

Describe the classroom as a clothing store. Explain to students that you are in _____ (name of store). Use a popular name of a store so students will recognize the context. Write

Men's Section on the board. Ask students to help you list clothing in the men's section. Then, ask students to look at the picture.

Ⓐ Listen and point.

Play the recording several times and help students with their pronunciation.

Look at the men's section. If there is an item that students didn't mention in Presentation 1, write it on the board. Ask students to write the words in their books in Exercise B in the column for the men's section.

Practice 1   10-15 mins.

Ⓑ Write the clothes you see in Exercise A.

Ask students to complete the table.

🎧 **Listening Script**   CD 1, Track 63

Men's	Women's	Children's
Teen Boys'	Teen Girls'	Fitting Room

Evaluation 1   3 mins.

Recreate the table on the board and ask volunteers to complete it.

STANDARDS CORRELATIONS

CASAS: 1.3.9 (See CASAS Competency List on pages 167–173.)
SCANS: **Basic Skills** Reading, writing, listening, speaking
Resources Allocate materials and facility resources
Information Acquire and evaluate information, interpret and communicates information

Interpersonal Participate as a member of a team, teach others
Thinking Skills Think creatively, make decisions
EFF: **Communication** Speak so others can understand, listen actively
Decision Making Solve problems and make decisions, plan
Interpersonal Cooperate with others

Presentation 2   15-20 mins. ▮▮▯

In the introduction, you put an article of clothing in a corner. Now, ask students where it is. For example, ask: *Where's the sweater?* Several students may know the word *corner*. Help them use it in a complete sentence. On the board, write: *It's in the corner.*

C Read.

Ask students to open their books and read the grammar box together. Don't assume students will understand the concept of prepositions of location without more explanation. For some students, this concept may be unclear. Confirm understanding by doing Exercise D together as a class. Make sure students are able to make a distinction between *in* and *on*.

Some students may be ready for more complicated phrases. If your class is ready, you might introduce the sentence: *It's in the front, right corner.* Receptive practice with combined forms will be introduced in Presentation 3.

D Answer the questions. Look at page 64.

Pronunciation

Minimal pairs *in/on*

One form of pronunciation practice that deals with sounds is called minimal pair practice. In this type of practice, students learn to distinguish sounds by contrasting them to other sounds. Usually, the practice involves two words that are almost the same, except for one sound. Sometimes this practice is referred to as the *ship/sheep* method. Drilling students on minimal pairs is good for awareness; however, it should be noted that pronunciation practice in context and using other techniques are important to gain fluency.

Many languages don't make the /I/ sound so a word like *in* /In/ may be pronounced /en/. At this level, such a small distinction is not essential to general comprehension. However, students should be led to understand the distinction between *in* and *on*. Show students how the jaw drops to pronounce *on*. By minimal pair practice, show them how the two words sound different.

E Listen and practice. (Student A looks at Exercise D and Student B looks at page 64.)

Prepare students for the practice by listening to dialog. Help them with proper intonation.

 Listening Script   CD 1, Track 64

The listening script matches the conversation in Exercise E.

Practice 2   7-10 mins. ▮▮

Student A asks the questions and Student B answers by looking at the picture on page 64. Student A checks Student B's answers by looking at Exercise D.

Evaluation 2   5-7 mins. ▮▮

Ask for volunteers to present the questions and answers in front of the class.

GOAL ➤ **Identify and find sections in a store**

Where's the women's section?

C Read.

Prepositions of Location	
a. It's **in the front of** the store. b. It's **in the corner of** the store. c. It's **in the middle of** the store. d. It's **in the back of** the store. e. It's **on the left side of** the store. f. It's **on the right side of** the store.	d b b e c f b b a

D Answer the questions. Look at page 64.

1. Where's the fitting room? It's in the back of the store.

2. Where's the men's section? It's in the corner of the store.

3. Where's the women's section? It's on the left side of the store.

4. Where's the children's section? It's in the middle of the store.

5. Where's the teen boys' section? It's in the back of the store.

6. Where's the teen girls' section? It's on the right side of the store.

E Listen and practice. (Student A looks at Exercise D and Student B looks at page 64.)

CD 1
TR 64

A: Can you help me?
B: Sure. What can I do for you?
A: Where's the fitting room?
B: It's in the back of the store.
A: Thank you.

  F Listen and point.

CD 1
TR 65

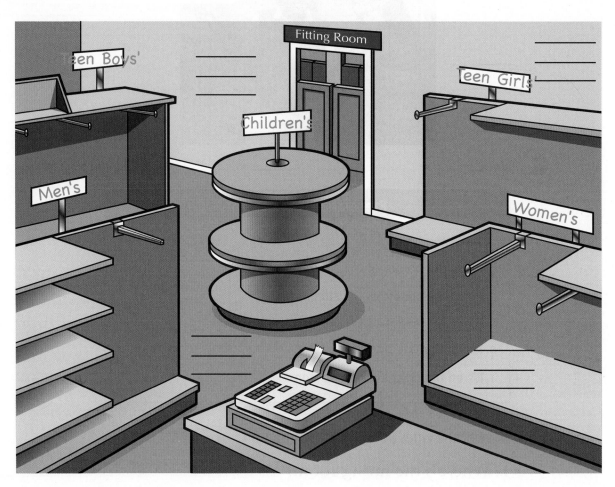

  G Listen and write the sections in the picture.

CD 1
TR 66

H In a group, write clothing in the picture for each section. (Answers will vary.)

Presentation 3

15–20 mins.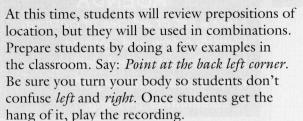

At this time, students will review prepositions of location, but they will be used in combinations. Prepare students by doing a few examples in the classroom. Say: *Point at the back left corner.* Be sure you turn your body so students don't confuse *left* and *right*. Once students get the hang of it, play the recording.

Note: Presentation 3, Practice 3, and the application all use the picture on this page. Monitor students and encourage them to stay on task and not to get ahead of the class.

(F) Listen and point.

This exercise is part of the presentation so do it as a class.

 Listening Script CD 1, Track 65

Point to the front right corner of the store.
Point to the middle of the store.
Point to the back left corner of the store.
Point to the right side of the store.
Point to the back of the store.
Point to the front of the store.
Point to the back right corner of the store.
Point to the front left corner of the store.

Practice 3

5 mins.

(G) Listen and write the sections in the picture.

Here students write the name of the section where designated. You may need to play the recording several times.

 Listening Script CD 1, Track 66

Conversation 1
A: *Excuse me, where is the fitting room?*
B: *It's in the back left corner of the store.*
A: *Thanks!*

Conversation 2
A: *Can I help you?*
B: *I'm looking for the women's section.*
A: *The women's section is in the front right corner of the store.*

Conversation 3
A: *I'm looking for the children's section.*
B: *The children's section is in the middle of the store. Do you need any help?*
A: *No, thank you.*

Conversation 4
A: *Excuse me. Where is the men's section?*
B: *It's in the front left side of the store.*
A: *Thanks.*

Conversation 5
A: *I need help.*
B: *Yes, what can I do for you?*
A: *I need to find my sister. She said she would be in the teen girls' section.*
B: *The teen girls' section is in the back right.*

Evaluation 3

3 mins.

Ask students to peer-edit each others' work.

Application

5–7 mins.

(H) In a group, write clothing in the picture for each section.

Encourage students to use words from the unit as well as any other words they would like to include. Monitor students' work and write new words on the board as needed.

Refer students to *Stand Out Basic Grammar Challenge*, Unit 4, Challenge 2 for more practice with prepositions of location.

Activity Bank

Lesson 2, Worksheet 1: Sections in a Store
Lesson 2, Worksheet 2: Locations

AT-A-GLANCE PREP

Objective: Identify colors and describe clothing
Grammar: *There is, there are*
Pronunciation: *Yes/No* intonation, rhythm, and prominence
Academic Strategy: Focused listening
Vocabulary: Clothing sizes, colors, *inventory, size, item, quantity*

RESOURCES

Activity Bank: Lesson 3, Worksheet 1
Reading and Writing Challenge: Unit 4
Grammar Challenge: Unit 4, Challenge 3

Audio: CD 1, Tracks 67–69
Heinle Picture Dictionary: Clothes, pages 104–105; Colors, pages 10–11; Describing Clothes, pages 110–111

 1.5 hour classes   2.5 hour classes   ▢ 3⁺ hour classes

AGENDA

Make a list of articles of clothing.
Identify colors and clothing.
Listen for colors and clothing.
Write a class inventory of classmates' clothing.

Warm-up and Review   10-15 mins.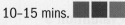

Ask groups to list all the types of clothing they see in the classroom. Ask each group to write their list on the board and then compare lists.

Introduction   5-7 mins.

Ask students to identify what you are wearing. Ask them *yes/no* questions, for example: *Is my shirt white or blue?* State the objective: *Today we will identify colors and describe clothing.*

Presentation 1   30-40 mins.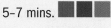

Ask students where they buy clothing. If they don't understand, give some examples of stores.

Ask students to listen to the conversation with their books closed. (CD 1, Track 67) On the board, write: *pants, shirts, socks,* and *shoes.* Ask students to identify what Yusuf is buying: *Is he buying a shirt, a pair of pants, socks, or shoes?*

(A) Talk about the picture with your teacher.

Ask the questions under the picture and a few others. Ask them to point to Yusuf, the shirts, and other details.

(B) Listen and read.

Play the recording and ask students to read along. Ask pairs of students to practice the exchange.

Listening Script   CD 1, Track 67

The listening script matches the conversation in Exercise B.

Ask students to do a Corners activity. Students go to different corners of the room, depending on their preferences. The preferences are *white, blue, red,* or *I don't like any of the colors.* Help students understand the negative of *like.* Write on the board: *I like blue. I don't like white or red.* Once they are in the corners, ask students to say the color they like and the colors they don't like.

Note: This is only an introduction to the negative form of the simple present. Students are not expected to master the use of this structure.

Practice 1   7-10 mins.

Have students practice this dialog. Have them say the color they chose in the Corners activity.

Student A: *Can I help you?*
Student B: *Yes, I want a shirt.*
Student A: *What color do you like?*
Student B: *I like blue.*

Evaluation 1   3-5 mins.

Ask for volunteers to present the conversation.

STANDARDS CORRELATIONS

CASAS: 1.1.9, 1.2.1, 1.3.9 (See CASAS Competency List on pages 167-173.)
SCANS: **Basic Skills** Reading, writing, listening, speaking
Resources Allocate materials and facility resources
Information Acquire and evaluate information, interpret and communicate information

Thinking Skills Make decisions
EFF: Communication Speak so others can understand, listen actively
Decision Making Solve problems and make decisions

What colors do you like?

GOAL ➤ Identify colors and describe clothing

A Talk about the picture with your teacher.

What is Yusuf doing?
What color shirt do you like for Yusuf?

Pronunciation

Yes/No Questions

➤ Can I help you?

➤ May I help you?

➤ Do you need help?

  B Listen and read.

CD 1
TR 67

Salesperson: Can I help you?
Yusuf: Yes, I want a shirt.
Salesperson: What color do you like—white, blue, or red?
Yusuf: I don't know, maybe blue.

 C Listen and repeat.

CD 1
TR 68

red   yellow   blue

green   white   black

| blue shirt (correct) |
| shirt blue (not correct) |

| S = Small | M = Medium | L = Large | XL = Extra Large |

 D Listen and point to the clothing items.

CD 1
TR 69

 E Look at Exercise D. Complete the chart.

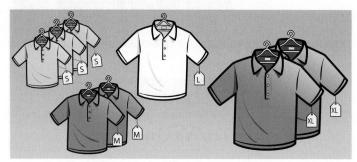

Adel's Inventory List			
Quantity (How many?)	Item	Size	Color
3	shirt	S	yellow
2	shirt	M	green
1	shirt	L	white
2	shirt	XL	blue

Presentation 2   20-30 mins.

C **Listen and repeat.**

Go over the new vocabulary with students. Make sure they understand the boxes below the colors, especially the box about word order. Some students will have a difficult time putting the adjective before the noun. They will have an opportunity to practice this in Practice 3.

> **Listening Script**   *CD 1, Track 68*
>
> red   yellow   blue   green   white   black

Teaching Tip

Error correction

We suggest that you correct students only on the concepts you are teaching or have taught. It is often more desirable to encourage peer-correcting over teacher-correcting because it can be less intimidating. It may also be useful to wait until you hear the error several times and explain the error to the class instead of identifying students who are making the error.

Finally, be careful to limit correcting in application stages and team projects. In these activities, students are taking ownership of their own language and overcorrecting can inhibit this process.

Look for things in the classroom and identify colors. For example, you may say: *The door is blue.* Also, to practice word order, you may say: *The blue door is over there.* Drill students on the color vocabulary by prompting them to listen and repeat. Then have them substitute by pointing to an object and asking them to add the color: *The door is _____.*

Discuss the picture in Exercise D with students. Write *small, medium, large,* and *extra large* on the board. Drill students on the new vocabulary and then say the sizes and colors. Have them identify the shirts by pointing to them in their books.

For shorter classes, ask students to do Exercise E for homework.

D **Listen and point to the clothing items.**

This recording allows students to practice sifting through a conversation and identifying the new vocabulary. When they hear the color, they point to the item.

> **Listening Script**   *CD 1, Track 69*
>
> **Salesperson:** *We have many sizes and colors in our store. For example, in this shirt, we have two extra-large blue shirts.*
> **Yusuf:** *I don't need that size. Do you have any large white shirts?*
> **Salesperson:** *Sure, we have one in the back. I can get it for you.*
> **Yusuf:** *OK, and while you're at it, could you get me a medium green shirt for my brother?*
> **Salesperson:** *OK, but are you sure he might not want a small yellow shirt? We have three of those on sale.*
> **Yusuf:** *Yes, I'm sure.*

Practice 2   7-10 mins.

E **Look at Exercise D. Complete the chart.**

Help students understand what *inventory* means. Ask them to complete the information.

Teaching Tip

Critical thinking

Students at this level are often asked to repeat or to copy. However, students should be introduced to ways of thinking critically when they are ready and given enough information and resources to do so. Activities that force students to complete a puzzle in the context of the given objective are very useful. As students think critically, they become independent learners.

Evaluation 2   3-5 mins.

Ask questions about the chart in Exercise E such as: *How many white shirts are there?*

Presentation 3   10-15 mins. ■■■

Review singular and plural nouns with students. Ask them the *how many* questions from Exercise E again. Review the verb *be* with students. You may want to do this first with books closed to see how much students remember from Unit 1, Lesson 3. Re-create the chart from page 8 on the board. Leave out the forms of *be*. Ask for volunteers to complete the chart.

(F) Read.

Teach *there is* and *there are* and prepare students to do Exercise G for practice. Show them how to substitute the information underlined with other information from the inventory on the previous page. Make sure you remind students about adjective order.

Go over the pronunciation of the sentences. Show students that using the contraction is more common than not.

Pronunciation

Rhythm and prominence

English sentence rhythm does not follow a consistent pattern. Various aspects of the language affect it. English has a series of stops and starts based on prominent words and the pauses that sometimes follow. In this case, one could pronounce the sentence *There is one white shirt*, in various ways.

If, in the context, a speaker is making a distinction between a white shirt and another color, he might emphasize *one*—making it prominent. In this case, the speaker is answering the question *How many?* Hence, the number is emphasized.

Changing the phrase *there is* to a contraction also changes the rhythm from a steady, even pace to a more natural one. The speaker will generally emphasize the number and follow it with a slight pause.

Practice 3   7-10 mins. ■

(G) Read and practice. Use the information in Exercise E.

Help as needed.

Evaluation 3   3 mins. ■

Ask for volunteers to present the conversation to the class.

Application   15-25 mins. ■■

(H) Write an inventory for your class. Write about your classmates' clothing.

In groups, have students make a class inventory. Put the inventories on the board. Then, in pairs, have students practice the dialog from Exercise G again, using their new class inventory for the information.

(I) Active Task. Go home and write an inventory of the clothes in your closet.

Refer students to *Stand Out Basic Grammar Challenge*, Unit 4, Challenge 3 for more practice with *there is* and *there are*. Also see *Extension Challenge 2* for more practice with the negative simple present.

Activity Bank

Lesson 1, Worksheet 1: Colors and Clothing

Instructor's Notes

_____

_____

_____

_____

_____

_____

_____

_____

_____

_____

_____

_____

_____

_____

GOAL ➤ Identify colors and describe clothing

F Read.

Singular	Plural
There **is** one green shirt.	There **are** two black shirts.
There**'s** one green shirt.	

G Read and practice. Use the information in Exercise E.

A: How many <u>white</u> shirts are there?
B: There's <u>one</u>.

H Write an inventory for your class. Write about your classmates' clothing.
(Answers will vary.)

Class Inventory		
Quantity (How many?)	**Item**	**Color**

I Active Task. Go home and write an inventory of the clothes in your closet.

That's $5.00.

GOAL ➤ Make purchases and count money

CD 1
TR 70

A Listen and read the cash registers.

1.

2.

3.

B Bubble in the number from Exercise A.

1. one dollar   1 2 3
                       ● ○ ○

2. ten dollars and forty-one cents   1 2 3
                                      ○ ○ ●

3. six dollars and twenty-five cents 1 2 3
                                      ○ ● ○

C Practice the conversation with a partner.

A: How much is the <u>comb</u>?
B: It's $1.00.
A: Thanks.

AT-A-GLANCE PREP

Objective: Make purchases and count money
Grammar: Review *How much is / How much are*
Academic Strategies: Focused listening, test-taking skills
Vocabulary: *dollar, quarter, dime, nickel, penny, receipts, price, cash register*

RESOURCES

Activity Bank: Lesson 4, Worksheets 1 and 2
Reading and Writing Challenge: Unit 4
Grammar Challenge: Unit 4, Challenge 4

Audio: CD 1, Tracks 70–77
Heinle Picture Dictionary: Money and Shopping, pages 8–9

■ 1.5 hour classes   ■ 2.5 hour classes   ■ 3⁺ hour classes

AGENDA
Review clothing and make a list.
Read cash register totals.
Learn about U.S. money.
Read receipts.
Write a receipt.

Warm-up and Review   15-20 mins. ■■■

Ask groups to list clothing without using a dictionary or their books. Then ask them to write the words in alphabetical order. Ask each group to write their list on the board. If students introduce new words, acknowledge them and briefly practice their pronunciation.

Introduction   3-5 mins. ■■■

Ask students to identify clothes in the classroom by color and name. Ask where they buy clothing. State the objective: *Today we will learn how to make purchases and count money.*

Presentation 1   15-20 mins. ■■■

 Listen and read the cash registers.

Practice saying *cash register*. Play the recording. Ask students to point to which cash register is being talked about. Have them repeat the money amount with you.

> **Listening Script**   CD 1, Track 70
>
> **1. Cashier:** *Let's see. You want this comb.*
> *That's $1.00.*
> **Tien:** *$1.00?*
> **Cashier:** *That's right.*
> **Tien:** *OK, here you go.*
>
> **2. Cashier:** *OK, that's one red t-shirt.*
> **Tien:** *How much is it?*
> **Cashier:** *That's $6.25 with tax.*
>
> **3. Cashier:** *Let's see. The shorts are $10.41.*
> **Tien:** *OK, do you have change?*
> **Cashier:** *Sure.*
> **Tien:** *Thanks!*

B Bubble in the number from Exercise A.

Do this exercise with students. Remind students to fill in the entire "bubble."

Prepare students to do the practice. Show them how to substitute information. Ask students to write the items being purchased in Exercise A next to the cash registers. You may choose to play the recording again (CD 1, Track 70). Item 1 is a comb; Item 2 is a t-shirt; and Item 3 is a pair of shorts.

Practice 1

C Practice the conversation with a partner.

Help as needed.

Evaluation 1   3-5 mins. ■■■

Ask volunteers to present the conversation.

STANDARDS CORRELATIONS

CASAS: 1.1.6, 1.3.9, 4.8.1, 6.1.1 (See CASAS Competency List on pages 167–173.)
SCANS: Basic Skills Reading, writing, arithmetic, listening, speaking
Resources Allocate money
Information Acquire and evaluate information, organize and maintain information, interpret and communicate information
Systems Understand systems
EFF: Communication Read with understanding, convey ideas in writing, speak so others can understand, listen actively
Decision Making Use math to solve problems and communicate

Presentation 2 10–15 mins. ■■■

D Listen and read with your teacher.

If you have samples of bills and coins, use them. This is also a good place to use "play" money. Put money together in different combinations and see if students can give you the totals.

Listening Script   CD 1, Track 71

The listening script matches the list in Exercise D.

Review numbers 1–100 with students.

Practice using *have* and *has* in this presentation as a review. You may choose to refer back to page 63. Say: *Kim has $35.00—one 20-dollar bill, one 10-dollar bill, and one 5-dollar bill.* Do a short dictation and give students four amounts. After checking to make sure everyone understood the same number, ask students what bills and coins they might need.

Note: At this level, students need consistency. Insist that they insert *and* between the dollars and cents. They should say *six dollars and twenty-five cents*, not *six dollars, twenty-five cents*. Also, make sure that students do not drop the plural *s* when saying *dollars*.

For shorter classes, ask students to do Exercise E for homework.

Practice 2   5–7 mins. ■■

E Match.

Ask students when they finish drawing the lines to speak to a partner and recite the type of money (quarter, nickel, etc.) they see in the right column.

Evaluation 2   5–7 mins. ■■

Check students' book work. Practice saying the amounts with students. Make sure they pronounce the *s* in *dollars*. Also, ask students the names of the types of money (quarter, nickel, etc.) in the right column.

Instructor's Notes

_____
_____
_____
_____
_____
_____
_____
_____
_____
_____
_____
_____
_____
_____
_____
_____
_____
_____
_____
_____
_____
_____

GOAL ➤ **Make purchases and count money**

 D Listen and read with your teacher.

CD 1
TR 71

a dollar bill /
a dollar coin
$1.00

a quarter
$.25

a dime
$.10

a nickel
$.05

a penny
$.01

E Match.

a.

1. $.50

b.

2. $15.08

c.

3. $35.10

LESSON  4   **GOAL** ➤ **Make purchases and count money**

 F Listen and write.

CD 1
TR 72-77

1.

$32.50

2.

$24.50

3.

$44.00

4.

$18.00

5.

$82.50

6.

$22.50

Singular	Plural
How much **is** the dress?	How much **are** the shoes?

G Ask a classmate for the prices in Exercise F. Write.

Adel's
Clothing Emporium

shirt	$24.50
shoes	$44.00
Total	$68.50
Customer Copy

Adel's
Clothing Emporium

dress	$82.50
shorts	$18.00
blouse	$22.50
Total	$123.50
Customer Copy

Adel's
Clothing Emporium

pants	$32.50
Total	$32.50
Customer Copy

H Write a receipt. Buy three items. (Answers will vary.)

Adel's
Clothing Emporium

Total

Customer Copy

Presentation 3   10–15 mins. ■■□

F Listen and write.

Review *How much is?* and *How much are?* Then play the six brief conversations and ask students to write the prices they hear in their books.

Prepare students for the practice by modeling how to do Exercise G. This is an information-gap activity. Student A covers Exercise F and asks: *How much is the shirt?* Student B looks at Exercise F and responds. Student A writes the information on the receipt in Exercise G. Then students reverse roles.

Practice 3   7–10 mins. ■

G Ask a classmate for the prices in Exercise F. Write.

Evaluation 3   5–7 mins. ■

Together as a class, add the prices on the receipts. See if everyone gets the same results.

Application   10–15 mins. ■■■

H Write a receipt. Buy three items.

Have students choose three of the items from Exercise F. A receipt can also be found on the Activity Bank CD-ROM.

 Refer students to *Stand Out Basic Grammar Challenge,* Unit 4, Challenge 4 for more practice with singular and plurals and the *be* verb.

Activity Bank

Lesson 4, Worksheet 1: Money and Totals
Lesson 4, Worksheet 2: Counting Money
Lesson 4, Worksheet 3: Writing Receipts

Instructor's Notes

_____

_____

_____

_____

_____

_____

_____

_____

Objective: Read advertisements

Grammar: *How much / How many*, subject pronoun *they*

Academic Strategies: Focused listening, asking for information, predict information

Vocabulary: *how much, each, ad, save*

RESOURCES

Activity Bank: Lesson 5, Worksheets 1 and 2
Reading and Writing Challenge: Unit 4
Grammar Challenge: Unit 4, Challenge 5

Audio: CD 1, Track 78
Heinle Picture Dictionary: Money and Shopping, pages 8–9

■ 1.5 hour classes   ■ 2.5 hour classes   ■ 3⁺ hour classes

AGENDA

Review writing receipts.
Read an ad.
Practice asking for information.
Take orders.
Compare stores.
Create an ad.

Warm-up and Review   10-15 mins.

Ask students to turn back to page 69, Exercise G, and do the exercise again with a partner.

Teaching Tip

Review

Students should be encouraged to do activities over again after a few days or weeks so the book becomes a tool for learning. This activity is a good example. At this level, you will find that students learn and forget readily.

Introduction   5 mins.

Ask students questions using *what*. For example, you may ask: *What color is your shirt?* State the objective: *Today we will read advertisements.*

Presentation 1   15-20 mins.

Talk a little about clothing stores and where you shop. Ask students where they shop for clothes. Go over the advertisement and review sizes, colors, and prices. Ask questions using *how much*. Remind students what *save* means.

Prepare students for the listening activity by asking them to predict the omitted prices.

Practice 1   7-10 mins.

(A) **Read, listen, and write.**

Play the recording and ask students to listen for the omitted prices. Ask them to write what they hear. Then, ask them to do Exercise B.

> 🎧 **Listening Script**   CD 1, Track 78
>
> *Here at Adel's Clothing Emporium, we have great sales. Come in and see for yourself. Men's shirts in all sizes are only $22.50. You will be happy to see women's dresses in sizes 6 to 12 are only $33.00. We have men's sweaters on sale for $33.00. Men's pants are only $28.00 this week. Women's shoes are now only $24.00. Save $4.00! Blouses are a bargain at $18.00! We will be waiting for you. Remember Adel's Clothing Emporium for great savings!*

(B) **Write.**

Give students a chance to write the information.

Evaluation 1   2-5 mins.

(C) **Ask a classmate the questions in Exercise B.**

Ask students to read and respond to the information in Exercise B in pairs.

STANDARDS CORRELATIONS

CASAS: 1.1.9, 1.2.1, 1.3.9, 4.8.3 (See CASAS Competency List on pages 167–173.)
SCANS: Basic Skills Reading, writing, arithmetic, listening, speaking
Resources Allocate time, allocate money
Information Acquire and evaluate information, organize and maintain information, interpret and communicate information

Interpersonal Participate as a member of a team, teach others, serve clients and customers
Thinking Skills Think creatively, make decisions, solve problems
EFF: Communication Read and understand, convey ideas in writing, speak so others can understand, listen actively
Decision Making Use math to solve problems and make decisions, plan
Interpersonal Cooperate with others, guide others

How much are the shoes?

GOAL ➤ Read advertisements

  A Read, listen, and write.

CD 1
TR 78

All Sizes

Save $5.00

$22.50

Save $12.00

Sizes 6-12

$33.00

SALE

$33.00
All Sizes

SALE

All Sizes

Save $4.00

SALE

$24.00

Save $5.00

$18.00   All Sizes

All Sizes

$28.00

Adel's
CLOTHING EMPORIUM

 B Write.

1. How much are the shirts? __$22.50__
2. How much are the dresses? __$33.00__
3. How much are the shoes? __$24.00__
4. How much are the blouses? __$18.00__

 C Ask a classmate the questions in Exercise B.

LESSON **5**

GOAL ➤ **Read advertisements**

 Read.

How much and How many		
Question		**Answer**
How much	(money) is the sweater?	It is $33.00.
How many	coats do you want?	I want three coats.

E **Read and practice.**

A: Can I help you?
B: Yes, I want some <u>shirts</u>.
A: How many shirts do you want?
B: I want two shirts. How much are they?
A: They are <u>$22.50</u> each.

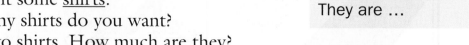

The sweaters are ...

They are ...

F **Practice taking orders from four classmates. Write. (Use the ad on page 73.)**

(Answers will vary.)

Name	Quantity (How many?)	Product	Price
Yusuf	two	shirts	$22.50

Presentation 2

D Read.

Go over questions carefully with students. Review the *be* verb.

Show students that when asked in general terms, the questions are always in the plural: *How much are the shirts?* When it is about a specific shirt, the speaker would say: *How much is the shirt?* Don't spend too much time on this point.

Teaching Tip

Addressing student levels

Students come to any ESL class at various levels. Formal multilevel classes are very common. In the formal multilevel class, students are designated at different levels within the same classroom.

Even if not formally designated, all classes are multilevel to some extent. Students come to classes with a variety of experience in schooling and in English training or exposure, and they also come with different abilities. Some may be good speakers but may have trouble writing while others might be just the opposite.

In the *Stand Out* approach, our philosophy is not to hold a student back if he or she is ready for additional information. The instructor should be aware of what individual students can handle. We often suggest limiting exposure to certain concepts in order to avoid overwhelming students with too much information. However, some students might be ready for more. Be aware of this and help those students when appropriate. Use *Stand Out* ancillaries to further challenge these students.

E Read and practice.

Go over the dialog with students. Drill them in different ways. Help them to see that *each* means for one item.

Teaching Tip

Presentation *vs.* practice

Here, students are preparing to do the practice. Even though in the instruction line we say *practice*, students are not doing anything that requires thinking skills—like getting new or different information from a partner. We say that *presentation* is teacher-centered, practice is teacher-guided, and *application* is completely student-centered where students have taken ownership of the task.

Therefore, this task is best categorized as part of a presentation stage in lesson planning.

Prepare students for the practice by showing them how to make the substitutions.

Practice 2

F Practice taking orders from four classmates. Write. (Use the ad on page 73.)

This activity can be extended or made more difficult by asking students to complete the chart without following the dialog in Exercise E.

Evaluation 2

Ask volunteers to demonstrate the conversation in front of the class.

Presentation 3    10-15 mins. ■■■

G **Read.**

Go over the new advertisement with students. Introduce students to *sale price* and *regular price*. Ask them to help you calculate the regular price of the shirt and the dress. Now have them look at page 73 and compare certain items. Ask them which store has a better price for shirts. Students might think Norma's Fine Clothing does because shoppers save more, but Adel's has a cheaper price.

For shorter classes, ask students to do Exercise H for homework.

Practice 3   5-10 mins. ■

H **Compare Norma's Fine Clothing to Adel's Clothing Emporium (page 73). Write two receipts.**

Students are to write the same items on both receipts applying different prices.

Evaluation 3   7-10 mins. ■

Check students' work and ask which store has better prices. Depending on what items students choose, either store could have better prices. Although there is no clear right answer, note that the prices for men's clothing are cheaper at Adel's while the prices for women's clothing are cheaper at Norma's.

Application   20-30 mins. ■■■

I **In a group, make an advertisement for a new clothing store. Practice the conversation from Exercise E.**

In this activity, make sure students form a conversation using the dialog from Exercise E. Monitor each group well. Ask students to share their conversations and ads with the class.

Activity Bank

> Lesson 5, Worksheet 1: Asking Questions
> Lesson 5, Worksheet 2: Create an Advertisement

 Refer students to *Stand Out Basic Grammar Challenge*, Unit 4, Challenge 5 for more practice with *How much* and *How many*.

GOAL ➤ **Read advertisements**

G Read.

H Compare Norma's Fine Clothing to Adel's Clothing Emporium (page 73). Write two receipts. (Answers will vary.)

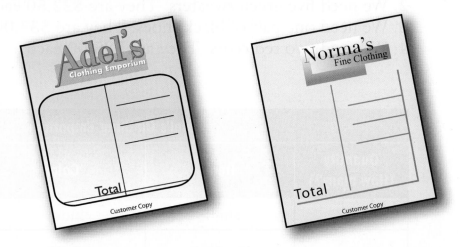

I In a group, make an advertisement for a new clothing store. Practice the conversation from Exercise E.

Review

A Write the words. (Lesson 1)

1.

___shirt___

2.

___shoes___

3.

___socks___

4.

___pants___

5.

___shorts___

6.

___dress___

7.

___blouse___

8.

___sweater___

B Read and write. (Lessons 3–5)

1. We need three blue shirts. They are $18.59 each.
2. We need five green sweaters. They are $22.50 each.
3. We need one pair of black shoes. They are $33.00 each.
4. We need two red coats. They are $85.00 each.

Adel's Clothing Emporium			
Quantity (How many?)	Item	Color	Price
1. 3	shirt	blue	$55.77
2. 5	sweater	green	$112.50
3. 1	shoes	black	$33.00
4. 2	coat	red	$170.00

Objective: All unit objectives
Grammar: All unit grammar
Academic Strategies: Focused listening,
reviewing, evaluating, developing study skills
Vocabulary: All unit vocabulary

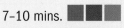 1.5 hour classes   2.5 hour classes   3+ hour classes

AGENDA
Discuss unit objectives.
Complete the review.
Do My Dictionary.
Evaluate and reflect on progress.

Warm-up and Review   7–10 mins.

Ask students what new clothes they want to buy.
Make a list on the board of all the vocabulary
students can come up with from the unit.

Introduction   5 mins.

Write all the objectives on the board from Unit
4. Show students the first page of every lesson
so they understand that today will be review.
Complete the agenda.

Note: Depending on the length of the term,
you may decide to have students do Presentation
and Practice 1 for homework and then review
student work as the warm-up for another class
meeting.

Presentation 1   10–15 mins.

This presentation and practice will cover the
first three pages of the review. Quickly go to the
first page of each lesson. Discuss the objective of
each. Ask simple questions to remind students
what they have learned.

Practice 1   15–20 mins.

A Write the words. (Lesson 1)

B Read and write. (Lessons 3–5)

Teaching Tip

Recycling/Review

The review process and the project that
follows are part of the recycling/review
process. Students at this level often need to be
reintroduced to concepts to solidify what they
have learned. Many concepts are learned and
forgotten while learning other new concepts.
This is because students learn but are not
necessarily ready to acquire language concepts.

Therefore, it becomes very important to review
and to show students how to review on their
own. It is also important to recycle the new
concepts in different contexts.

STANDARDS CORRELATIONS

CASAS: 1.1.9, 1.2.1, 1.3.9, 7.4.1, 7.4.2, 7.4.3 (See CASAS Competency
List on pages 167–173.)
SCANS: **Basic Skills** Reading, writing, listening, speaking
Information Acquire and evaluate information, organize and maintain
information, interpret and communicate information

Thinking Skills See things in the mind's eye
EFF: **Communication** Speak so others can understand
Lifelong Learning Take responsibility for learning, reflect and evaluate

Practice 1 (continued)

C Write the locations. (Lesson 2)

D What money do you need? Write. (Lesson 4)

Write the locations. (Lesson 2)

a. It's in the corner of the store.

b. It's in the front of the store.

c. It's on the right side of the store.

d. It's in the back of the store.

e. It's in the middle of the store.

f. It's on the left side of the store.

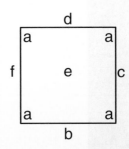

D **What money do you need? Write. (Lesson 4)** (Answers may vary.)

Total	$20 bills	$10 bills	$5 bills	$1 bills	quarters	dimes	nickels	pennies
$69.00	3		1	4				
$22.50	1			2	2			
$56.90	2	1	1	1	3	1	1	
$132.00	6	1		2				
$153.75	7	1		3	3			
$113.80	5	1		3	3		1	

Review

E Read the ad. (Lesson 5)

F Write the information from the ad. (Lesson 5)

Item	Price	Savings
green pants	$28.50	$5.00
black pants	$17.50	$5.00
white shirts	$17.50	$2.00
blouses	$23.50	$3.00
socks	$3.50	$1.00
coats	$44.50	$5.00

Practice 1 *(continued)*

E Read the ad. (Lesson 5)

F Write the information from the ad.
(Lesson 5)

Evaluation 1   15-20 mins. ■■■

Go around the room and check on students'
progress. Help individuals when needed. If you
see consistent errors among several students,
interrupt the class and give a mini lesson
or review to help students feel comfortable
with the concept.

Presentation 2 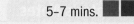 5-7 mins.

My Dictionary

Review with students what My Dictionary is and help them see the value of it.

Practice 2 7-10 mins.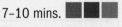

Ask students to complete My Dictionary.

Evaluation 2 5 mins.

Ask students to share their cards with the class.

Presentation 3

Learner Log

Review the concepts of the Learner Log. Make sure students understand the concepts and how to do the log including the check marks.

Teaching Tip

Learner Logs

Learner logs function to help students in many different ways.

1. They serve as part of the review process.

2. They help students to gain confidence and document what they have learned. In this way, students see that they are progressing and want to move forward in learning.

3. They provide students with a tool that they can use over and over to check and recheck their understanding. In this way, students become independent learners.

Practice 3 10-15 mins.

Ask students to complete the Learner Log.

Evaluation 3 2 mins.

Go over the log with students.

Application

Ask students to write down their favorite lesson or page in the unit.

My Dictionary

Make flash cards to improve your vocabulary.

1. Choose four new words from this unit.
2. Write each word on an index card or on a piece of paper.
3. On the back of the index card or paper, draw a picture, find a sentence from the book with the word, and write the page number.
4. Study the words.

How much are the shoes?
page 73

Learner Log

Write the page number(s).

	Page Number	I can do it. ✓
1. Identify types of clothing.	61	
2. Find sections in a store.	64	
3. Describe clothing.	67	
4. Count money.	70	
5. Read advertisements.	73	

My favorite page in this unit is (Answers will vary.)

Open a clothing store!

Carrie's Clothing Store

Quantity (how many)	Item	Color	Price
1 50	shirts	blue, red, yellow	$27.00
2 30	pants	blue, green, black	$35.99
3 22 pairs	shoes	black, brown	$40.00
4 15	sweaters	white, pink, red	$30.50

SALE
All Sizes
$25.00

1. Form a team with four or five students. In your team, you need:

POSITION	JOB	STUDENT NAME
Student 1: Team Leader	See that everyone speaks English. See that everyone participates.	
Student 2: Writer	Make an inventory list.	
Student 3: Artist	Make an ad for a clothing store.	
Students 4/5: Spokespeople	Prepare a presentation.	

2. Open a store. What is the name? Design the store.

3. Make an ad.

4. Write an inventory list.

5. Present your store to the class.

Introduction   5 mins.

In this project, students will work in teams to create a clothing store. They will use the vocabulary from the unit. They may choose to use Worksheets 8 and 9 from the Activity Bank CD-ROM as templates.

Stage 1   15-20 mins.
Form a team with four or five students.

Set the scene and form teams of four or five. Show students examples of the project if you have one.

Help students to assign positions by asking the leaders to all stand. On the spot, students will have to choose who will be the leader of their group. Review the responsibility of a leader and ask students to write the name of their leader in their books. Do the same with all positions.

Stage 2   10-15 mins.
Open a store. What is the name of the store? Design the store.

Ask students to create a clothing store and choose a name for it. Try to encourage them to be original and not to use a name of a clothing store they may already know about.

Stage 3   40-50 mins.
Make an ad.

The team creates an advertisement. You may bring in magazines for teams to cut up and use in their ads. Another approach would be to have students find pictures on the Internet and use them. Yet another approach would be to have students draw the clothing for their advertisements.

Stage 4   10-30 mins.
Write an inventory list.

Ask students to create the inventory list.

Stage 5   10-30 mins.
Present your store to the class.

Ask groups to present their projects. This can be particularly effective if you videotape the presentations.

STANDARDS CORRELATIONS

CASAS: 1.3.9, 4.8.1 (See CASAS Competency List on pages 167–173.)
SCANS: Basic Skills Reading, writing, listening, speaking
Resources Allocate time, allocate money, allocate materials and facility resources, allocate human resources
Information Acquire and evaluate information, organize and maintain information, interpret and communicate information, use computers to process information
Interpersonal Participate as a member of a team, teach others, serve clients and customers, exercise leadership, negotiate to arrive at a decision, work with cultural diversity
Systems Understand systems, monitor and correct performance, improve and design systems

Thinking Skills Think creatively, make decisions, solve problems, see things in the mind's eye
Personal Qualities Responsibility, sociability, self management
EFF: Communication Read with understanding, convey ideas in writing, speak so others can understand, listen actively, observe critically
Decision Making Solve problems and make decisions, plan
Interpersonal Cooperate with others, advocate and influence, resolve conflict and negotiate, guide others
Lifelong Learning Take responsibility for learning, reflect and evaluate

Objective: Identify and ask about locations
Grammar: *Yes/No* questions and answers, *which*
Pronunciation: Question intonation
Academic Strategy: Focused listening
Vocabulary: Community locations, *which*

RESOURCES

Activity Bank: Lesson 5, Worksheet 1
Reading and Writing Challenge: Unit 5
Grammar Challenge: Unit 5, Challenge 1

■ 1.5 hour classes ■ 2.5 hour classes ■ 3⁺ hour classes

AGENDA

Talk about shopping.
Identify stores.
Identify places in the community.
Ask questions about the community.

Audio: CD 2, Tracks 1–7
Heinle Picture Dictionary: Shops and Stores, pages 48–49

Stand Out Basic Assessment CD-ROM with Exam*View*®

Preassessment *(optional)*

Use the Stand Out Basic Assessment CD-ROM with Exam*View*® to create a pretest for Unit 5.

Warm-up and Review   7–10 mins. ■■■

Tell students where you shop. List on the board things you need to buy or rent. Include: *shoes, food for dinner, a hot dog, a video or CD,* and *medicine.* As a class, list stores where you might buy or rent these items. Use specific store names.

Introduction   7–10 mins. ■■■

Draw a map of your school's community. Label cross streets. Ask students to point to locations mentioned in the warm-up. State the objective: *Today we will identify and ask about locations.*

Presentation 1   30–45 mins. ■■■

(A) Listen and point.

Play the recording. Help students identify the types of stores with the stores you listed in the warm-up. Drill students by asking questions such as: *Where do I buy a shirt? Where do I buy food?* There may be more than one answer.

> 🎧 **Listening Script**   CD 2, Track 1
>
> 1. *clothing store*   5. *video store*
> 2. *shoe store*   6. *convenience store*
> 3. *pharmacy*   7. *department store*
> 4. *supermarket*

Use the new vocabulary in context. Ask students to point to the location.

Practice 1   5–7 mins. ■■■

(B) Listen and write the number of the conversation.

> 🎧 **Listening Script**   CD 2, Tracks 2–6
>
> 1. **A:** *We need to go to the store.*
>   **B:** *Why? What do we need?*
>   **A:** *We need lots of things. We need milk, apples, and bread.*
>   **B:** *Then we need to go to the supermarket right away.*
>   **A:** *You said it!*
>
> 2. **A:** *My feet hurt.*
>   **B:** *It's those shoes you're wearing.*
>   **A:** *These things are old, but I love them.*
>   **B:** *I think if we were to go to a shoe store, you would feel a lot better.*
>   **A:** *OK, let's go.*
>
> 3. **A:** *I need a new dress for the party.*
>   **B:** *What size do you wear?*
>   **A:** *I wear a size 9.*
>   **B:** *I think the clothing store on the corner has a good selection.*
>   **A:** *Really? That's great. Let's go.*
>
> 4. **A:** *We need some medicine.*
>   **B:** *Yes, I know. We need to buy some aspirin and cough syrup.*
>   **A:** *Sounds like a good idea. Let's get some bandages, too.*
>   **B:** *OK. Let's go to the pharmacy down the street.*
>
> 5. **A:** *There is a new movie on video. You've got to see it.*
>   **B:** *Is it good?*
>   **A:** *Yeah, it's great.*
>   **B:** *OK, let's rent it. The video store is still open.*

Evaluation 1   3 mins. ■■■

Ask students to report their answers

Note: Standards Correlations are on the next page.

Our Community

GOALS

➤ **Identify and ask about locations**
➤ **Describe housing**
➤ **Identify types of transportation**

➤ **Express transportation preferences**
➤ **Give and follow directions**

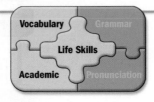

LESSON **1**

Where we live

GOAL ➤ **Identify and ask about locations**

A Listen and point.

CD 1
TR 1

1.

5.

2.

6.

3.

7.

4.

B Listen and write the number of the conversation.

CD 2
TR 2-6

_1_ supermarket
_2_ shoe store
_4_ pharmacy

_5_ video store
_3_ clothing store

CD 2
TR 7

C Listen and point to the signs.

D Write the places in Exercise C.

Place to sleep	Places to eat	Places to buy things
hotel	restaurant	clothing store
	fast-food restaurant	shoe store
		pharmacy
		video store

Presentation 2   10-15 mins. ■■□

Ask students to look at the New York street scene. Ask them to cover Exercise D so they are not tempted to move ahead. Go over the details in the scene.

C Listen and point to the signs.

 Listening Script   CD 2, Track 7

1. *Find the hotel.*
2. *Find the restaurant.*
3. *Find the fast-food restaurant.*
4. *Find the clothing store.*
5. *Find the shoe store.*
6. *Find the pharmacy.*
7. *Find the video store.*
8. *Find the bus stop.*
9. *Find the telephone.*

For shorter classes, have students do Exercise D for homework.

Teaching Tip

Art vs. Photographs

In *Stand Out,* we often choose art, especially at lower levels, to give the instructor more control of the vocabulary. The detail in photographs may provide more information than would be helpful at lower levels. Such detail can overwhelm students, especially if some students begin to ask about each item, detracting from the presentation.

Practice 2   15-20 mins. ■□

Ask students to drill each other on vocabulary. Student A says a location and Student B points to it in the picture.

D Write the places in Exercise C.

Ask students to write and categorize. Students may do this in pairs. Don't prepare students by giving them instructions for this activity. Allow them to figure out what to do.

Teaching Tip

Receptive vs. Productive vocabulary

The vocabulary in each lesson is limited to essential; however, each class is unique and vocabulary needed may vary. A lot of vocabulary may overwhelm students, especially if they are using picture dictionaries. Therefore, it is important to help students know what words they are responsible for. Make sure they are aware of the vocabulary lists in the appendix (pages 161-162). Students will also take more responsibility for their learning if you have regular spelling or vocabulary tests.

Evaluation 2   5-7 mins. ■■

Check students' book work by going over the answers as a class. Reproduce the chart on the board and ask students to come up and complete it. Add more items to the list if students come up with places that are not in the picture.

Teaching Tip

Preparation to practice and critical thinking

Students at all levels need to begin to think critically and make decisions about what they should be doing in a given activity. One important principle in the presentation stage of a lesson is to prepare students for practice. Occasionally, however, it is beneficial to allow students the opportunity to think through an activity and discover for themselves what to do. This activity is one of those cases. Some students may ask for help. Try to encourage them to take risks and do what makes sense to them.

STANDARDS CORRELATIONS

CASAS: 1.3.7, 7.2.3 (See CASAS Competency List on pages 167-173.)
SCANS: **Basic Skills** Reading, writing, listening, speaking
Information Acquire and evaluate information, organize and maintain information

EFF: **Communication** Speak so others can understand, listen actively

Presentation 3   15–20 mins.

E   Read.

Yes/no questions were introduced in the previous unit. However, students need to review asking and answering these questions with the appropriate intonation. Ask students to see if they can find where they learned this intonation (page 67). In this lesson, we will expand the answer from *yes* or *no* to *No, I don't*, and *Yes, I do*.

In previous lessons, students learned information questions. You may want to help them remember all the information question words they have learned: *how, where, when*, and *what*. As students progress through the book, they will add to the list. Show students how *which* is used when there is a choice between items and how it is followed by a noun. Be careful to avoid spending so much time on the grammar in this unit that students lose sight of the principal objective.

Teaching Tip

Grammar presentations

In the *Stand Out* approach, grammar is introduced many times before students are expected to acquire a structure. At the lower levels, structures are also presented little by little. Students begin to grasp context as more information is added from previous lessons.

It is important that the instructor is mindful of all the information being presented and the objective. The instructor should try to challenge students without overwhelming them. For example, forming questions is an important grammar focus that could have been included in this lesson, but students are not prepared at this level for such a presentation. If the instructor spends time trying to teach the formation of questions at this level, students will become confused and lose confidence.

At this level, it is far better to concentrate on the answers and intonation of the given questions.

Go over the conversations in Exercise F. Show students how they can substitute information from Exercise A. Model the activity with several students.

Practice 3   7–10 mins.

F   Practice with a partner. Ask about the places in Exercise A.

Help as needed.

Evaluation 3   5–7 mins.

Ask for volunteers to present the conversation in front of the class.

Application   10–15 mins.

G   Talk to four classmates. Write places they buy things.

 Refer students to *Stand Out Basic Grammar Challenge*, Unit 5, Challenge 1 for more practice with *yes/no* questions.

Activity Bank

Lesson 1, Worksheet 1: Locations in the Community

Instructor's Notes

_____

_____

_____

_____

_____

_____

_____

_____

_____

_____

_____

_____

_____

_____

_____

_____

E Read.

Yes/No Questions	
Question	**Answer**
Do you buy clothing at a department store?	Yes, I do.
Do you buy food at a supermarket?	No, I don't.
Do you buy shoes at a shoe store?	

Pronunciation

Yes/No **Questions**

➤ Do you buy shoes at a shoe store?

➤ Do you buy food at a supermarket?

F Practice with a partner. Ask about the places in Exercise A.

A: Peter, do you buy medicine at a pharmacy?
B: Yes, I do.
A: Which one?
B: Save-A-Lot Pharmacy.

> Which one? = Which store?

A: Maria, do you buy shoes at a shoe store?
B: No, I don't. I buy shoes at a department store.
A: Which one?
B: Marcy's.

G Talk to four classmates. Write places they buy things.   (Answers will vary.)

Name	Places
Peter	Jack's Supermarket, Rudolfo's Mexican Café

Where do you live?

GOAL ➤ Describe housing

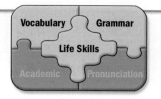
Vocabulary | Grammar
Life Skills
Academic | Pronunciation

A Talk about the map.

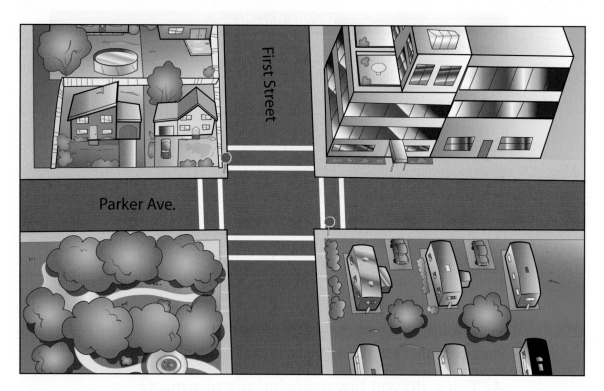

on / in
I live **on** First Street.
I live **in** a house.

a / an
a house
a mobile home
an <u>apartment</u>

 B Listen and practice.

CD 2
TR 8

A: Where do you live?
B: I live on First Street.
A: Do you live in a house or an apartment?
B: I live in a house.

AT-A-GLANCE PREP

Objective: Describe housing
Grammar: *in/on, a/an*
Academic Strategies: Focused listening,
  test-taking strategies
Vocabulary: housing words, *avenue, park, bedroom, rent*

AGENDA
Review stores and make a list.
Read a map.
Read a classified ad.
Learn about different types of housing.

RESOURCES

Activity Bank: Lesson 2, Worksheet 1
Reading and Writing Challenge: Unit 5
Grammar Challenge: Unit 5, Challenge 2

Audio: CD 2, Tracks 8–10
Heinle Picture Dictionary: Types of Homes, pages 62–63

■ 1.5 hour classes ■ 2.5 hour classes ■ 3⁺ hour classes

Warm-up and Review 10-12 mins.

Ask groups to list all the places they buy from. Then ask groups to report to the class.

Introduction 7-10 mins.

Ask individuals where they live. Prompt students to ask you. Respond: *I live in a house/ condominium/apartment in _____* (your city). State the objective: *Today we will learn how to describe housing.*

Presentation 1 30-40 mins.

Write *apartment, house,* and *mobile home* on the board. Help students understand through pictures what each type of home is like. Ask a few students if they live in a house or an apartment. If students live in condominiums or other kinds of housing, write these on the board.

Write *in* and *on* on the board. Remind students that they are pronounced differently. Help students understand that *in* would mean they live inside a building while *on* literally means that the building rests on top of the street.

Ask questions and encourage students to use the correct words. Teacher: *Do you live in a house or an apartment?* Student: *I live in a house.*

This is the first time students are introduced to *an.* If they are ready, you may expand this explanation beyond *an* with *apartment.*

However, most examples will be out of context so don't spend too much time on it.

A Talk about the map.

Talk about the streets the houses, apartments, and mobile homes are on. Ask questions: *Where are the mobile homes?* (They are on Parker Avenue.) Write questions and answers on the board.

B Listen and practice.

Ask students to listen to the conversation. Help them hear the rhythm of the language. Have them say the conversation with you a few times.

> **Listening Script**   *CD 2, Track 8*
>
> The listening script matches the conversation in Exercise B.

Practice 1 7-10 mins.

Do a Corners activity. The corners represent *apartment, house, mobile home,* and *other types of housing.* Have students go to corners according to their housing. Ask students to practice the conversation from Exercise B in their corner.

Evaluation 1 3-7 mins.

Ask for volunteers from each group to present the conversation in front of the class.

STANDARDS CORRELATIONS

CASAS: 1.4.1, 1.4.2, 1.9.4 (See CASAS Competency List on pages 167–173.)
SCANS: Basic Skills Reading, writing, listening, speaking
Information Acquire and evaluate information, organize and maintain information

Interpersonal Participate as a member of a team, teach others
EFF: Communication Read with understanding, convey ideas in writing, speak so others can understand, listen actively, observe critically
Interpersonal Cooperate with others

Presentation 2　　　　15–20 mins. ■■■

C Read.

Help students with new vocabulary and prepare them for the practice in Exercise D by asking familiar questions about ads. Then ask students how many bedrooms their home has. Also, be sure you have added *condominium* to the vocabulary for this lesson if students didn't come up with it earlier.

Prepare students for a focused listening activity in Exercise E.

Practice 2　　　　7–10 mins. ■■

D Bubble in the correct answer.

Ask students to take five minutes and answer the questions on their own without help from other students. After five minutes, go over the answers and check students' work. Walk students through each question and help them find the answers in the classified ads.

E Listen and write.

Play the recording without pausing it, repeating it in its entirety if necessary.

 Listening Script　　　CD 2, Track 9

1. *I think that you will be very happy with our special this week. This is a fine three-bedroom house with new floors in a beautiful neighborhood. Please come and see it. It's on Parker Street.*
2. *My family and I live in a three-bedroom home in the city. It is on a big lot. We enjoy our mobile home. We have many friends who live in the park.*
3. *There is a great rental on Parker Avenue. I think it is under $1,000 a month. It is a two-bedroom apartment and there is a community pool.*

Evaluation 2　　　　5–7 mins. ■■

Go over the answers students have written in their books.

GOAL ➤ **Describe housing**

C Read.

FOR SALE	FOR SALE	FOR RENT
3-bedroom house 3114 Parker Ave. New York, NY 10003	**1-bedroom condominium** 212 First Street New York, NY 10003	**2-bedroom apartment** 3232 Parker Ave. New York, NY 10003
OPEN HOUSE		

D Bubble in the correct answer.

1. What home is on 3114 Parker Ave.?
   - ● the house
   - ○ the apartment
   - ○ the condominium

2. What home is for sale?
   - ○ the apartment
   - ○ the condominium
   - ● the house and the condominium

3. What home has only one bedroom?
   - ○ the apartment
   - ○ the house
   - ● the condominium

4. What home is for rent?
   - ● the apartment
   - ○ the house
   - ○ the house and the apartment

  E Listen and write.

CD 2
TR 9

   a house   an apartment   a mobile home

1. _____a house_____   2. _____a mobile home_____   3. _____an apartment_____

GOAL ➤ **Describe housing**

 CD 2
TR 10

F Listen and read.

1. I'm Chen.
   I'm from China.
   I live in a house.
   I live on First Street
     in Alpine City.

2. I'm Latifa.
   I'm from Saudi Arabia.
   I live in an apartment.
   I live in Casper Town
     on Parker Avenue.

3. I'm Natalia.
   I'm from Guatemala.
   I live in a condominium
     in Alpine City on
     First Street.

G Practice the conversation.

Chen: Hi, I'm Chen.
Latifa: Nice to meet you, Chen. I'm Latifa.
Chen: Where do you live?
Latifa: I live in Casper Town.
Chen: Do you live in an apartment, a condominium, or a house?
Latifa: I live in an apartment.

H Write a conversation. (Answers may vary.)

Latifa: Hi, I'm Latifa.

Natalia: Nice to meet you, Latifa. I'm Natalia.

Latifa: Where do you live?

Natalia: I live in Alpine City.

Latifa: Do you live in an apartment, a condominium, or a house?

Natalia: I live in a condominium.

I Write and practice a conversation about you and a partner. (Answers will vary.)

Presentation 3　　15-20 mins.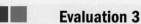

F Listen and read.

Have students listen one time with their books closed or with the information below the pictures covered. Then ask students to uncover the information and read along as they listen to the recording a second time.

> **Listening Script**　　*CD 2, Track 10*
>
> The listening script matches the statements in Exercise F.

Review the simple present tense. Remind students to use *does* + *live* when asking a question about each person and *lives* in the response. You might ask: *Where does Chen live?* The response should be: *He lives in a house, He lives on First Street,* or *He lives in Alpine City.* Write each answer on the board and show how students can respond.

Do a drill where you ask a student the questions. The student answers and then asks another student. Continue with this drill until all students have responded. You might prompt students to talk about different people on the page. If you want students to respond differently, point to one of the examples on the board.

G Practice the conversation.

Go over the conversation with students and help them with intonation and rhythm. Ask students to practice in pairs. Make sure students understand every word in the conversation.

For shorter classes, ask students to do Exercise H for homework.

Practice 3　　5 mins.

H Write a conversation.

This conversation may be very similar to the conversation in Exercise G. Make sure students know to put the information about Natalia into the conversation.

Evaluation 3　　3-5 mins.

Ask volunteers to present their conversations in front of the class.

Application　　5-7 mins.

I Write and practice a conversation about you and a partner.

Show students how they can use previous dialogs for models.

📖 **Refer students to *Stand Out Basic Grammar Challenge*, Unit 5, Challenge 3 for more practice with *come* and *go* and the simple present.**

Activity Bank 💿

Lesson 2, Worksheet 1: Housing

Instructor's Notes

_____
_____
_____
_____
_____
_____
_____
_____
_____
_____
_____
_____
_____
_____
_____
_____
_____

Objective: Identify types of transportation
Grammar: *come* and *go*
Pronunciation: Information question intonation
Academic Strategies: Focused listening,
  interpreting graphs
Vocabulary: Types of transportation, *cost,*
  transportation, come, go, drive, take, ride, walk

RESOURCES

Activity Bank: Lesson 3, Worksheets 1 and 2
Reading and Writing Challenge: Unit 5
Grammar Challenge: Unit 5, Challenge 3

■ 1.5 hour classes   ■ 2.5 hour classes   ■ 3⁺ hour classes

AGENDA

Review types of housing.
Read a map.
Learn about transportation and calculate cost.
Talk to other students about their
  transportation.

Audio: CD 2, Track 11
Heinle Picture Dictionary: Vehicles and Traffic Signs,
  pages 118–119; Public Transportation, 128–129

Warm-up and Review   10–15 mins.

Ask students again where they live. Review their
conversations in Exercise I on page 86. Have
students do the application activity from the
previous lesson with different people.

Ask students to have a conversation with four other
students and complete a chart like the one below.
You may choose to use the three-column template
on the Activity Bank CD-ROM.

Name	City	Type of Home

Introduction   5–7 mins.

Tell students about your schedule. Include how you
get to work. Describe briefly what transportation
you take to school. State the objective: *Today we will*
identify types of transportation.

Presentation 1   15–20 mins.

A **Look at the map.**

Look at the map with students. Explain the
map's scale. *Miles* and other parts of this
discussion are mostly receptive vocabulary at this

point. Get an idea from students how far they
travel to come to school. Pantomime driving and
ask: *Who drives to school?*

B **Listen and read.**

Go over the dialog with students and help
them feel comfortable with the rhythm of the
language. Prepare students to do Exercise C.

 Listening Script   CD 2, Track 11

The listening script matches the conversation in
Exercise B.

Practice 1   7–10 mins.

C **Ask four classmates.**

Circulate around the classroom and help as needed.

Evaluation 1   3–5 mins.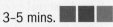

Take a class poll after students finish the activity.
Some students undoubtedly walk or come to
school by other means. This is to be expected.
Find out what students who don't drive or take
the bus use for transportation.

STANDARDS CORRELATIONS

CASAS: 1.1.3, 2.2.3, 2.2.5, 6.7.2 (See CASAS Competency List on
pages 167–173.)
SCANS: **Basic Skills** Reading, writing, arithmetic, listening, speaking
Resources Allocate time, allocate money
Information Acquire and evaluate information, organize and maintain
information, interpret and communicate information

Systems Understand systems
Thinking Skills Make decisions, solve problems, see things in the mind's eye
EFF: **Communication** Read with understanding, convey ideas in writing,
speak so others can understand, listen actively
Decision Making Use math to solve problems and communicate, solve
problems and make decisions, plan

I take the bus.

GOAL ➤ Identify types of transportation

A Look at the map.

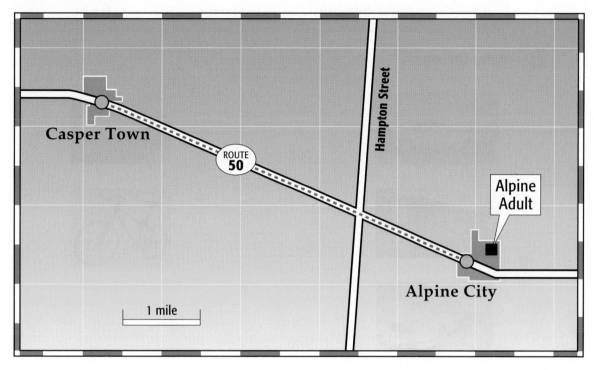

CD 2
TR 11

B Listen and read.

Chen: Do you drive to school?
Latifa: No, I don't. I take the bus.
Chen: How much is it?
Latifa: It's 75 cents.

C Ask four classmates. (Answers will vary.)

Name	Do you drive or take the bus?

GOAL ➤ **Identify types of transportation**

| car | bicycle | taxi | train | bus |

D Write the words.

car

train

bus

bicycle

taxi

E Read the bar graph.

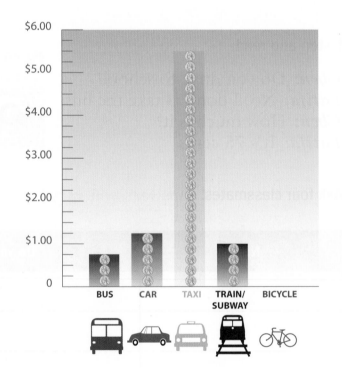

F Ask a partner, *"How much?"*

EXAMPLE: How much is it to travel by bus?

Presentation 2   20-30 mins.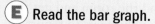

In Evaluation 1, you discussed other forms of transportation. Go over the types listed in the box and with students identify them by the pictures.

(D) Write the words.

(E) Read the bar graph.

Show students how to read the bar graph. Show them how each line is 25 cents. On the board, write: *How much is it to travel by car?* Substitute other forms of transportation and practice the question. Ask students to follow your lead and ask the questions. *Travel* will be a new word for students, but in context, they should understand it.

Remind students to say *and* between dollars and cents. If you need to, you can refer students to page 70 for review.

Teaching Tip

Graphs

Graphs are an excellent way to convey information so that most students with limited vocabulary will understand. Graphs are an especially good strategy when students are at multiple levels of proficiency. The lowest levels can understand the same information as the higher levels.

It is essential that the instructor help students get a feel for how to read and, later, create graphs. Students will use and develop critical thinking skills as they interpret and design graphs. Graphs are especially useful for the visual learner.

Practice 2   7-10 mins.

(F) Ask a partner, "How much?"

Ask students to drill one another. Because this might be difficult for some students, put students in groups of four instead of in pairs to do this activity.

Teaching Tip

Pair work in groups

The instructor cannot possibly be everywhere in the classroom at the same time. Certain students, however, will need special attention. One way to accommodate these students is to group them together in the classroom, as is done in many designated multilevel classes. Then the instructor can spend extra time with the group that needs more attention.

This strategy will work but sometimes it will present additional problems:

1. Students in the special group may feel isolated.
2. Students in the larger group may feel neglected.
3. Students in the special group may feel they are not as "good" as the other students.

Another strategy is to use student mentors. Group a stronger student with others who may need additional help.

For example, students will do a drill where Student 1 asks Student 2 a question. Student 2 answers and asks Student 3. Student 3 answers and asks Student 4. Student 4 answers and asks Student 1. This should be modeled several times before students start. Make sure there is one strong student who understands the process and the concepts in each group.

Evaluation 2   7-10 mins.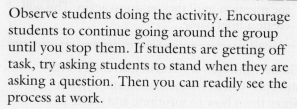

Observe students doing the activity. Encourage students to continue going around the group until you stop them. If students are getting off task, try asking students to stand when they are asking a question. Then you can readily see the process at work.

Presentation 3

10–15 mins.

G Read.

Ask the class to help you make a different pantomime for each vocabulary word. Students can be very creative. Get them started by pantomiming *drive a car* for them. Another way to do this, if there is time, is to play charades. Write each of the phrases on a 3-by-5 index card. Mix the cards up and ask for a volunteer to choose one of them. Ask the volunteer to pantomime the activity and allow the class to guess the phrase.

In this lesson, you will also introduce two new words. Help students understand the difference between *come* and *go*.

Pronunciation

Information questions

This lesson is a review from earlier lessons on information questions. Students used *how* to ask about the weather on page 34. Now, they will use it in a different context. Remind students that with information questions, the information word is often emphasized and is followed by a slight pause.

To help students understand this, ask them to stand every time they say *how* and to sit when saying the rest of the question. First, start by asking the class to stand when you say *how*. Then write the two questions from the lesson on the board. Ask each student to read the questions. Make sure students don't complete the question until they sit down again. This will create a brief pause.

Go over the conversation in Exercise H with students. Check for intonation and rhythm. Show them how to substitute and create new conversations using the information on page 88.

Practice 3

7–10 mins. ■

H Practice the conversation.

You might choose to do an alternative pairing activity such as inside/outside circle as described on page 63a, dialog cards on page 55a, or pair work in groups on page 88a.

Evaluation 3

3–7 mins. ■

Ask for volunteers to present the conversation in front of the class.

Application

10–15 mins. ■■■

I Ask four classmates.

Ask students to go around the room and get the information and then ask volunteers to report to the class. Make sure students report using the third person singular: *Natalia drives to school.*

J Active Task. How much does the bus cost to go from your home to school?

Students may need to research this or they can ask other students if they don't take the bus.

Refer students to *Stand Out Basic Grammar Challenge*, Unit 5, Challenge 3 for more practice with *come* and *go* and the simple present.

Activity Bank

Lesson 3, Worksheet 1: Transportation Vocabulary

Lesson 3, Worksheet 2: Transportation Prices

Instructor's Notes

_____

_____

_____

_____

_____

_____

_____

_____

_____

_____

_____

G   Read.

drive a car	take a bus
ride a bike	take a train
walk	take a taxi

Come and *Go*	
You are at school. You ask, "How do you **come** to school?"	You are at home. You ask, "How do you **go** to school?"
You are at school. You ask, "How do you **go** home?"	You are at home. You ask, "How do you **come** home?"

H   Practice the conversation.

Latifa: How do you come to school?
Natalia: I <u>drive</u>.
Latifa: When do you go home?
Natalia: I go home at <u>3:00</u>.

I   Ask four classmates.   (Answers will vary.)

Name	How do you come to school?	When do you go home?
Natalia	drives	3:00

J   **Active Task.** How much does the bus cost to go from your home to school? _____

(Answers will vary.)

4

She takes the train.

GOAL ➤ Express transportation preferences

A Listen and write.

CD 2
TR 12

1. I'm James.
   I'm from the
   United States.
   I live in a house.

   I take the ___bus___
   to school.

2. I'm Nga.
   I'm from Vietnam.
   I live in a house.

   I ___ride___ a bicycle
   to school.

3. I'm Carina.
   I'm from Cuba.
   I live in an

   ___apartment___.
   I drive to school.

B Write.

Name	Country	Housing	Transportation
James	United States	house	bus
Nga	Vietnam	house	bicycle
Carina	Cuba	apartment	drive

Objective: Express transportation preferences
Grammar: Simple present
Academic Strategy: Focused listening
Vocabulary: *housing, live, take, walk, drive, ride*

RESOURCES

Activity Bank: Lesson 4, Worksheet 1
Reading and Writing Challenge: Unit 5
Grammar Challenge: Unit 5, Challenge 4

Audio: CD 2, Track 12
Heinle Picture Dictionary: Road Trip, pages 122–123

■ 1.5 hour classes ■ 2.5 hour classes ■ 3⁺ hour classes

AGENDA
Take a class poll.
Listen and write about transportation.
Practice the simple present.
Write about yourself using the simple present.

Warm-up and Review   15-20 mins. ■■■

Take a class poll. What types of transportation do people take to school? Write the results on the board. Ask students to make a bar graph of the results. You may supply them with graph paper or use a template from the Activity Bank CD-ROM. If your students are ready, and if you have access to computers, you may use spreadsheet software to make graphs.

Introduction   3-5 mins. ■■■

Ask students questions about themselves on topics covered thus far. State the objective: *Today we will express transportation preferences.*

This lesson is primarily review.

Teaching Tip

Review

Reviewing and recycling past material are of particular importance at lower levels because students tend to focus so much on new information. On occasion, helping students catch up can be beneficial and give them more confidence. Returning to previously learned material reinforces what students have learned and develops confidence as well.

Presentation 1   15-20 mins. ■■■

This presentation is a review of many of the statements students have learned. Review the statements and ask students questions about themselves. If students have trouble, you might want to refer them back to the pages where the concepts were originally taught and ask them to review those pages for homework.

Before introducing Exercise A, ask students to cover Exercise B.

A Listen and write.

Play the recording and, as a class, listen and write the missing information.

 Listening Script   *CD 2, Track 12*

The listening script matches the statements in Exercise A.

Practice 1   15-20 mins.

B Write.

Ask students to cover Exercise A. In groups, ask them to see how much they can remember and write. Give them no more than ten minutes. Then, with Exercise A still covered, play the recording again and encourage students to edit their work. Finally, ask students to uncover Exercise A and complete the activity.

Evaluation 1   3-5 mins. ■■■

Recreate the chart on the board and ask students to come up and fill in the information.

STANDARDS CORRELATIONS

CASAS: 0.1.2, 0.2.4 (See CASAS Competency List on pages 167-173.)
SCANS: **Basic Skills** Reading, writing, listening, speaking
Information Acquire and evaluate information
EFF: **Communication** Read with understanding, convey ideas in writing, speak so others can understand, listen actively, observe critically

Presentation 2   10–15 mins. ■■■■

C Read.

Go over the simple present with students. Help them understand that they can use any of the available pronouns in the box on the left to form a sentence. The simple present is being recycled again to reinforce what students have already learned. Help them understand that they will be exposed to it many times before they can say that they have acquired it, and that this is a normal part of the process.

Students have previously been introduced to the simple present on pages 6, 35, 52, 54, and 63.

For shorter classes, ask students to do Exercises D and E for homework.

Practice 2   7–10 mins. ■■

D Write about James, Carina, and Nga.

Help as needed.

E Write about Leslie and Briana.

Help as needed.

Evaluation 2   5–7 mins. ■■

Check students' book work.

GOAL ➤ **Express transportation preferences**

C Read.

Simple Present		
Subject	**Verb**	**Example sentence**
I, you, we, they	live	I **live** in Mexico.
	take	We **take** the bus.
	ride	You **ride** a bicycle.
	walk	They **take** a train.
he, she, it	live**s**	He **takes** the bus.
	take**s**	She **rides** a bicycle.
	ride**s**	
	walk**s**	

D Write about James, Carina, and Nga.

1. James _____ **lives** _____ in a house.

2. He _____ takes _____ the bus to school.

3. Carina _____ lives _____ in an apartment.

4. She _____ drives _____ to school.

5. Nga _____ lives _____ in a house.

6. She _____ rides _____ a bicycle to school.

7. James and Nga _____ live _____ in a house.

E Write about Leslie and Briana.

1. Leslie and Briana _____ live _____ in Cambodia.

2. Leslie _____ takes _____ the bus to work every day.

3. Briana _____ drives _____ a car to work.

4. They _____ live _____ in a house.

GOAL ➤ Express transportation preferences

F Read.

Simple Present: *Be* Verb		
Subject	***Be* Verb**	**Example sentence**
I	am	I **am** Nga.
he, she, it	is	She **is** from China.
we, you, they	are	They **are** married.

G Read the chart.

Name	Country	Housing	Transportation to school
Karen	United States	house	bus
Sang	China	apartment	bus

H Write.

1. Karen _____is_____ from the United States.

2. Karen _____lives_____ in a house.

3. She _____takes_____ the bus.

4. Sang _____is_____ from China.

5. He _____lives_____ in an apartment.

6. Karen and Sang _____take_____ the bus.

I Answer the questions. (Answers will vary.)

1. What's your name?

   My name _____.

2. Where are you from?

   I _____ from

   _____.

3. Do you live in a house?

   I _____ in a(n)

   _____.

4. How do you come to school?

   I _____ to school.

Presentation 3   10-15 mins. ■■■ ■

F Read.

Remind students that the *be* verb has been introduced in previous lessons. This is the first time in the book that students will have a choice to use the *be* verb with other verbs.

G Read the chart.

Show students how the chart is similar to the one they completed on page 90. Ask them questions about the chart. Encourage them to use pronouns.

For shorter classes, ask students to do Exercise H for homework.

Practice 3   10-20 mins. ■

H Write.

After students have written the correct verbs for the statements, ask them to write the complete sentences in their notebooks.

If you believe your students are ready, you might also give them a dictation of the sentences they have just completed.

Evaluation 3   10 mins. ■

Check students' work.

Application   7-10 mins. ■■■ ■

I Answer the questions.

Again, ask students to write the completed sentences in their notebooks.

Refer students to *Stand Out Basic Grammar Challenge*, Unit 5, Challenge 4 for more practice with the simple present.

Activity Bank 🔘

Lesson 4, Worksheet 1: Simple Present

Objective: Give and follow directions

Grammar: *the*, imperatives, review prepositions of location

Academic Strategy: Dictation

Vocabulary: *stop, turn, right, left, go straight, bank, post office, hospital*

RESOURCES

Activity Bank: Lesson 5, Worksheet 1

Reading and Writing Challenge: Unit 5

Grammar Challenge: Unit 5, Challenge 5

■ 1.5 hour classes ■ 2.5 hour classes ■ 3⁺ hour classes

AGENDA

In groups, make a list.

Talk about a map.

Learn and practice giving directions.

Write directions to a location from school.

Audio: CD 2, Tracks 13–15

Heinle Picture Dictionary: Road Trip, pages 122–123

Warm-up and Review   10-15 mins. ■■■

In groups, ask students to list all the locations (stores, schools, streets, etc.) they can think of in their community. Ask them to write their lists on the board and go over them briefly. Ask them to point in the direction of where each location is. For example, ask: *Where's the post office?*

Introduction   5 mins. ■■■

Remind students what *next to* means. You may use a person who is sitting next to another as an example. You may also want to use some locations students mentioned in the warm-up. For example, say: *The post office is next to...,* allowing them to complete the sentence. State the objective: *Today we will give and follow directions.*

Presentation 1   15-20 mins. ■■■

 Talk about the map of Alpine City.

There is a lot of vocabulary in this lesson. Most of the locations are review from Lesson 1 of this unit. Practice using *next to* and ask students questions about the map. Introduce new vocabulary when it is appropriate.

 Learn the new words.

Go over the new vocabulary carefully with students. Then ask them to point to locations when you identify them. Start by using the names of the places. Then change to sentences that describe the locations. For example, you might say: *This is a place where people go when they are sick.* Write important words on the board, such as *sick.* Ask more questions and see if students can identify the places by their description. Do the same drill again. This time, identify locations by what they are next to.

Go over the grammar box with students. There are some exceptions to this rule, but following the rule will help students avoid many common errors. Some students might incorrectly say: *I live on the First Street.* Use the definite article *the* with most general words for places, but don't use *the* with proper nouns. Names of streets would not use *the*. There is no need to discuss the exceptions with students at this time.

Practice 1   7-10 mins. ■■■

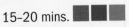 **Match. Draw a line.**

After students complete this activity, ask them to ask each other the questions in pairs. Students answering should cover Exercise C.

Evaluation 1   5-7 mins. ■■■

Ask all students to cover Exercise C and ask individuals or the class the same questions.

STANDARDS CORRELATIONS

CASAS: 1.1.3, 1.9.1, 1.9.4, 2.2.1, 2.2.2, 2.5.4 (See CASAS Competency List on pages 167-173.)

SCANS: **Basic Skills** Reading, writing, listening, speaking **Information** Acquire and evaluate information

Thinking Skills Think creatively, solve problems, see things in the mind's eye

EFF: **Communication** Read with understanding, convey ideas in writing, speak so others can understand, listen actively, observe critically

LESSON 5

Where's the store?

GOAL ➤ Give and follow directions

A Talk about the map of Alpine City.

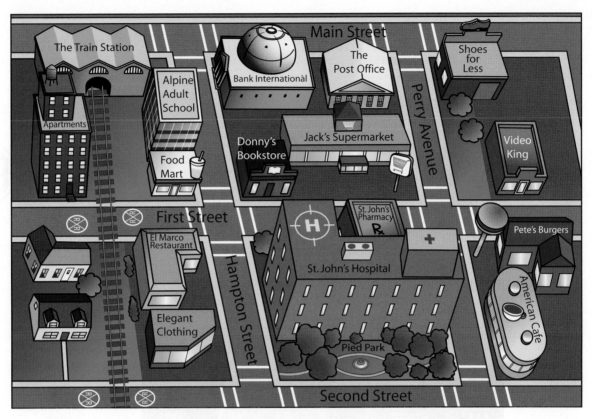

B Learn the new words.

bank   post office   hospital

the
the post office
~~**the**~~ Shoes for Less
~~**the**~~ First Street

C Match. Draw a line.

1. Where is the adult school?
2. Where is the video store?
3. Where is the bookstore?
4. Where is the post office?

a. It's on Perry Avenue next to Shoes for Less.
b. It's on First Street next to the supermarket.
c. It's on Main Street next to the bank.
d. It's on Hampton Street next to Food Mart.

GOAL ➤ **Give and follow directions**

CD 2
TR 13

D Listen and repeat.

stop	go straight	turn right	turn left

E Write the correct words.

___turn left___   ___go straight___   ___turn right___   ___stop___

F Read the map.

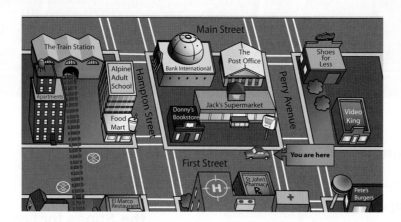

G Where is the adult school? Complete the directions.

1. ⬆ ___Go straight___ on First Street.

2. ↱ ___Turn right___ on Hampton Street.

3. 🛑 ___Stop___ at the adult school.

H Write directions to the bookstore. (Answers will vary.)

Presentation 2 15–25 mins.

D Listen and repeat.

Play the recording several times.

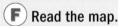 **Listening Script** CD 2, Track 13

The listening script matches the words in the box in Exercise D.

E Write the correct words.

After going over the road signs and the new vocabulary, ask a student to come to the front of the class. Ask the student to follow the directions you give him or her. The student will walk around the room. Try to do the same thing with other students. Finally, see if the whole class can do it.

F Read the map.

Go over signs and stores with students. Give them some directions and see if they can follow them.

G Where is the adult school? Complete the directions.

Do this activity as a class. Point out that they will use *at* in the last sentence. If you have time, ask students to close their books and do a dictation of the three sentences.

For shorter classes, ask students to do Exercise H for homework.

Practice 2 7–10 mins.

H Write directions to the bookstore.

This activity might be difficult for students. Here they are asked to string more than one sentence together. Have them work in pairs or groups to complete the sentences. During the activity, interrupt them occasionally to remind them to start with capital letters and to end with periods.

Evaluation 2 5–7 mins.

Ask volunteers to write their directions on the board.

Teaching Tip

Dictation

There are several ways to do dictation. In higher levels, it is very productive to give dictation where students haven't been exposed to the exact sentences you will be giving. At this level, students don't have a lot of experience so a dictation can be one-word or very short sentences that they have already seen. The objective of this kind of dictation is not to check student ability but rather to allow students more opportunities to practice what they are learning.

Because this type of dictation is not for evaluative purposes, you may decide in some cases, such as this one, to read a sentence out loud two or three times and then to ask students to compare what they have written with one another, allowing for a type of peer-editing. Afterwards, give the sentence a final time.

Remember that at the beginning and intermediate levels, students tend to try to write while the instructor is speaking. They need to be taught to listen first, repeat the sentence in their heads, and then write. To help them learn this strategy, you should avoid giving sentence dictation one word at a time.

Finally, some dictation includes words that are intimidating or difficult for students, especially when proper nouns are given. Students tend to focus on these words, which may affect their performance. To avoid this problem, it is wise to write difficult words and names on the board in preparation for the dictation.

Presentation 3   7–10 mins. ▪▪▫▫

 Listen and read.

Have students practice the dialog in pairs. Help
them to hear the intonation and the rhythm. Ask
students to trace the route with their fingers on
the map. You may want to make a transparency
of this page and do it on an overhead projector.

🎧 **Listening Script**   *CD 2, Track 14*

The listening script matches the conversation in
Exercise I.

Practice 3   5–10 mins. ▪

J **Listen and follow the directions.**
Number the locations 1–4.

The directions on the recording are numbered
1–4. Ask students to write the corresponding
number on each final location.

🎧 **Listening Script**   *CD 2, Track 15*

1. *Go straight. Turn right on Perry Avenue. It's*
    next to Pete's Burgers.
2. *Turn right on Hampton Street. Turn left on*
    Second Street. It's next to Ned's Shoes.
3. *Turn right on Hampton Street. It's next to El*
    Marco Restaurant.
4. *Go straight. Turn right on Perry Avenue. Turn*
    right on Second Street. It's next to Big's Foods.

Evaluation 3   5–7 mins. ▪

Go over the answers with students.

Application   20–30 mins. ▪▪▪

K **Write three stores in your community.**

Help as needed.

L **Write directions to one store from**
your school.

Ask students to use the phrases on page 94. You
may choose to give students a starting point such
as the school itself.

 Refer students to *Stand Out Basic Grammar*
Challenge, **Unit 5, Challenge 5 for more**
practice with imperatives.

Instructor's Notes

GOAL ➤ **Give and follow directions**

  I **Listen and read.**

CD 2
TR 14

Carina: Excuse me, where's American Café?
Nga: It's on Perry Avenue.
Carina: Can you give me directions?
Nga: Yes. Go straight on First Street. Turn right on Perry Avenue. It's next to Pete's Burgers.

  J **Listen and follow the directions. Number the locations 1–4.**

CD 2
TR 15

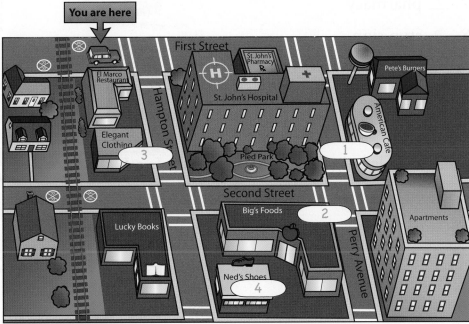

K **Write three stores in your community.** (Answers will vary.)

1. _____ 2. _____ 3. _____

L **Write directions to one store from your school.** (Answers will vary.)

_____

_____

_____

_____

A Write the correct letter. (Lessons 1–5)

1. _d_ apartment
2. _e_ bank
3. _k_ bus
4. _a_ car
5. _i_ hospital
6. _g_ house
7. _f_ pharmacy
8. _b_ stop sign
9. _l_ supermarket
10. _h_ taxi
11. _c_ train
12. _j_ turn left sign

a.

g.

b.

h.

c.

i.

d.

j.

e.

k.

f.

l.

B Practice with a partner. (Lesson 1)

1. Where do you live?
2. Where do you buy clothing?
3. Where do you buy shoes?
4. Where do you eat?

AT-A-GLANCE PREP

Objective: All unit objectives
Grammar: All unit grammar
Academic Strategies: Focused listening, reviewing, evaluating, developing study skills
Vocabulary: all unit vocabulary

AGENDA
Discuss unit objectives.
Complete the review.
Do My Dictionary.
Evaluate and reflect on progress.

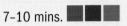 1.5 hour classes   2.5 hour classes 3⁺ hour classes

Warm-up and Review   7-10 mins.

With their books closed, ask students to help you make a list on the board of all the vocabulary they can come up with from the unit. Then have a competition where students in groups look through the unit and write the page numbers for each item on the list. The first group to have the correct page number for each item wins.

Introduction   5 mins.

Write all the objectives on the board from Unit 5. Show students the first page of every lesson so they understand that today will be review. Complete the agenda.

Note: Depending on the length of the term, you may decide to have students do Presentation and Practice 1 for homework and then review student work as the warm-up for another class meeting.

Presentation 1   10-15 mins.

This presentation and practice will cover the first three pages of the review. Quickly go to the first page of each lesson. Discuss the objective of each. Ask simple questions to remind students what they have learned.

Practice 1   15-20 mins.

(A) Write the correct letter. (Lessons 1-5)

(B) Practice with a partner. (Lesson 1)

Teaching Tip

Recycling/Review

The review process and the project that follows are part of the recycling/review process. Students at this level often need to be reintroduced to concepts to solidify what they have learned. Many concepts are learned and forgotten while learning other new concepts. This is because students learn but are not necessarily ready to acquire language concepts.

Therefore, it becomes very important to review and to show students how to review on their own. It is also important to recycle the new concepts in different contexts.

STANDARDS CORRELATIONS

CASAS: 2.2.3, 7.4.1, 7.4.2, 7.4.3 (See CASAS Competency List on pages 167-173.)
SCANS: Basic Skills Reading, writing, listening, speaking
Information Acquire and evaluate information, organize and maintain information, interpret and communicate information

Thinking Skills See things in the mind's eye
EFF: Communication Speak so others can understand
Lifelong Learning Take responsibility for learning, reflect and evaluate

Practice 1 *(continued)*

C Write and practice a conversation.
(Lessons 2 and 4)

D Write. (Lesson 4)

1. I'm Aki.
   I'm from Japan.
   I live in an apartment.
   I live in New York on
     Second Street.
   I drive to school.

2. I'm Adriano.
   I'm from Italy.
   I live in a house.
   I live in New York on Broadway.
   I take the bus to school.

C Write and practice a conversation. (Lessons 2 and 4)   (Answers will vary.)

Aki: Hi, Adriano. Where do you live? _____

Adriano: _____

Aki: _____

Adriano: _____

Aki: _____

Adriano: _____

D Write. (Lesson 4)

1. Aki _____drives_____ to school.

2. Adriano __takes the bus__ to school.

3. They _____live_____ in New York.

Review

 E **Read the map. (Lesson 5)**

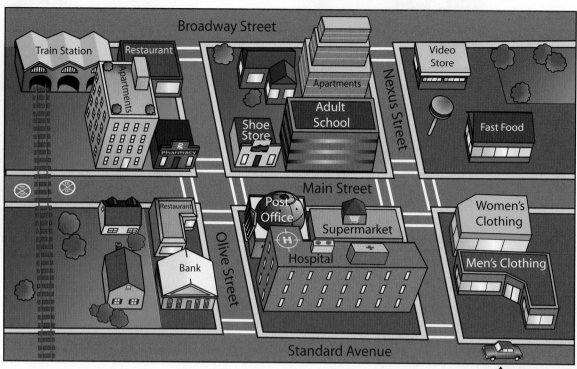

You are here

 F **Write the place. (Lesson 5)**

Place	Directions
the post office	Turn right on Nexus. Turn left on Main. It's next to the supermarket.
the bank	Go straight. Turn right on Olive Street. It's next to the houses.
the shoe store	Go straight. Turn right on Olive Street. Turn right on Main Street. It's next to the adult school.
the train station	Turn right on Nexus. Turn left on Broadway. It's next to the restaurant.

Practice 1 (continued)

(E) Read the map. (Lesson 5)

(F) Write the place. (Lesson 5)

Evaluation 1   15 mins.

Go around the room and check on student
progress. Help individuals when needed. If you
see consistent errors among several students,
interrupt the class and give a mini lesson
or review to help students feel comfortable
with the concept.

Presentation 2

My Dictionary

Review with students what My Dictionary is and help them see the value of it.

Practice 2   7–10 mins.

Ask students to complete My Dictionary.

Evaluation 2   2 mins. ■■

Ask students to share their cards.

Presentation 3

Learner Log

Review the concepts of the Learner Log. Make sure students understand the concepts and how to do the log including the check marks.

> ## Teaching Tip
>
> ### Learner Logs
>
> Learner Logs function to help students in many different ways.
>
> 1. They serve as part of the review process.
> 2. They help students to gain confidence and document what they have learned. In this way, students see that they are progressing and want to move forward in learning.
> 3. They provide students with a tool that they can use over and over to check and recheck their understanding. In this way, students become independent learners.

Practice 3   10–15 mins.

Ask students to do the learner log.

Evaluation 3   2 mins. ■■■

Go over the log with students.

Application

Ask students to write down their favorite lesson or page in the unit.

My Dictionary

Make flash cards to improve your vocabulary.

1. Choose four new words from this unit.
2. Write each word on an index card or on a piece of paper.
3. On the back of the index card or paper, draw a picture, find and write a sentence from the book with the word, and write the page number.
4. Study the words.

I live in a condominium.

page 86

Learner Log

Write the page number(s).

	Page Number	I can do it. ✓
1. Identify and ask about locations.	81–83	
2. Describe housing.	84–86	
3. Identify types of transportation.	87–89	
4. Express transportation preferences.	90–92	
5. Give and follow directions.	93–95	

My favorite lesson in this unit is (Answers will vary.) .

Team Project

Describe your community.

1. Form a team with four or five students. In your team, you need:

POSITION	JOB	STUDENT NAME
Student 1: Team Leader	See that everyone speaks English. See that everyone participates.	
Student 2: Writer	Write directions.	
Student 3: Artist	Make a map.	
Students 4/5: Spokespeople	Prepare a presentation.	

2. Make a list of types of transportation in your community.

3. Make a map of your community with the school in the middle. Write the names of stores and other places near your school.

4. Write directions from your school to three places in your community.

5. Present your project to the class.

Introduction
5 mins.

For this project, tell students they will work in teams to create a map of the community surrounding their school, incorporating the vocabulary from this unit. They may choose to use templates from the Activity Bank CD-ROM to help them.

Stage 1
15-20 mins.

Form a team with four or five students.

Show students examples of the project, if you have some, or discuss the art on the Student Book page.

Help students to assign positions by asking the leaders to stand. On the spot, students will have to choose who will be the leader of their group. Review the responsibility of a leader and ask students to write the name of their leader in their books. Do the same with all positions.

Stage 2
10-15 mins.

Make a list of types of transportation in your community.

Ask students to make a list of types of transportation. Ask them to draw pictures of the means of transportation they listed or to use magazine, newspaper, or Internet pictures.

Stage 3
10-30 mins.

Make a map of your community with the school in the middle. Write the names of stores and other places near your school.

Ask students to work together and to be as accurate as possible.

Stage 4
10-30 mins.

Write the directions from your school to three places in the community.

Ask students to write out directions to three places in the community. Ask them to create dialogs that demonstrate in what situations they could be asked to give these directions. This can be part of the group presentation if they decide to use them.

Stage 5
10-30 mins.

Present your project to the class.

Ask groups to present their projects. This can be particularly effective if you videotape the presentations.

STANDARDS CORRELATIONS

CASAS: 2.2.3, 4.8.1 (See CASAS Competency List on pages 167-173.)
SCANS: Basic Skills Reading, writing, listening, speaking
Resources Allocate time, allocate money, allocate materials and facility resources, allocate human resources
Information Acquire and evaluate information, organize and maintain information, interpret and communicate information, use computers to process information
Interpersonal Participate as a member of a team, teach others, serve clients and customers, exercise leadership, negotiate to arrive at a decision, work with cultural diversity
Systems Understand systems, monitor and correct performance, improve and design systems

Thinking Skills Think creatively, make decisions, solve problems, see things in the mind's eye
Personal Qualities Responsibility, sociability, self management
EFF: Communication Read with understanding, convey ideas in writing, speak so others can understand, listen actively, observe critically
Decision Making Solve problems and make decisions, plan
Interpersonal Cooperate with others, advocate and influence, resolve conflict and negotiate, guide others
Lifelong Learning Take responsibility for learning, reflect and evaluate

AT-A-GLANCE PREP

Objective: Identify body parts
Grammar: Imperatives
Pronunciation: Voiced and voiceless consonants
Academic Strategy: Focused listening
Vocabulary: Basic body parts

RESOURCES

Activity Bank: Lesson 1, Worksheet 1
Reading and Writing Challenge: Unit 6
Grammar Challenge: Unit 6, Challenge 1

 1.5 hour classes ■ 2.5 hour classes □ 3⁺ hour classes

AGENDA
Draw a map to the hospital.
Learn about the doctor's office and body parts.
Follow directions in the doctor's office.

Audio: CD 2, Tracks 16–17
Heinle Picture Dictionary: The Human Body, pages 132–133

Stand Out Basic Assessment CD-ROM with Exam*View*®

 Preassessment *(optional)*

Use the Stand Out Basic Assessment CD-ROM with Exam*View*® to create a pretest for Unit 6.

Warm-up and Review   10-15 mins.

Ask students where the nearest hospital is. Have groups draw a map from the school to the hospital. See if all groups chose the same route.

Introduction   10-15 mins.

Write *health* on the board. See if students can figure out what it means. Pantomime minor symptoms such as coughing and sneezing. Say: *Right now my health is bad.* Point to the word when you say it. Demonstrate some exercises and say: *Exercise is good for your health.*

Ask students to open their books and briefly go over the goals at the top of the page. Show them how each goal relates to health. State the objective: *Today we will identify body parts.*

Presentation 1   20-25 mins.

A **Look at the picture.**

Ask students the questions at the bottom of the picture. Ask them to identify things they see. Write *checkup* on the board. Ask: *How many times do you get a checkup every year?* They may not understand, but if you say *I go one time a year,* they may begin to.

B **Listen and write.**

Ask students to close their books and listen to the paragraph. Then ask students to open their

books and listen while reading along. Have students complete the paragraph by filling in the missing words. Tell students that they will do a dictation of the paragraph.

>  **Listening Script**   CD 2, Track 16
>
> The listening script matches the paragraph in Exercise B.

To prepare for the dictation, write *Chicago* and *Guillermo* on the board for students to refer to. Ask students to underline any difficult or new words. Go over the words, discuss their meaning, and ask students to write each word several times in their notebooks.

Practice 1   7-10 mins.

Give a dictation of the paragraph.

Teaching Tip

Multilevel dictation

To give a dictation to a multilevel class, provide students who will struggle the most a handout of the paragraph with key words missing. Another level might have most words missing, and another blank paper.

Evaluation 1 3-5 mins.

Go over the dictations carefully and allow students to self-correct.

STANDARDS CORRELATIONS

CASAS: 3.1.1, 3.1.3 (See CASAS Competency List on pages 167-173.)
SCANS: **Basic Skills** Reading, writing, listening, speaking
Information Acquire and evaluate information, organize and maintain information, interpret and communicate information

EFF: **Communication** Read with understanding, convey ideas in writing, speak so others can understand, listen actively

Healthy Living

GOALS

➤ **Identify body parts**
➤ **Describe symptoms and illnesses**

➤ **Identify medications**
➤ **Describe healthy habits**
➤ **Identify actions in a waiting room**

LESSON 1

I need a checkup.

GOAL ➤ **Identify body parts**

A Look at the picture.

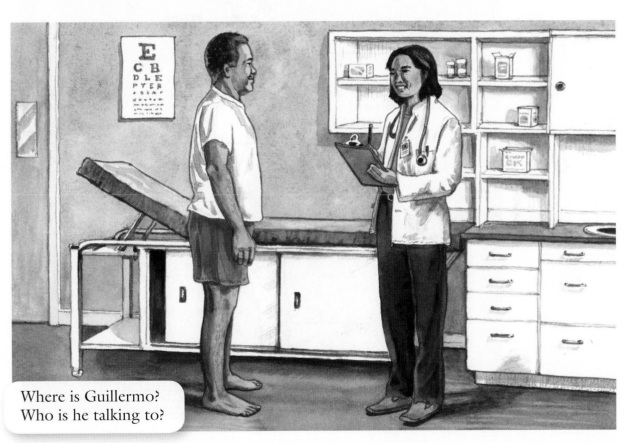

Where is Guillermo?
Who is he talking to?

B Listen and write.

CD 2
TR 16

My name is Guillermo. _____I_____ live in Chicago. I _____am_____ 61 years old. I _____see_____ the doctor once a year for a checkup. I'm very healthy.

C Read the new words.

head	back	hand	foot
neck	arm	leg	nose

D Write the new words in the picture.

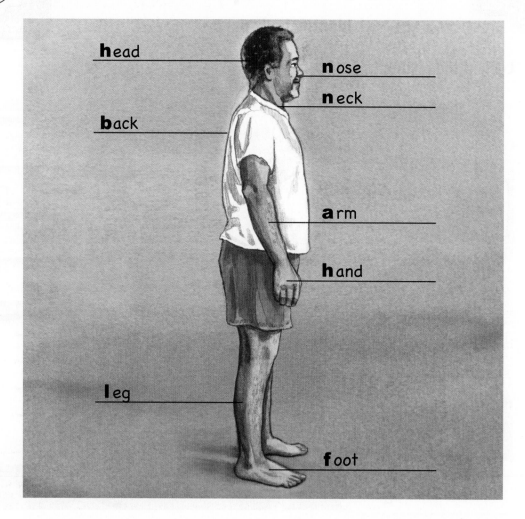

head

nose

neck

back

arm

hand

leg

foot

E Talk to a partner.

A: Where's the nose?
B: It's here. (points to own nose)

Presentation 2

10-15 mins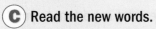

C Read the new words.

Go over each word and the pronunciation with students. Make sure students pronounce the final consonants and release them when they say the words in isolation. With *head, hand,* and *foot,* the tongue releases and there is a very brief and quiet *ah* with the release after the articulation of the final sound. Try exaggerating at first so students understand. With *back, neck,* and *leg,* the throat closes to pronounce the sound and then relaxes. Again there is a very brief and quiet *ah.* With *arm,* the mouth opens after the /m/ is produced, and with *nose,* the /z/ is produced followed by the mouth opening slightly.

This is also a good opportunity to ask what other body-part vocabulary your students would like to learn. Possibilities include the following: *shoulders, elbows, knees, wrists,* and *waist.*

For shorter classes, ask students to do Exercise D for homework.

Practice 2

7-10 mins.

D Write the new words in the picture.

Have students write the parts of the body.

Evaluation 2

5-7 mins.

E Talk to a partner.

Observe students doing this activity.

Pronunciation

Voiced and voiceless consonants

Many pronunciation features, like grammar structures, are learned over time and not immediately acquired. Students, for the most part, can be understood without understanding the difference between voiced and voiceless consonants. The following practice might be done as a way to help students become aware of different sounds.

Ask students to put two fingers on their throats, that is, on their voice boxes. Ask students to pronounce an /m/ for an extended period of time. Demonstrate what you want them to do. Ask them what they feel. They may make a fluttering motion with their hands. Then ask students to sing a melody using only this sound. Choose a song they all know.

Next ask them to do the same with /d/ and /g/. Now ask them to pronounce *head, hand, arm,* and *leg.* Show them how each word ends and how the voice box flutters or vibrates.

Do the same with /t/, and /k/. Show them how with these sounds they can't sing a melody because the voice box doesn't vibrate. Contrast the /k/ and the /g/ sounds. Then contrast the /t/ and the /d/ sounds. Have students then pronounce *back, neck,* and *foot.* Finally, have them contrast the endings by practicing the following:

hand—foot
head—foot
neck—leg

Don't expect students to immediately incorporate this concept into their speech. Review it occasionally to help students pronounce sounds correctly.

Presentation 3   10-15 mins. ■■□

F Read.

Go over the grammar chart with students. Help them to see how imperatives (or commands) imply the subject pronoun *you*, but the pronoun is not used. Take this opportunity to go over the new vocabulary with students as well. Say the statements and see if they can point to the body part each statement implies. Ask students to close their books and say the statements again. Point to your eyes, ears, and mouth and ask students to call out the vocabulary.

Ask students to open their books and say the statements when you say the body part. Then ask them to close their books and do the same.

G Listen and practice the conversation.

Go over the conversation with students and help them use proper intonation and rhythm. Show them how to use the other statements in the conversation from Exercise F.

 Listening Script   *CD 2, Track 17*

The listening script matches the conversation in Exercise G.

Practice 3   7-10 mins. ■■□

H Practice the conversation with a partner. Use new sentences.

Have students walk around and switch partners often. Have them substitute different actions with each partner. Remind them to do the actions.

Evaluation 3   2-7 mins. ■■□

Ask volunteers to present the conversation in front of the class.

Application   7-10 mins. ■■□

I What body parts are most important to you? Take a class poll.

Show students how to do ranking. Ask students to report their findings and attempt to do a class poll.

Refer students to *Stand Out Basic Grammar Challenge*, Unit 6, Challenge 1 for more practice with imperatives.

Activity Bank

Lesson 1, Worksheet 1: Body Parts

Instructor's Notes

GOAL ➤ **Identify body parts**

F Read.

Imperatives		
	Subject	**Verb**
Please	~~you~~	read open let me (look) sit down stand up

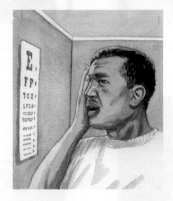

Please read the chart.

Please open your
mouth and say "Ah."

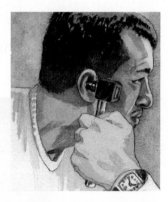

Let me look
in your ear.

CD 2
TR 17

G Listen and practice the conversation.

Doctor: Please sit down.
Guillermo: OK.
Doctor: Please open your mouth and say, "Ah."
Guillermo: Ah.

H Practice the conversation with a partner. Use new sentences.

I What body parts are most important to you? Take a class poll. (Answers will vary.)

1. _____   3. _____

2. _____   4. _____

I'm sick!

GOAL ➤ **Describe symptoms and illnesses**

  A Listen and repeat.

CD 2
TR 18

headache   backache   stomachache

cold and runny nose   cough and sore throat   fever

   B Listen and point.

CD 2
TR 19-24

C Read the conversation. Practice it with a partner. Use new words.

Maritza: How are you?
Shan: I'm sick!
Maritza: What's the matter?
Shan: I have <u>a headache</u>.

Objective: Describe symptoms and illnesses
Grammar: Simple present
Academic Strategies: Focused listening, test-taking skills
Vocabulary: *headache, backache, stomachache, fever, cold, runny nose, sick, ailment, once*

AGENDA
Practice identifying body parts.
Identify symptoms and illnesses.
Practice stating symptoms.
Use the simple present to describe illnesses and symptoms.
Listen to people talking about illnesses.

RESOURCES

Activity Bank: Lesson 2, Worksheets 1 and 2
Reading and Writing Challenge: Unit 6
Grammar Challenge: Unit 6, Challenge 2

Audio: CD 2, Tracks 18–28
Heinle Picture Dictionary: Illnesses, Injuries, Symptoms, and Disabilities, pages 134–135

■ 1.5 hour classes   ■ 2.5 hour classes   ■ 3⁺ hour classes

Warm-up and Review   7-10 mins. ■■■

Ask students to do Exercise E from Lesson 1.

Introduction   5-7 mins. ■■■

Pantomime a stomachache. Write on the board: *What's the matter?* Pantomime again and point to the question. When students ask, say: *I have a stomachache.* State the objective: *Today we will describe symptoms and illnesses.*

Presentation 1   15-20 mins. ■■■

Present the symptoms by pantomiming.

 Listen and repeat.

Go over each picture with students. Ask them to identify each illness as you describe it.

 Listening Script   CD 2, Track 18

The listening script matches the list of words in Exercise A.

 Listen and point.

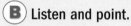 **Listening Script**   CD 2, Tracks 19–24

1. **Doctor:** *It is good to see you.*
   Man: *It's good to see you, too.*
   Doctor: *What's the matter today?*
   Man: *I have a terrible stomachache. Maybe I ate something bad yesterday.*

2. **Doctor:** *You look like you are in a lot of pain today.*
   Man: *I sure am. Every day I get these terrible headaches. What can I do about it?*
   Doctor: *For headaches, we usually prescribe pain relievers, but maybe we should check this out with some tests.*
   Man: *Thanks, Doctor.*

3. **Doctor:** *How can I help you?*
   Woman: *I think I have a high fever.*
   Doctor: *Let's check it out.*
   Woman: *Thanks, Doctor. I hope I'm not too sick.*

4. **Doctor:** *You must be feeling terrible.*
   Woman: *I sure am. I think I've only got a cold, but it is causing so many problems.*
   Doctor: *I know you want to go to work, but sometimes, even with a cold, you need to take it easy for a few days.*
   Woman: *I guess you're right. I just hate staying home!*

5. **Doctor:** *Can I help you?*
   Woman: *Yes, I can hardly move.*
   Doctor: *What seems to be the trouble?*
   Woman: *I have a terrible backache.*

6. **Doctor:** *How are you feeling today?*
   Woman: *Not very well. I think I have a cold. I have a bad cough and a sore throat.*
   Doctor: *Let me take a look.*
   Woman: *Thanks, Doctor.*

 Read the conversation. Practice it with a partner. Use new words.

Show students how to substitute illnesses.

Practice 1   7-10 mins. ■■■

Ask students to choose an illness and practice the conversation with several students.

Evaluation 1   3-5 mins. ■■■

Ask for volunteers to present the conversation.

Note: Standards Correlations are on the next page.

Presentation 2   10–15 mins.

D Read the charts.

Lesson 5 introduces the present continuous. This lesson includes a recap of the simple present. Most students have learned the simple present throughout the book but probably have not acquired it yet. It is important to reinforce and review it from time to time so students don't confuse the two structures once the present continuous has been introduced. The charts include everything students have learned thus far. They have had less experience with verb *have* than the other verbs, so emphasize it here.

For shorter classes, ask students to do Exercise E for homework.

Practice 2   10–15 mins.

E Write.

Go over the first example with students and ask them to complete the exercise by themselves. When they have finished, ask them to share their answers with a partner and peer-edit their work.

Evaluation 2   3–5 mins.

Check students' book work and ask for volunteers to write the answers on the board.

Teaching Tip

Grammar presentation

There are many ways to present grammar. In this case, the structure has already been covered so it will be a student-centered review. It is important to stay within the context. Students, especially at lower levels, are working with new vocabulary, new structures, and all the other skills they need to develop to learn English. If you stray from the context to give grammar explanations, you ask students to deal with new or different vocabulary while learning the structures. It is advisable to teach and review the same structures later in future lessons in different contexts. In this way, students learn to transfer the structure to new contexts.

In this case, with books closed, you might write the verbs from the chart: *see* and *visit*. Ask students what the words have to do with the lesson. Guide them to the sentences in the chart. You might recreate the chart on the board and put in some information including one sample sentence.

Encourage students to come to the board and complete the chart. Then compare the chart to what is in the book.

STANDARDS CORRELATIONS

CASAS: 0.1.2, 0.2.1, 3.1.1 (See CASAS Competency List on pages 167–173.)
SCANS: **Basic Skills** Reading, writing, listening, speaking
Information Acquire and evaluate information, organize and maintain information, interpret and communicate information

EFF: **Communication** Read with understanding, convey ideas in writing, speak so others can understand, listen actively

GOAL ➤ **Describe symptoms and illnesses**

D Read the charts.

Simple Present (Regular)		
Subject	**Verb**	**Example sentence**
I, you, we, they	see	I **see** the doctor once a year.
	visit	We **visit** the doctor once a year.
he, she, it	sees	He **sees** the doctor once a week.
	visits	She **visits** the doctor once a week.

Simple Present (Irregular)		
Subject	**Be**	**Example sentence**
I	am	I **am** sick.
you, we, they	are	We **are** sick.
he, she, it	is	He **is** sick.

Simple Present (Irregular)		
Subject	**Have**	**Example sentence**
I, you, we, they	have	I **have** a headache.
he, she, it	has	She **has** a runny nose.

E Write.

1. He ___has___ (have) a headache.

2. She ___is___ (be) very sick.

3. We ___see___ (see) the doctor.

4. I ___am___ (be) sick.

5. You ___have___ (have) a cold.

6. Oscar ___has___ (have) a stomachache.

7. Maritza ___visits___ (visit) the doctor once a year.

8. You ___are___ (be) sick.

9. We ___are___ (be) tired.

10. I ___like___ (like) my doctor.

11. The student ___has___ (have) a fever.

12. He ___is___ (be) a good doctor.

GOAL ➤ **Describe symptoms and illnesses**

(F) **Listen and bubble in the correct answer.**

CD 2
TR 25-28

1. Maritza has
   ○ a cold.
   ● a headache.
   ○ a fever.

2. Shan has
   ○ a backache.
   ● a fever.
   ○ a cold.

3. John has
   ● a runny nose.
   ○ a fever.
   ○ a headache.

4. Anakiya has
   ● a fever.
   ○ a runny nose.
   ○ a backache.

(G) **How many times a year are you sick? Write.**   (Answers will vary.)

Headache	Stomachache	Backache	Fever	Cold

(H) **Talk to four classmates. Then, fill in the chart.**

A: <u>John</u>, how often do you have a <u>headache</u>?
B: I have a <u>headache four times a year</u>.

How often?	
once	a year
two times	a month
three times	a week
four times	a day

(Answers will vary.)

Name	Headache	Stomachache	Backache	Fever	Cold

Presentation 3

10-15 mins.

Go over each symptom again by having students identify your pantomiming. Write each ailment on the board and put a number next to it. Then talk about each symptom. Ask students to tell you which symptom you are talking about by holding up the corresponding number of fingers.

Look at Exercise F. Pantomime each of the answers in order and ask students to do it with you. Prepare students for focused listening.

Teaching Tip

Focused listening

Focused listening has been discussed throughout the book. The recordings are at an authentic speed and are filled with language students may not understand. The purpose of the task is to help students develop the ability to pull meaning out of complex and natural conversations by identifying key words.

It's important to remind students of this every time you do a focused listening activity so they don't become frustrated and stop listening altogether.

Practice 3

7-10 mins. ■■■

F Listen and bubble in the correct answer.

Tell students that you will only play the recording for each question two times.

Listening Script   CD 2, Tracks 25–28

1. *Maritza is a good student. She can't come to school today because she has a headache. I hope she comes back tomorrow.*
2. *Shan works all day and comes to school at night. He isn't at school today. He called me and told me he would be out because he had a fever of around 102 degrees. I hope he is all right and will get better soon.*
3. *Hi, John! This is your teacher, Rob. I hear you are having a hard time with a cold and a runny nose. It's no fun to be sick. Get well soon! Bye.*
4. *Anakiya is new in the United States. She arrived Tuesday. I hope she will be OK. She is already sick. She has a fever.*

Evaluation 3

3-5 mins.

Check students' book work. Play the recording for each conversation one more time if necessary.

Application

10-15 mins. ■■■

G How many times a year are you sick? Write.

Demonstrate this activity for students by filling out the chart on the board for yourself.

H Talk to four classmates. Then, fill in the chart.

Copy the table on the board and perform the dialog with a few students to show the class how to complete the activity. Teach students the new information question phrase *how often* and show them how to use it with frequency phrases.

📖 **Refer students to *Stand Out Basic Grammar Challenge*, Unit 6, Challenge 2 for more practice with the simple present.**

Activity Bank

Lesson 2, Worksheet 1: Symptoms and Illnesses
Lesson 2, Worksheet 2: *How often?*

Instructor's Notes

_____

_____

_____

_____

_____

_____

_____

_____

_____

_____

AT-A-GLANCE PREP

Objective: Identify medications
Grammar: Simple present
Academic Strategy: Focused listening
Vocabulary: *medicine, sore throat, cough, aspirin, antacid, pain relievers, cough syrup, illness, caution*

RESOURCES

Activity Bank: Lesson 3, Worksheets 1 and 2
Reading and Writing Challenge: Unit 6
Grammar Challenge: Unit 6, Challenge 3

Audio: CD 2, Track 29
Heinle Picture Dictionary: Pharmacy, pages 142–143

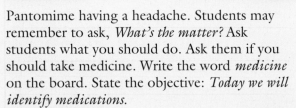 1.5 hour classes   2.5 hour classes   3⁺ hour classes

AGENDA

Review time.
Read an appointment book.
Talk about medicine and illnesses.
Discuss what medicine you have at home.

Warm-up and Review   10-15 mins.

Ask students what time it is. Write this dialog on the board and ask students to practice it in pairs.

A: *What time do you eat lunch?*
B: *I eat lunch at 12:00.*
A: *What time do you eat dinner?*
B: *I eat dinner at 6:00.*

Ask students to do the dialog with four students and complete this chart.

Name	Dinner	Lunch

Introduction   10-15 mins.

Pantomime having a headache. Students may remember to ask, *What's the matter?* Ask students what you should do. Ask them if you should take medicine. Write the word *medicine* on the board. State the objective: *Today we will identify medications.*

Presentation 1   40-50 mins.

(A) Read, listen, and write the missing words.

Go over the appointment book carefully. Review phone numbers. Tell students that they will listen to a recording to get the missing information. Play the recording.

Listening Script   CD 2, Track 29

Doctor: *I'm a little late. I will be there soon. What patients do we have today? Oh, and can you give me their numbers, too? I might want to call a few before I get to the office.*

Nurse: *No problem, Doctor. Let's see. Julio Rodriguez has an appointment at 3:30. He has a headache. His number is 555-1395. Huong Pham is coming in at 4:00. He has a high fever. His phone is 555-3311. Richard Price has an appointment at 4:30. He has a stomachache. His number is 555-2323. Mele Ikahihifo has a sore throat. She's coming in at 5:00. You can reach her at 555-5511. Fred Wharton's number is 555-9764. He has a cold. Ayumi Tanaka is coming in at 6:00 with a backache. Her number is 555-8765.*

Doctor: *Thanks.*

Practice 1   10-15 mins.

(B) Write the problems.

Ask students to complete the chart.

(C) Write sentences.

Before you help them, see if students can use the proper form of *have*.

Evaluation 1   5-7 mins.

Ask students to write their sentences on the board.

STANDARDS CORRELATIONS

CASAS: 2.3.1, 3.1.2, 3.3.1 (See CASAS Competency List on pages 167–173.)
SCANS: Basic Skills Reading, writing, listening, speaking
Resources Allocate time
Information Acquire and evaluate information, organize and maintain information, interpret and communicate information
Interpersonal Participate as a member of a team, teach others

Systems Understand systems
EFF: Communication Read with understanding, speak so others can understand, listen actively
Decision Making Solve problems and make decisions
Interpersonal Cooperate with others

You need aspirin.

GOAL ➤ Identify medications

**CD 2
TR 29**

A Read, listen, and write the missing words.

February 18			
Name	Time	Problem	Phone
Julio Rodriguez	3:30	headache	(777) 555-1395
Huong Pham	4:00	fever	(777) 555-3311
Richard Price	4:30	stomachache	(777) 555-2323
Mele Ikahihifo	5:00	sore throat and cough	(777) 555-5511
Fred Wharton	5:30	cold	(777) 555-9764
Ayumi Tanaka	6:00	backache	(777) 555-8765

B Write the problems.

fever

sore throat and cough

stomachache

Have	
I, you, we, they	have
he, she	has

backache

headache

cold

C Write sentences.

1. Julio has a headache.
2. Richard has a stomachache.
3. Ayumi has a backache.

GOAL ➤ Identify medications

D Look at the medicine bottles.

Caution: Do not take more than four times a day.

E Write other types of medicine you take. (Answers will vary.)

_____   _____   _____

F In a group, write a medicine for each illness. (Answers will vary.)

Illness	Medicine
headache	
fever	
stomachache	
sore throat and cough	
cold	

Presentation 2

10-12 mins.

D Look at the medicine bottles.

Ask students to listen as you read the caution box. Tell them that the bottle might also say *warning* and that this is very important to read and understand. Ask: *Can I take this medicine five times a day?*

Go over the medicines and make sure students understand the vocabulary.

E Write other types of medicine you take.

Help students with the vocabulary words needed to describe the types of medicine they take.

Practice 2

15-20 mins. ■■

F In a group, write a medicine for each illness.

Allow students to come up with medicines within their groups. Encourage them to give brand names as well as general medicine terms. After ten minutes, ask one student from each group to visit other groups and compare answers.

Teaching Tip

Group work

Students should be getting more comfortable working in groups. It may be a good idea to have the groups choose a leader whose job it is to make sure all group members speak English. Also, they should have a secretary who writes down the information. Some students may want to work on their own. Tell the groups that you will only accept answers if all members of the group agree and have discussed their answers.

Try to avoid managing the teams yourself. Encourage group interaction and monitor progress by asking questions as you walk from group to group.

Evaluation 2

5-7 mins. ■■

Ask the groups to report to the class.

Instructor's Notes

_____
_____
_____
_____
_____
_____
_____
_____
_____
_____
_____
_____
_____
_____
_____
_____
_____
_____
_____
_____
_____
_____
_____
_____
_____
_____
_____
_____
_____
_____
_____
_____
_____
_____

Presentation 3   10–15 mins. ■■■

G Read.

Students will once again review the simple present. It is important to avoid making the mistake of thinking that most students have acquired the simple present tense at this point. You may also choose to review earlier presentations of the structure or ask students to find those presentations in their books.

Go over the chart with students. You are now introducing the verb *need* for the first time; however, many students will already understand it because of the contexts they have heard or seen it used in.

For shorter classes, ask students to do Exercise H for homework.

Teaching Tip

Earlier pages in the book

The technique of showing students where they learned something earlier will help reinforce your teaching, and help them to identify the book as a tool that they can refer to during class and even after they advance to a higher level.

Practice 3   15–20 mins. ■

H Write sentences. Use *need*.

Ask students to complete the sentences.

If your students are ready, you may also choose to give them a dictation of the same sentences once they have completed them.

Evaluation 3   7–10 mins. ■

Ask students to write their sentences on the board.

Application   15–20 mins. ■■■

I What types of medicine do you have at home? Write.

After students write the information, ask them to share their work with a group.

J Active Task: Go to a pharmacy. Look for more types of medicines. Make a list and share it with the class.

 Refer students to *Stand Out Basic Grammar Challenge*, Unit 6, Challenge 3 for more practice with the simple present.

Activity Bank

Lesson 3, Worksheet 1: Medicine

Lesson 3, Worksheet 2: Medicine for Ailments

Instructor's Notes

_____

_____

_____

_____

_____

_____

_____

_____

_____

_____

_____

_____

_____

_____

_____

_____

_____

_____

_____

_____

_____

_____

GOAL ➤ **Identify medications**

G Read.

Simple Present		
I, you, we, they	need	aspirin
he, she, it	need**s**	antacid

H Write sentences. Use *need*. (Suggested answers are below.)

1. Julio has a headache. He needs aspirin.
2. Huong has a fever. He needs aspirin .
3. Richard has a stomachache. He needs antacid .
4. Mele has a sore throat and cough. She needs cough syrup .
5. Fred has a cold. He needs aspirin .
6. Ayumi and Sue have backaches. They need aspirin .
7. Tami and I have stomachaches. We need antacid .
8. Shiuli and Sang have sore throats. They need aspirin .
9. You have a cold. You need aspirin .
10. You have a headache. You need aspirin .
11. We have sore throats. We cough syrup .
12. We have fevers. We need aspirin .

I What types of medicine do you have at home? Write. (Answers will vary.)

_____ _____ _____ _____

J **Active Task.** Go to a pharmacy. Look for more types of medicine. Make a list and share it with the class.

Exercise every day!

GOAL ➤ Describe healthy habits

A Read and listen.

CD 2
TR 30

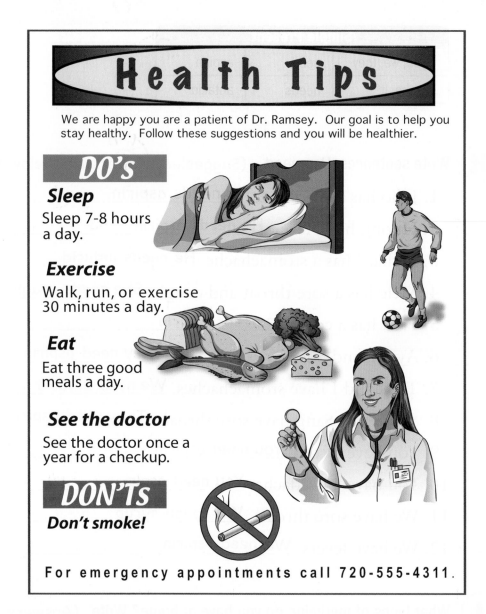

Health Tips

We are happy you are a patient of Dr. Ramsey. Our goal is to help you stay healthy. Follow these suggestions and you will be healthier.

DO's

Sleep
Sleep 7-8 hours a day.

Exercise
Walk, run, or exercise 30 minutes a day.

Eat
Eat three good meals a day.

See the doctor
See the doctor once a year for a checkup.

DON'Ts

Don't smoke!

For emergency appointments call 720-555-4311.

B Practice with a partner.

Dr. Ramsey: How many hours do you sleep a day?
Hasna: I sleep five hours a day.
Dr. Ramsey: That is not healthy. You need to sleep seven to eight hours.

AT-A-GLANCE PREP

Objective: Describe healthy habits
Grammar: Negative simple present
Academic Strategies: Focused listening, interpreting graphs
Vocabulary: *tip, exercise, see, smoke, meal, healthy, per day, per month, per year.*

RESOURCES
Activity Bank: Lesson 4, Worksheets 1 and 2
Reading and Writing Challenge: Unit 6
Grammar Challenge: Unit 6, Challenge 4

| ■ 1.5 hour classes | ■ 2.5 hour classes | ■ 3⁺ hour classes |

AGENDA
Review illnesses.
Read about healthy practices.
Write about healthy habits.

Audio: CD 2, Tracks 30–31
Heinle Picture Dictionary: Daily Activities, pages 34–35

Warm-up and Review   10-15 mins.

Ask students what medicine they take for various illnesses and symptoms. List them on the board. Write the following conversation on the board and ask students to practice it:

Doctor: *What's the matter?*
Julio: *I have a headache.*
Doctor: *You need aspirin.*

Ask them to put in their own information and complete this chart about four classmates.

Name:	
Illness	**Medicine**
Headache	
Stomachache	
Backache	
Cold	
Sore throat	
Fever	

Introduction   15-20 mins.

Ask how many hours each student sleeps every night. Make a bar graph as a class. State the objective: *Today we will describe healthy habits.*

Presentation 1   15-20 mins.

A **Read and listen.**

Help students learn the new vocabulary by asking them questions about the brochure. Teach them that *every day* and *a day* mean almost the same thing. Play the recording one time and ask them to read along as they listen.

> 🎧 **Listening Script**   CD 2, Track 30
>
> The listening script matches the brochure in Exercise A.

As a class, decide on things for each category on the brochure that would not be healthy. Show students how to use this information in the conversation in Exercise B.

Practice 1   5-7 mins.

B **Practice with a partner.**

Ask students to practice the conversation with a partner substituting information.

Evaluation 1   5-7 mins.

Ask volunteers to present the conversation.

STANDARDS CORRELATIONS

CASAS: 3.1.1 (See CASAS Competency List on pages 167–173.)
SCANS: **Basic Skills** Reading, writing, listening, speaking
Resources Allocate time, allocate materials and facility resources
Information Acquire and evaluate information, organize and maintain information, interpret and communicate information

Personal Qualities Responsibility, sociability, self-management
EFF: **Communication** Read with understanding, convey ideas in writing, speak so others can understand, listen actively, observe critically
Lifelong Learning Take responsibility for learning, reflect and evaluate

Presentation 2   15-20 mins.

C **Listen and read Huong's story. Why is Huong healthy?**

Ask students to first listen to Huong's story with their books closed. Write the four categories on the board. Ask students to see if they can hear the information that goes which each one.

Sleep	
Eat	
Exercise	
Smoke	

🎧 **Listening Script**   CD 2, Track 31

The listening script matches the paragraph in Exercise C.

D **What does Huong do? Fill in the chart.**

Ask students to open their books, read Exercise C, and complete the chart with little if any explanation from you. Encourage students to try to figure out what to do on their own, but be careful not to allow students to get frustrated.

E **Read the charts.**

Read the charts with students. Review the third-person singular and then help them to see that the verb in the negative is the base form.

Review the second chart carefully where the *s* is deleted. Point out the use of *don't* and *doesn't*.

Work with students by doing some choral, substitution, and transformational drills.

Teaching Tip

Metalanguage

Students don't need metalanguage to speak English well or to understand grammar. Some English speakers may never know what the *third-person singular* is. However, sometimes when working with adults, some labeling of grammar structures can help them to identify things they have learned earlier and apply them to new structures.

The chart in the book does not identify the base (*simple* or *root*) form of the verb by name. It merely shows that it no longer carries the *s* in the negative. You may choose to introduce the term *base* and/or *root* at this time if you feel students will understand the concept. (*Base* is the term used in *Stand Out* Levels 1–5.)

Practice 2   7-10 mins.

F **Write about Huong.**

Make sure that students refer to Exercise C so that they know when to use the negative.

Evaluation 2   5 mins.

Check students' sentences. Ask students to write their sentences on the board.

 LESSON 4   **GOAL** ➤ **Describe healthy habits**

CD 2
TR 31

 C Listen and read Huong's story. Why is Huong healthy?

I'm healthy. I exercise one hour every day. I eat breakfast, lunch, and dinner. I don't eat a lot of candy. I don't smoke. I sleep seven hours every night.

D What does Huong do? Fill in the chart.

What does Huong do?	What doesn't Huong do?
exercise	eat a lot of candy
eat breakfast, lunch, and dinner	smoke
sleep seven hours every night	

 E Read the charts.

Simple Present		
Subject	**Verb**	**Example sentence**
I, you, we, they	eat	I **eat** three meals a day.
he, she, it	sleep**s**	She **sleeps** seven hours a night.

Negative Simple Present			
Subject	**Verb**		**Example sentence**
I, you, we, they	**don't**	eat	We **don't eat** three meals a day.
he, she, it	**doesn't**	sleep~~s~~	He **doesn't sleep** seven hours a day.

F Write about Huong.

1. Huong _____exercises_____ (exercise) one hour every day.

2. Huong _____sleeps_____ (sleep) seven hours every night.

3. Huong _____eats_____ (eat) breakfast, lunch, and dinner.

4. Huong ___doesn't smoke___ (smoke).

5. Huong ___doesn't eat___ (eat) a lot of candy.

Unit 6   Lesson 4   **111**

G Read.

Name: Julia
Sleep: 8 hours
Meals: breakfast,
      lunch, dinner
Exercise: 30 minutes
      a day
Checkup: 1 time a year
Smoke: no

Name: Hasna
Sleep: 5 hours
Meals: lunch, dinner
Exercise: 0 minutes
      a day
Checkup: 1 time a year
Smoke: no

Name: Dalmar
Sleep: 8 hours
Meals: breakfast,
      lunch, dinner
Exercise: 20 minutes
      a day
Checkup: 0 times a year
Smoke: yes

H Write.

1. Julia and Hasna _____don't smoke_____ (smoke).

2. Hasna _____doesn't eat_____ (eat) breakfast.

3. Dalmar and Julia _____sleep_____ (sleep) eight hours every day.

4. Hasna _____doesn't exercise_____ (exercise).

5. Julia and Hasna _____see_____ (see) the doctor for a checkup.

6. Dalmar _____doesn't see_____ (see) the doctor for a checkup.

I Write. (Answers will vary.)

Your name: _____   Exercise: _____

Sleep: _____   Checkup: _____

Meals: _____   Smoke: _____

Presentation 3   10-15 mins. ■■■□

G Read.

Go over the pictures with students. Ask questions and ask them to answer. Practice the negative when appropriate.

For shorter classes, ask students to do Exercise H for homework.

Practice 3   10-15 mins. ■□□□

H Write.

After students finish doing the exercise, have them write the entire sentences on another sheet of paper.

If you have time, you may consider using these sentences as a modified multilevel dictation as described on page 101a.

Evaluation 3   5-7 mins. ■□□□

Ask students to write the complete sentences on the board.

Application   20-30 mins. ■■□□

I Write.

After students put in their personal information, ask them to share their information with a group. They might say: *I exercise one hour every day.*

Activity Bank AB

Lesson 4, Worksheet 1: Personal Inventory
Lesson 4, Worksheet 2: Negative Simple Present

Refer students to *Stand Out Basic Grammar Challenge*, Unit 6, Challenge 4 for more practice with the negative simple present.

AGENDA
Review illnesses.
Talk about waiting rooms.
Describe waiting rooms.

Objective: Identify actions in a waiting room
Grammar: Present continuous
Pronunciation: /g/
Academic Strategy: Focused listening
Vocabulary: *wait, read, answer, talk, sleep, reception, magazine*

RESOURCES

Activity Bank: Lesson 5, Worksheet 1
Reading and Writing Challenge: Unit 6
Grammar Challenge: Unit 6, Challenge 5

Audio: CD 2, Track 32
Heinle Picture Dictionary: Medical Center, pages 140–141

■ 1.5 hour classes ■ 2.5 hour classes ■ 3⁺ hour classes

Warm-up and Review   7–10 mins. ■■■

Divide the class into two. One half will pretend that they are sick. Ask students who are not "sick" to look for students pantomiming an illness and ask them: *What's the matter?* Students continue this activity with several partners.

Introduction   3–5 mins. ■■■

Ask students if they go to the hospital or the doctor's office when they are sick. Go through the ailments on page 104. Ask students where they think is the best place to go for each symptom. Ask students if they wait at the doctor's office or hospital. Pantomime *waiting* impatiently. State the objective: *Today we will discuss actions in a waiting room.*

Presentation 1   20–30 mins. ■■■

Ask students to open their books. Point to the picture and say: *She has a doctor's appointment.* Point again and say: *She is waiting.* Point to people in the picture and ask questions: *Where is she? What are they doing?* Help students hear the /ing/ sound when you say it. Don't expect students to use the present continuous yet.

(A) Use the words in the box to talk about the picture.

Make sure students know what each word means. Write many of the sentences students say on the board. Don't overcorrect individuals, but always write the sentences correctly.

Go over the words in Exercise B. Explain that verbs can take different forms. Ask students to repeat the words in parentheses. Emphasize *-ing*. Prepare students for focused listening.

Practice 1   5–7 mins. ■■■

(B) Listen to the conversation. What words do you hear first? Write 1–5.

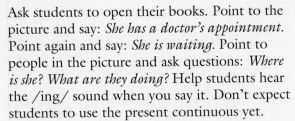

🎧 Listening Script   CD 2, Track 32

Doctor: *I'm a little late. I will be there in ten minutes. How many patients are there?*
Receptionist: *There are four. They are all waiting. Mrs. Hill and Mrs. Johnson are talking, and Guillermo Espinosa is reading a magazine. Mr. Masters is sleeping in a chair.*
Doctor: *What are you doing?*
Receptionist: *I'm answering the phone and writing patient information in their files.*
Doctor: *OK, I'll see you in a few minutes.*

Evaluation 1   7–10 mins. ■■■

Ask students to go to the appendix of their books and find the listening script. Ask them to underline the words from the list and check to see if they have them in the correct order.

STANDARDS CORRELATIONS

CASAS: 3.1.3 (See CASAS Competency List on pages 167-173.)
SCANS: Basic Skills Reading, writing, listening, speaking
Resources Allocate materials and facility resources
Information Acquire and evaluate information

Interpersonal Participate as a member of a team, teach others
EFF: Communication Read and write, convey ideas in writing, speak so others can understand, listen actively, observe critically
Interpersonal Cooperate with others, guide others

I have an appointment.

GOAL ➤ **Identify actions in a waiting room**

Vocabulary · Grammar
Life Skills
Academic · Pronunciation

A Use the words in the box to talk about the picture.

| talk | wait | read | answer | sleep |

RECEPTIONIST

B Listen to the conversation. What words do you hear first? Write 1–5.

CD 2
TR 32

_2_	talk (are talking)
_1_	wait (are waiting)
_3_	read (is reading)
_5_	answer (am answering)
_4_	sleep (is sleeping)

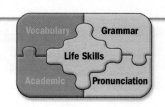

C Read the chart.

Present Continuous (right now)			
Subject	*Be* **verb**	**Base + *ing***	**Example sentence**
I	am	talking	I **am talking**.
he, she, it	is	sleeping	He **is sleeping**.
we, you, they	are	waiting	They **are waiting**.

Pronunciation

/g/
ing

D Look at the picture on page 113. Write.

1. The receptionist _is_ _answering_ (answer) the phone now.

2. The man in the white shirt _is_ _sleeping_ (sleep) in the chair now.

3. The people _are_ _waiting_ (wait) for the doctor now.

4. The women _are_ _talking_ (talk) about their children now.

5. Guillermo _is_ _reading_ (read) a magazine now.

E Talk to a partner.

What is the receptionist doing now?
What is the man in the white shirt doing now?
What are the people doing now?
What are the women doing now?
What is Guillermo doing now?

Presentation 2　　　20-30 mins.

C Read the chart.

As you go over the chart, remind students that these structures, like the others learned in this book (with the exception of the imperative), can have other subjects besides the pronouns. Substitute other names and words in place of the pronouns.

Students may also be confused about *people, men,* and *women.* Show them how the plural works with these words.

Pronunciation

/ing/

The present continuous is used a great deal in English. Students will tend to hear the /ing/ as it runs together with other words in discourse. The /g/ is sometimes difficult to hear if it is present at all in native speech.

There is a relationship between what students hear, what they say, and what they write. Some students, after learning the structure, may leave off the *g* when writing the word much like students often leave off the *s* when writing the plural. Therefore, it is to students' advantage to stress the /ing/ in practice.

D Look at the picture on page 113. Write.

Since this is the first real exposure to the present continuous, do this activity as a class as part of the presentation. Show students the role *now* plays with the present continuous.

Prepare students for the practice.

Practice 2　　　7-10 mins.

E Talk to a partner.

Exercise D contains the answers to the questions in Exercise E. Ask students who might be ready to do this activity with Exercise D covered.

Evaluation 2　　　5-7 mins.

Observe the activity.

Presentation 3   8–10 mins.

F **Look at the picture.**

Look at the picture with students and discuss all the verbs that might be used with the picture. Write the verbs in the base form on the board. Refer students to page 113 to remind them of what verbs might be used.

Review again using the present continuous. Write one appropriate sentence using the present continuous on the board.

Practice 3   10–15 mins. ■

G **Talk about the picture with a partner.**

Ask one student to point to an action in the picture while the other responds with a sentence in the present continuous.

After they have talked about the picture for a sufficient amount of time, ask them to write sentences.

Evaluation 3   3 mins. ■

Ask for volunteers to write their sentences on the board.

Application   10–15 mins. ■■

H **Imagine you are in a waiting room. Write sentences.**

You will have to convey to students the meaning of *imagine* before they can do this exercise.

 Refer students to *Stand Out Basic Grammar Challenge*, Unit 6, Challenge 5 for more practice with the present continuous.

Activity Bank

Lesson 5, Worksheet 1: Present Continuous

F Look at the picture.

G Talk about the picture with a partner.

H Imagine you are in a waiting room. Write sentences.   (Answers will vary.)

1. I'm _____

2. _____

3. _____

4. _____

Review

A Write the body parts. (Lesson 1)

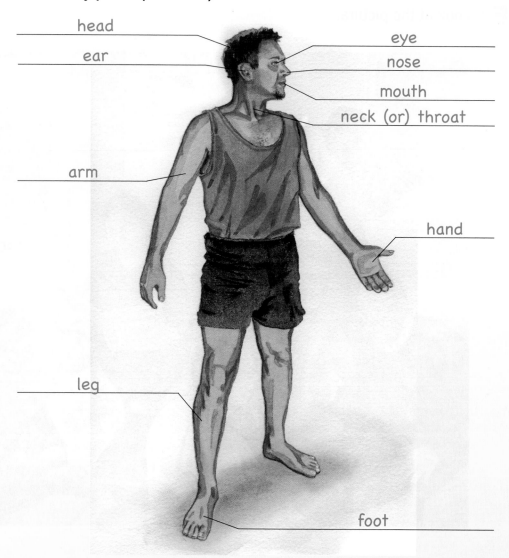

head

ear

eye

nose

mouth

neck (or) throat

arm

hand

leg

foot

B Write the symptom or illness. (Lesson 2)

stomach _____ stomachache _____

head _____ headache _____

back _____ backache _____

throat _____ sore throat _____

nose _____ runny nose _____

Objective: All unit objectives
Grammar: All unit grammar
Academic Strategies: Focused listening, reviewing, evaluating, developing study skills
Vocabulary: All unit vocabulary

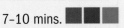 1.5 hour classes   2.5 hour classes ▨ 3⁺ hour classes

AGENDA
Discuss unit objectives.
Complete the review.
Do My Dictionary.
Evaluate and reflect on progress.

Warm-up and Review   7-10 mins. ◼◼▨

With their books closed, ask students to help you make a list on the board of all the vocabulary they can come up with from the unit. Then have a competition where students in groups will find and write page numbers for each item on the list. The first group to have the correct page number for each item, wins.

Introduction   5 mins. ◼◼▨

Write all the objectives on the board from Unit 6. Show students the first page of every lesson so they understand that today will be review. Complete the agenda.

Note: Depending on the length of the term, you may decide to have students do Presentation and Practice 1 for homework and then review student work as the warm-up for another class meeting.

Presentation 1   10-15 mins. ◼◼▨

This presentation and practice will cover the first three pages of the review. Quickly go to the first page of each lesson. Discuss the objective of each. Ask simple questions to remind students what they have learned.

Practice 1   15-20 mins. ◼◼▨

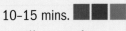 Write the body parts. (Lesson 1)

B Write the symptom or illness. (Lesson 2)

Teaching Tip

Recycling/Review

The review process and the project that follows are part of the recycling/review process. Students at this level often need to be reintroduced to concepts to solidify what they have learned. Many concepts are learned and forgotten while learning other new concepts. This is because students learn but are not necessarily ready to acquire language concepts.

Therefore, it becomes very important to review and to show students how to review on their own. It is also important to recycle the new concepts in different contexts.

STANDARDS CORRELATIONS

CASAS: 3.1.1, 3.1.2, 3.1.3, 3.3.1 (See CASAS Competency List on pages 167-173.)
SCANS: Basic Skills Reading, writing, listening, speaking
Information Acquire and evaluate information, organize and maintain information, interpret and communicate information

Thinking Skills See things in the mind's eye
EFF: Communication Speak so others can understand
Lifelong Learning Take responsibility for learning, reflect and evaluate

Practice 1 (continued)

C Complete the sentences with the present continuous. (Lesson 5)

D Write. (Lesson 3)

E Read and write in the chart. (Lesson 5)

C Complete the sentences with the present continuous. (Lesson 5)

1. The receptionist _is_ _talking_ (talk) on the phone.

2. The patient _is_ _sleeping_ (sleep).

3. The people _are_ _waiting_ (wait) for the doctor.

4. The women _are_ _asking_ (ask) about their children.

5. Hector _is_ _reading_ (read) a magazine.

D Write. (Lesson 3)

1. Richard has a headache. What does he need? (Answers will vary.)

   Medicine: _____

2. Orlando has a stomachache. What does he need?

   Medicine: _____

3. Hue has a fever. What does she need?

   Medicine: _____

4. Chan has a sore throat. What does he need?

   Medicine: _____

E Read and write in the chart. (Lesson 4)

Jeremiah is not very healthy. He smokes ten cigarettes a day. He doesn't exercise. He eats one meal a day. He doesn't sleep eight hours a night. He doesn't drink water. He sees the doctor once a year.

What does Jeremiah do?	What doesn't Jeremiah do?
smoke	exercise
eat one meal a day	sleep eight hours a night
see the doctor once a year	drink water

Review

F Complete the sentences with the simple present. (Lessons 2 and 4)

1. She _____ has _____ (have) a headache.

2. They _____ need _____ (need) medicine.

3. We _____ are _____ (be) sick.

4. I _____ am _____ (be) healthy.

5. You _____ exercise _____ (exercise) every day.

6. Mario and Maria _____ visit _____ (visit) the doctor.

7. He _____ sleeps _____ (sleep) eight hours a day.

8. Alfonso _____ smokes _____ (smoke) cigarettes.

G Complete the sentences with the negative simple present. (Lesson 4)

1. He _____ doesn't smoke _____ (smoke) every day.

2. They _____ don't eat _____ (eat) breakfast.

3. We _____ don't need _____ (need) medicine.

4. They _____ don't exercise _____ (exercise).

5. Nga _____ doesn't have _____ (have) a headache.

6. She _____ doesn't visit _____ (visit) the doctor.

7. I _____ don't want _____ (want) lunch.

8. You _____ don't exercise _____ (exercise).

Practice 1 (continued)

F Complete the sentences with the simple present. (Lessons 2 and 4)

G Complete the sentences with the negative simple present. (Lesson 4)

Evaluation 1

15 mins. ■■■■

Go around the room and check on students' progress. Help individuals when needed. If you see consistent errors among several students, interrupt the class and give a mini lesson or review to help students feel comfortable with the concept.

Presentation 2   5-7 mins.

My Dictionary

Review with students what My Dictionary is and help them see the value of it.

Practice 2   7-10 mins.

Ask students to complete My Dictionary.

Evaluation 2   7 mins.

Observe students work while they complete My Dictionary.

Presentation 3   5 mins.

Learner Log

Review the concepts of the Learner Log. Make sure students understand the concepts and how to do the log including the check marks.

Practice 3   10-15 mins.

Ask students to do the Learner Log.

Evaluation 3   2 mins.

Go over the log with students.

Application   5-7 mins.

Ask students to write down their favorite lesson or page in the unit.

Teaching Tip

Learner Logs

Learner Logs function to help students in many different ways.

1. They serve as part of the review process.
2. They help students to gain confidence and document what they have learned. In this way, students see that they are progressing and want to move forward in learning.
3. They provide students with a tool that they can use over and over to check and recheck their understanding. In this way, students become independent learners.

My Dictionary

Make flash cards to improve your vocabulary.

1. Choose four new words from this unit.
2. Write each word on an index card or on a piece of paper.
3. On the back of the index card or on a paper, draw a picture, find and write a sentence from the book with the word, and write the page number.
4. Study the words.

Julio has a headache.

page 109

Learner Log

Write the page number(s).

	Page Number	I can do it. ✓
1. Identify body parts.	101–103	_____
2. Describe symptoms and illnesses.	104–106	_____
3. Identify medications.	107–109	_____
4. Describe healthy habits.	110–112	_____
5. Identify actions in a waiting room.	113–115	_____

My favorite lesson in this unit is (Answers will vary.).

Team Project

Write conversations and create an appointment book page.

February 18			
Name	Time	Problem	Phone
Julio Rodriguez	3:30		(777) 555-1395
Huong Pham	4:00	fever	(777) 555-3311
Richard Price	4:30		(777) 555-2323
Mele Ikahihifo	5:00	sore throat and cough	(777) 555-5511
Fred Wharton	5:30		(777) 555-9764
Ayumi Tanaka	6:00	backache	(777) 555-8765

1. Form a team with four or five students.
   In your team, you need:

POSITION	JOB	STUDENT NAME
Student 1: Team Leader	See that everyone speaks English. See that everyone participates.	
Student 2: Writer	Write conversations to act out.	
Student 3: Artist	Make an appointment book page.	
Students 4/5: Spokespeople	Prepare a presentation.	

2. Prepare your roles.

   Who is the doctor? _____

   Who is Patient 1? _____

   Who is Patient 2? _____

   Who is the receptionist? _____

3. Make an appointment book page.

   What is Patient 1's name?
   When is the appointment?
   What is the problem?
   Write a conversation between the receptionist and Patient 1.
   Write a conversation between the doctor and Patient 1.

4. Write conversations for Patient 2.

5. Present your conversations and appointment book page to the class.

Introduction

In this project, students will work in teams to create a role play about two patients visiting the doctor's office. The role play should incorporate the vocabulary and some of the conversations they have learned in this unit.

Stage 1   15–20 mins.

Form a team with four or five students.

Show students examples of the project if you have one or discuss the art on the student book page.

Help students to assign positions in their groups. On the spot, students will have to choose who will be the leader of their group. Review the responsibility of a leader and ask students to write the name of their leader in their books. Do the same with all positions: artist, writer, and spokesperson.

Stage 2   10–15 mins.

Prepare your roles.

Help students understand that all of them will be part of the conversations. They should write their role assignments in their books.

Stage 3   40–50 mins.

Make an appointment book page.

Together, team members write the conversations between doctor, patient, and receptionist. They may use their books as a resource. The artist will also make an appointment book page as a prop with everyone's assistance.

Stage 4   10–30 mins.

Write conversations for Patient 2.

Ask students to prepare a set of conversations.

Stage 5   10–30 mins.

Present your conversations and appointment book page to the class.

Ask teams to practice their presentations before they give them. Videotaping can greatly enhance the learning experience.

STANDARDS CORRELATIONS

CASAS: 1.3.9, 4.8.1 (See CASAS Competency List on pages 167–173.)
SCANS: **Basic Skills** Reading, writing, listening, speaking
Resources Allocate time, allocate money, allocate materials and facility resources, allocate human resources
Information Acquire and evaluate information, organize and maintain information, interpret and communicate information, use computers to process information
Interpersonal Participate as a member of a team, teach others, serve clients and customers, exercise leadership, negotiate to arrive at a decision, work with cultural diversity
Systems Understand systems, monitor and correct performance, improve and design systems

Thinking Skills Think creatively, make decisions, solve problems, see things in the mind's eye
Personal Qualities Responsibility, sociability, self management
EFF: **Communication** Read with understanding, convey ideas in writing, speak so others can understand, listen actively, observe critically
Decision Making Solve problems and make decisions, plan
Interpersonal Cooperate with others, advocate and influence, resolve conflict and negotiate, guide others
Lifelong Learning Take responsibility for learning, reflect and evaluate

Objective: Identify occupations
Grammar: Simple present
Pronunciation: /r/
Academic Strategy: Focused listening
Vocabulary: *job, student, occupations*

RESOURCES

Activity Bank: Lesson 1, Worksheet 1
Reading and Writing Challenge: Unit 7
Grammar Challenge: Unit 7, Challenge 1

 1.5 hour classes ■ 2.5 hour classes ■ 3+ hour classes

Audio: CD 2, Tracks 33–34
Heinle Picture Dictionary: Jobs 1, pages 146–147; Jobs 2, pages 148–149

Stand Out Basic Assessment CD-ROM with Exam*View*®

AGENDA

Interview classmates.
Talk about Emilio's job.
Learn about jobs.
Practice writing about jobs.
Ask a classmate about jobs.

Preassessment *(optional)*

Use the Stand Out Basic Assessment CD-ROM with Exam*View*® to create a pretest for Unit 7.

Warm-up and Review   15–20 mins. ■■■

Ask students their names, addresses, and phone numbers. Write the three questions and any others you would like on the board and ask students to interview one another.

Introduction   3–7 mins. ■■■

Write *teach* on the board. Ask: *What do I do?* Lead students to the response *teach*, and say: *I teach. I'm a teacher.* Add *-er* to *teach.* State the objective: *Today we will identify occupations.*

Presentation 1   40–50 mins. ■■■

Talk about the picture.

Ask students questions and pull out as many nouns as you can.

Listen and read.

Have students close their books and listen. Then have them open their books and read along.

> **Listening Script**   *CD 2, Track 33*
>
> The listening script matches the paragraph in Exercise B.

Write. What does Emilio do?

Teach that *What do you do?* is often asked to find out one's job. Ask students what they do. Make sure they understand that they can answer *student, homemaker,* or a paid job.

Practice 1   15–20 mins. ■■■

Ask students to copy the paragraph in Exercise B. Show them how it is indented.

Write on the board the following two sentences: *I have a job. I don't have a job.* Ask students to write a paragraph about themselves based on the model in Exercise B. If students don't finish in class, ask them to finish their paragraphs for homework.

In this unit, students will be introduced to several paragraphs. This activity will prepare them for this exposure.

A paragraph for a student who doesn't have a job might look like the following:

> *My name is Lidia. I live in Sacramento, California. I don't have a job. I'm a student at Oak Haven Adult School.*

Evaluation 1   3–5 mins. ■■■

Check students' writing. Focus on indenting, capital letters, periods, and the comma before the state. Make sure students understand that state names are usually not abbreviated in paragraphs.

STANDARDS CORRELATIONS

CASAS: 0.2.1, 4.1.8 (See CASAS Competency List on pages 167-173.)
SCANS: **Basic Skills** Reading, writing, listening, speaking
Information Acquire and evaluate information

EFF: **Communication** Read with understanding, speak so others can understand, listen actively

Work

GOALS

➤ Identify occupations
➤ Give information about work
➤ Identify job duties

➤ Read evaluations
➤ Read signs and follow directions

LESSON 1

Do you work?

GOAL ➤ Identify occupations

A Talk about the picture.

B Listen and read.

CD 2
TR 33

My name is Emilio. I live in Dallas, Texas. I have a new job. I'm a cashier at Ultra Supermarket on Broadway! This is a picture of my English class.

C Write. What does Emilio do?

He's a student, and he's also a ___cashier___.

GOAL ➤ **Identify occupations**

CD 2
TR 34

D Listen and repeat the words. What do these people do?

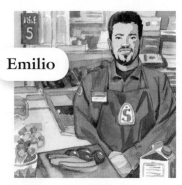
Emilio

Hue

Chan

cashier   doctor   bus driver

Carolina

Vache

Pete

student   salesperson   teacher

E Practice the conversation with a partner. Use the words in Exercise D.

A: What does <u>Emilio</u> do?
B: He's a <u>cashier</u>.

F Write sentences about the people in Exercise D.

1. Emilio is a cashier.
2. Hue is a doctor.
3. Chan is a bus driver.
4. Carolina is a student.
5. Vache is a salesperson.
6. Pete is a teacher.

Presentation 2   10–15 mins. ■■□

Ask students to close their books. Play charades by using 3-by-5 index cards with the six occupations in Exercise D on them. Give six student volunteers each a card and have them act out the occupation on that card.

(D) Listen and repeat the words. What do these people do?

Ask the students to point as you say: *He's a cashier. She's a doctor.*

 Listening Script   CD 2, Track 34

cashier
doctor
bus driver
student
salesperson
teacher

Prepare students to do the practice by going over the dialog as a class. Show them how to substitute information.

/r/

The /r/ sound in English is problematic for many students. Many languages don't pronounce the *r* like Americans do. When they see it, students will often tend to try to pronounce it as they would in their own language.

Help students to see that the /r/ in *doctor, driver, cashier,* and *teacher* is pronounced with little if any tongue movement and the lips are rounded. Exaggeration can help students see how it is done.

In this presentation, you may choose to expand the lesson, and in turn, the pronunciation portion, by showing students how adding *-er* to most any verb will change it to a noun indicating someone who performs this verb. Use the following examples:

teach-teacher
drive-driver
clean-cleaner
walk-walker
talk-talker
drink-drinker
run-runner
play-player

Practice 2   7–10 mins.

(E) Practice the conversation with a partner. Use the words in Exercise D.

Evaluation 2   7–10 mins.

(F) Write sentences about the people in Exercise D.

Check students' work.

Presentation 3   10–15 mins. ▪▪▪

Go over the vocabulary with students. Help them with the pronunciation. Pay particular attention to the final consonants. Make sure they release on the /n/ of *custodian*, the /k/ in *cook*, and the /s/ in *nurse*. Also, make sure they round their lips with the /r/ in *manager* and *carrier*.

(G) **Who works here? Write the jobs in the chart.**

Write *where* on the board. Show students how the information they write in Exercise G will help them do the practice, Exercise H. Do Exercise G as a class. The first words in the chart are from page 122. The second entries can be the new words in the box above. See if students can come up with one more word for each category. Notice that the categories relate to the topics covered in Units 1–6. Show students how they can go back in their books and discover more job titles.

Prepare students for the practice by going over the dialog in Exercise H. Remind students how to use the simple present in the affirmative and in the negative.

Practice 3   7–10 mins. ▪

(H) **Practice the conversation. Make new conversations.**

Evaluation 3   2–7 mins. ▪

Ask volunteers to present their new conversations in front of the class.

Application   7–10 mins. ▪▪▪

(I) **Read the conversation.**

Go over the conversation and show students how they will change it to do Exercise J.

(J) **Practice the conversation with four classmates.**

(K) **Active Task.** What do your friends and family do? Make a list.

📖 Refer students to *Stand Out Basic Grammar Challenge*, Unit 7, Challenge 1 for more practice with the simple present.

Instructor's Notes

Vocabulary Grammar
Life Skills
Academic Pronunciation

cook	custodian	mail carrier	manager	nurse

G Who works here? Write the jobs in the chart.

School	Restaurant	Clothing store	Community	Doctor's office
teacher	cashier	salesperson	bus driver	doctor
custodian	cook	manager	mail carrier	nurse

(Additional answers will vary.)

H Practice the conversation.
Make new conversations.

A: Where does <u>a teacher</u> work?
B: He works in <u>a school</u>.

Simple Present	
I work.	I don't work.
He works.	He doesn't work.
She works.	She doesn't work.

I Read the conversation.

A: Do you work?
B: Yes, I work. I'm a cashier. How about you? Do you work?
A: No, I don't work. I'm a student.

J Practice the conversation with four classmates. (Answers will vary.)

Name	Occupation

K Active Task. What do your friends and family do? Make a list. (Answers will vary.)

When do you go to work?

GOAL ➤ Give information about work

 **A** Listen.

CD 2
TR 35

1.

2.

Name: Isabel
Title: receptionist
Company: Johnson Company
Supervisor: Martin
Hours: 9 A.M.–6 P.M.
Break: 12 P.M.–1 P.M.
Days: Monday–Friday

Name: Colleen
Title: manager
Company: Freedman's Foods
Supervisor: Amelia
Hours: 2 P.M.–10 P.M.
Break: 6 P.M.–7 P.M.
Days: Wednesday–Sunday

3.

Name: Fred
Title: custodian
Company: America Bank
Supervisor: Mary
Hours: 10 P.M.–7 A.M.
Break: 1 A.M.–2 A.M.
Days: Sunday–Friday

  B Listen and write the names of the people from Exercise A.

CD 2
TR 36

1. Colleen   2. Fred   3. Isabel

AT-A-GLANCE PREP

Objective: Give information about work
Grammar: Information questions
Academic Strategies: Focused listening, making graphs
Vocabulary: *receptionist, custodian, manager, nurse, supervisor, when, where, what, who*

RESOURCES

Activity Bank: Lesson 2, Worksheet 1
Reading and Writing Challenge: Unit 7
Grammar Challenge: Unit 7, Challenge 2

Audio: CD 2, Tracks 35–39
Heinle Picture Dictionary: Working, pages 150–151

■ 1.5 hour classes   ■ 2.5 hour classes   ■ 3⁺ hour classes

AGENDA

Review occupations.
Listen to information about jobs.
Ask what, when, where, and who.
Read about a nurse.
Answer questions about your job or school.

Warm-up and Review   15-20 mins.

Take a class poll of jobs, including *students* and *homemakers*. Make a bar graph of the results.

Introduction   5-7 mins.

Write *when* and *where* on the board. Use these words to ask about work. State the objective: *Today we will learn to give information about work.*

Presentation 1   15-20 mins.

Help students to understand the information below the pictures. Ask questions about it.

 Listen.

Play the recording. Ask students to follow along.

> **Listening Script**   *CD 2, Track 35*
>
> Hello, I'm Isabel. I have a great job. I am a receptionist. I work for the Johnson Company and my supervisor's name is Martin. I work from 9:00 A.M. to 6:00 P.M., Monday through Friday. I take a one-hour lunch break at 12:00.
>
> My name is Colleen. I am the manager of Freedman's Foods. My supervisor is Amelia. I work Wednesday through Sunday from 2:00 P.M. to 10:00 P.M. I take a one-hour break at 6:00.
>
> I'm Fred. My friends call me Freddy. I work late at night. I work from 10:00 P.M. to 7:00 A.M., Sunday to Friday. I'm a custodian at America Bank. My supervisor's name is Mary.

Practice 1   15-20 mins.

 Listen and write the names of the people from Exercise A.

The people in these conversations are the same ones as in Exercise A. Students will write *Isabel, Colleen,* or *Fred* in the blanks.

> **Listening Script**   *CD 2, Track 36*
>
> 1. **Manager:** *Please take care of the customer over there.*
>   **Employee:** *OK. You are the boss.*
>   **Manager:** *Oh, and please write down any problems she is having.*
>   **Employee:** *I can do that.*
>   **Manager:** *You can go home after you take care of those two things.*
>   **Employee:** *Thanks!*
> 2. **Custodian:** *Excuse me, I need to mop under your desk.*
>   **Coworker:** *OK, I'll move for a few minutes.*
>   **Custodian:** *Thanks. I need to mop the whole bank every day.*
> 3. **Manager:** *My name is Martin. I am your new supervisor.*
>   **Receptionist:** *Nice to meet you, Martin.*
>   **Manager:** *Nice to meet you, too. When do you come to work?*
>   **Receptionist:** *I work from 9:00 A.M. to 6:00 P.M. every weekday.*

Evaluation 1   3-5 mins.

Check students' work.

Note: Standards Correlations are on the next page.

Presentation 2   10–15 mins.

C Read.

Go over the uses of *what, where, when* and *who*. The first three words have been previously introduced. You may ask some questions such as: *Where do you live? When do you come to school? What do you do?* Remind students of questions they have been exposed to throughout *Stand Out Basic*. Show them the difference between each word by identifying what kind of information is being asked for.

D Match the questions and answers about Colleen.

This is still at the presentation stage, so do the exercise as a class. After you finish, ask the same questions about Colleen once again.

Practice 2   7–10 mins.

E With a partner, answer the questions. Take turns being Fred.

Ask students in pairs to imagine one of them is Fred. Student A uses the questions in Exercise E. Student B, or Fred, answers by looking at the information on page 124. Have students reverse roles.

F Ask and answer questions about Isabel.

Evaluation 2   3–5 mins.

Ask for volunteers to demonstrate the questions and answers in front of the class.

Teaching Tip

Stages in grammar acquisition

It is important at this level that students don't get overwhelmed with too much information. Learning one objective well is often more important than having a weak grasp of many things.

Teaching grammar becomes problematic when instructors expect students to acquire the structure after introducing it to them only a few times. Consider the order of the following:

1. Exposure
2. Instruction
3. Application outside of the classroom
4. Acquisition

A lot of what students see in *Stand Out Basic* is exposure and instruction. Students do receive instruction at various times on the same structures in different contexts and are given the opportunity to apply what they have learned, but few students at this level will use the structures outside of the classroom. This is because they don't have the other necessary tools (vocabulary, competencies, etc.) to be able to use them regularly. This is why we repeat and recycle the structures so often in *Stand Out Basic*. Acquisition will come as students take the language they are using in the classroom outside of the classroom. *Stand Out 1* and *2* review most of these same structures while adding more in preparation for language acquisition.

In this lesson, students are not ready to form questions. This process is somewhat complicated. They are, however, ready to answer questions. The formation of questions, therefore, is merely necessary exposure.

STANDARDS CORRELATIONS

CASAS: 0.1.6, 4.8.1 (See CASAS Competency List on pages 167–173.)
SCANS: **Basic Skills** Reading, writing, listening, speaking
Information Acquire and evaluate information, organize and maintain information, interpret and communicate information

EFF: **Communication** Read with understanding, speak so others understand, listen actively, observe critically

GOAL ➤ **Give information about work**

C Read.

Information Questions	
Question word	**Type of answer**
What	information (receptionist)
Where	a place (Johnson Company)
When	a time or day (9–6) (Monday–Friday)
Who	a person (Martin)

D Match the questions and answers about Colleen.

1. What do you do?
2. Where do you work?
3. Who is your supervisor?
4. When do you work?
5. When is your break?

a. I work at Freedman's Foods.
b. It's from 6:00 P.M.–7:00 P.M.
c. I work Wednesday through Sunday.
d. I'm a manager.
e. Amelia.

E With a partner, answer the questions. Take turns being Fred.

1. What do you do, Fred?
2. Where do you work?
3. Who is your supervisor?
4. When do you work?
5. When is your break?

F Ask and answer questions about Isabel.

EXAMPLE: **A:** *What* does Isabel do?
B: She's a receptionist.

LESSON 2

GOAL ➤ **Give information about work**

G Read.

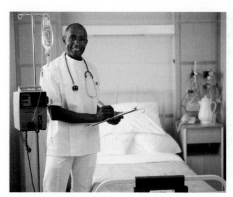

My name is Ben. I'm a nurse. I work at a hospital from 7:00 A.M. to 7:00 P.M. I work Monday through Thursday. I help the doctors and talk to patients. My supervisor is Mrs. O'Malley.

H Answer the questions.

1. What does Ben do? **He's a** nurse .

2. When does he start work? **He starts work at** 7:00 A.M. .

3. Where does he work? **He works at** a hospital .

4. Who is Ben's supervisor? **She is** Mrs. O'Malley .

I Listen. Fill in the chart about Tan, Maria, and Alfredo.

CD 2
TR 37–39

	What	**When**	**Where**
Tan	custodian	3:00 P.M. (or) at night	school
Maria	manager	Monday–Friday	restaurant
Alfredo	nurse	6:00 P.M.	hospital

J Answer the questions. (Answers will vary.)

1. What do you do? _____

2. Where do you work or go to school? _____

3. Who is your supervisor or teacher? _____

4. When do you work or go to school? _____

Presentation 3 · 10–15 mins.

G Read.

Allow students time to read the paragraph about Ben silently. After 30 seconds, have students close their books. Ask students the questions in Exercise H. See how much students remember. Then ask students to open their books again.

H Answer the questions.

Do this activity as a class. Remind students about the differences between the question words, especially *when* and *where*. Sometimes, students have a problem distinguishing between these two words.

Prepare students for the listening practice in Exercise I. Remind them of the principles of focused listening. This activity is much harder than the previous focused listening activities because students are listening for three pieces of information for each person.

Practice 3 · 7–10 mins.

I Listen. Fill in the chart about Tan, Maria, and Alfredo.

Play the recording four times. Allow students to discuss among themselves between tracks.

 Listening Script CD 1, Tracks 37–39

What does Tan do? When and where does he work?

My name is Tan. I have a great job. I work late at night and sleep during the day. I'm a custodian. I start work at 3:00 P.M. I work at a school.

What does Maria do? When and where does she work?

My name is Maria. I'm a manager at a restaurant. I work Monday through Friday. I work with customers and all the employees.

What does Alfredo do? When and where does he work?

My name is Alfredo. I'm a nurse. I work at a hospital. I take care of patients and help the doctors on the fifth floor. I start work at 6:00 P.M.

Evaluation 3 · 5–7 mins.

Check students' answers as a class. Play the recording again if necessary.

Application · 10–15 mins.

J Answer the questions.

Ask students to answer the questions and report to a group. One student in each group will stand and give his or her answers. Then a new student stands and does the same.

Refer students to *Stand Out Basic Grammar Challenge*, Unit 7, Challenge 2 for more practice with answering information questions.

Activity Bank

Lesson 2, Worksheet 1: *When, Where, and What*

Instructor's Notes

Lesson Planner: Unit 7, Lesson 2 **126a**

AT-A-GLANCE PREP

Objective: Identify job duties
Grammar: *Can*
Academic Strategy: Focused listening
Vocabulary: *worker, salesperson, administrative assistant, floor, file, type, customer, on time*

RESOURCES

Activity Bank: Lesson 3, Worksheets 1 and 2
Reading and Writing Challenge: Unit 7
Grammar Challenge: Unit 7, Challenge 3

■ 1.5 hour classes ■ 2.5 hour classes ■ 3⁺ hour classes

Audio: CD 2, Tracks 40–41
Heinle Picture Dictionary: Working, pages 150–151

> ## AGENDA
> *Talk about jobs.*
> *Learn about job actions.*
> *Listen and answer yes/no questions.*
> *Use can to describe what you are able to do.*

Warm-up and Review 7-10 mins. ■■■

Do a Corners activity. Assign these categories to the corners: *employed, unemployed but looking, unemployed and not looking, retired.* Ask students to ask each other these questions in their corners:

Employed: *Where do you work? When do you start work?*
Unemployed: *What job do you want? Where do you want to work?*
Not employed, Retired: *What do you do? Where do you live?*

Introduction 3-5 mins. ■■■

Tell students that you teach. Also, tell them that you take roll and talk to students. Write these two duties on the board. Write *duties* above the phrases. State the objective: *Today we will identify job duties.*

Presentation 1 12-15 mins. ■■■

Go over the pictures in Exercise A and help students with the vocabulary, especially verbs. Review the simple present. Point out that it is necessary in these sentences to use the final *s.*

 **A** Listen and point.

> **Listening Script**   CD 2, Track 40
>
> 1. *Receptionists have many responsibilities. They file and talk to customers. They also answer the phone.*
> 2. *Administrative assistants are very important. They do many things. One of the important things they do is type letters. Some secretaries can type more than 100 words a minute.*
> 3. *A salesperson is important. He or she talks to customers and answers their questions.*

> 4. *Custodians work in many different places. The custodian at the elementary school mops the floor, cleans the rooms, and helps the teachers.*

Practice 1 7-10 mins. ■■■

 B What do they do? Listen and write.

Have students cover Exercise A. Teach the expression *What do you do?* Explain that sometimes we answer with a job title and sometimes describe our duties. Play the recording for the example. Then have students complete the chart as they listen.

> **Listening Script**   CD 2, Track 41
>
> 1. *An administrative assistant has important responsibilities. He or she types letters, for one thing.*
> 2. *Custodians work in many different places. The custodian at an elementary school mops floors.*
> 3. *Receptionists have many responsibilities. For example, a receptionist in an office answers phones.*
> 4. *A salesperson is important. He or she talks to customers and does many other things.*
> 5. *Cashiers are usually in the front of a store or business. A cashier in a supermarket makes change as well as many other things.*
> 6. *A manager is responsible for seeing that all goes well in a business. He or she supervises other employees.*
> 7. *A nurse in a hospital helps the doctors as much as possible.*

Evaluation 1 3-7 min s. ■■■

Re-create the chart on the board and ask students to complete it.

Note: Standard Correlations are on page 128a.

LESSON 3

What do you do?

GOAL ➤ Identify job duties

  A Listen and point.

CD 2
TR 40

1.

answers the phone

3.

talks to customers

2.

types letters

4.

mops the floor

supervises employees   helps the doctor   makes change

  B What do they do? Listen and write.

CD 2
TR 41

Occupation	Job description
1. administrative assistant	types letters
2. custodian	mops floors
3. receptionist	answers phones
4. salesperson	talks to customers
5. cashier	makes change
6. manager	supervises other employees
7. nurse	helps the doctors

C Read.

A receptionist files papers.

Sometimes workers take breaks.

	mops	answers phones	talks to customers	types letters	takes breaks	files papers
salesperson		X	X		X	
administrative assistant		X		X	X	X
receptionist		X	X		X	X
custodian	X				X	

Pronunciation

Yes/No Questions

➤ Does he file?
➤ Does she type?
➤ Does he talk to customers?

D Answer the questions. Check (✓) *Yes* or *No*. Practice with a partner.

	Yes	No
1. Does a salesperson file?		✓
2. Does an administrative assistant take breaks?	✓	
3. Does a custodian talk to customers?		✓
4. Does a receptionist talk to customers?	✓	
5. Does a salesperson mop the floors?		✓

Presentation 2   15-20 mins.

C Read.

Help students learn the new vocabulary. Show students how a receptionist can have more than one duty (file and answer phones). Ask students what else a receptionist might do. Encourage students to look at the chart.

Go over the chart with students and make sure they understand how to read it. To make sure they understand, ask them comprehension questions such as: *What does an administrative assistant do?*

If you feel your students are ready, you might teach them how to use *and* as well as when to use commas. Write sentences on the board. Here are two example sentences: *A receptionist answers phones, talks to customers, and files papers. A custodian mops and takes breaks.*

Now ask *yes/no* questions. Remind students of the intonation. Go over the examples as a class.

Practice 2   10-15 mins.

D Answer the questions. Check (✓) *Yes* or *No*. Practice with a partner.

Evaluation 2   3-5 mins.

Go over the answers as a class by having different students ask and answer the questions.

STANDARDS CORRELATIONS

CASAS: 4.1.3, 4.1.8, 4.4.4 (See CASAS Competency List on pages 167–173.)
SCANS: **Basic Skills** Reading, writing, listening, speaking
Resources Allocate human resources
Information Acquire and evaluate information, interpret and communicate information

EFF: **Communication** Read with understanding, convey ideas in writing, speak so others understand, listen actively, observe critically
Lifelong Learning Reflect and evaluate

Presentation 3   7-10 mins. ■■■□

E Read.

Go over the charts with students. You may wish to introduce some grammar terminology at this point, such as *base form* and *negative*.

For shorter classes, ask students to do Exercises F and G for homework.

Practice 3   10-15 mins. ■

F Complete the sentences with *can* + the verb.

G Complete the sentences with *can't* + the verb.

Evaluation 3   5-7 mins. ■

Check the students' book work and go over the answers as a class.

Application   15-20 mins. ■■□■

H Write what you *can* and *can't* do. Use words from this lesson.

This activity is to help students evaluate what they might be able to do in a job setting. Encourage them to use vocabulary from this lesson.

Refer students to *Stand Out Basic Grammar Challenge*, Unit 7, Challenge 3 for more practice with *can* and *can't*.

Activity Bank

Lesson 3, Worksheet 1: Duties
Lesson 3, Worksheet 2: Using *can* and *can't*

GOAL ➤ **Identify job duties**

E Read.

Can			
Subject	**Can**	**Verb (base)**	**Example sentence**
I, you, he, she, it, we, they	can	type	I can type.
		mop	He can mop floors.

Can't			
Subject	**Can't**	**Verb (base)**	**Example sentence**
I, you, he, she, it, we, they	can't	type	I can't type.
		mop	He can't mop floors.

F Complete the sentences with *can* + the verb.

1. He _____ can file _____ (file) papers.
2. They _____ can type _____ (type) letters.
3. I _____ can mop _____ (mop) the floor.
4. You _____ can answer _____ (answer) phones.

G Complete the sentences with *can't* + the verb.

1. We _____ can't take _____ (take) breaks.
2. They _____ can't type _____ (type).
3. I _____ can't talk _____ (talk) to customers.
4. She _____ can't file _____ (file).

H Write what you *can* and *can't* do. Use words from this lesson. (Answers will vary.)

1. I can _____.   1. I can't _____.
2. _____   2. _____

You're doing great!

GOAL ➤ Read evaluations

Vocabulary · Grammar · Life Skills · Academic · Pronunciation

A Read.

Work Evaluation

Name: __Emilio Sanchez__

Helps customers	**Yes**	No
Comes to work on time	**Yes**	No
Speaks English well	**Yes**	No
Follows directions well	**Yes**	No

Manager Signature: __Calvin Carter__

B What does a good student do? Circle. (Answers will vary.)

files	practices English
listens	takes lunch breaks
cleans the office	follows directions
types letters	writes in class
does homework	reads in class
talks to customers	speaks in class
comes to school on time	answers phones

Objective: Read evaluations
Grammar: Negative and affirmative with the verb *be*
Academic Strategy: Focused listening
Vocabulary: *well, on time, signature, friendly, helpful, careful, cheerful*

RESOURCES

Activity Bank: Lesson 4, Worksheet 1
Reading and Writing Challenge: Unit 7
Grammar Challenge: Unit 7, Challenge 4

Audio: CD 2, Track 42
Heinle Picture Dictionary: Working, pages 150–151

■ 1.5 hour classes   ■ 2.5 hour classes   ■ 3⁺ hour classes

Warm-up and Review   10-15 mins.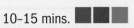

Review *can* and *can't*. Ask students to get in groups of four or five and report what they *can* do well and what they *can't* do well.

Then ask students to identify what jobs they might be able to do. You may want to write other skills, not taught in the previous lesson, that students might be able to do on the board. For example, you might write: *cook, serve food, clean,* and *speak another language.* Write jobs that might be associated with these words.

Introduction   15-20 mins. ■■■

Ask students what they can do to be a better student. Make a list on the board of their ideas. These ideas might include listening carefully and coming to class on time. State the objective: *Today we will read employment evaluations.*

Presentation 1   15-20 mins. ■■■

Ⓐ Read.

Go over the evaluation with students. Make sure they understand all the new vocabulary. Ask them questions about Emilio. Talk about the word *well*. This lesson is about doing things well, but you might also want to introduce *not well* here. Ask students which one of the four areas they think are most important.

Ask students to get into groups and rank the four areas from most important to least important. Every one in the group must agree. When students finish, take a class poll. There is no correct answer so validate all student answers.

Practice 1   7-10 mins.

Ⓑ What does a good student do? Circle.

Ask students to do this in their groups as well and then rank their answers like they did in Presentation 1.

Evaluation 1   10-12 mins.

Ask groups to report to the class. Write a sentence on the board to facilitate this: *We think* listens *is number one.*

STANDARDS CORRELATIONS

CASAS: 4.4.4 (See CASAS Competency List on pages 167–173.)
SCANS: Basic Skills Reading, writing, listening, speaking
Information Acquire and evaluate information, organize and maintain information, interpret and communicate information

EFF: Communication Read with understanding, convey ideas in writing, speak so others can understand, listen actively, observe critically
Lifelong Learning Reflect and evaluate

Presentation 2   15-20 mins. ■■■

Write *friendly* on the board. Ask students who they think is the friendliest student in the class. If they don't know the word, help them understand it. Have a class vote and make a class award for the person voted to be the friendliest.

C Read.

Ask students to open their books. Go over the new vocabulary and how to use it in a sentence. Review the *be* verb in both the affirmative and the negative.

Reinforce the example sentences by asking questions about who in the class is cheerful and who is helpful. Ask students what jobs would require a person to be careful. You might encourage them to go back in the unit to find examples of jobs. Add more jobs to their list like police officers, fire fighters, accountants, etc.

D Write the *be* verb.

This is still presentation so go over the activity as a class to make sure all students understand the basic structure.

Look at the Evaluation form for Exercise E. Ask students to evaluate themselves. They don't have to write or say anything, but some students may volunteer the information. Make sure they use *am*. Reinforce what they say with *we* when you share a characteristic with them.

Prepare students for practice by reviewing the principles of focused listening.

Practice 2   7-10 mins. ■■□

E Listen and circle.

Play the recording three times. Allow students to discuss answers between the times you play the recordings.

Listening Script   CD 2, Track 42

I evaluated Chan Chin today. He is a very good worker, and I think he is a good employee because, overall, his attitude is very good.

He is always happy and cheerful. This is important because the customers see this and it helps them to feel good about our store. Chan is not always helpful, though, because he is new and doesn't know very much about the job. In time, he will get better. Sometimes, Chan and Jim are not careful enough. They were responsible for the lamp being broken in the lighting section. I have asked Chan to work on being more careful around the displays. Chan has a good attitude. He talks to the customers and is very friendly. Overall, I am happy with Chan's work.

Evaluation 2   5-10 mins. ■■□

Go over the answers with students. You may need to play the recording again to confirm the answers. Ask students more about the listening excerpt to identify how much more they understand.

Teaching Tip

Evaluating student levels

There are times throughout instruction when you may choose to ask questions and find out if students can perform at a higher level. Some students may be learning at a faster rate than others, and you may find it useful to identify them.

In focused listening activities, students are expected to identify key words. They are not expected to understand the entire passage. Nevertheless, some students may understand more than what is required.

GOAL ➤ Read evaluations

Vocabulary · Grammar · Life Skills · Academic · Pronunciation

C Read.

Simple Present: *Be*		
Subject	***Be***	**Example sentence**
I	am	I **am** friendly.
he, she, it	is	She **is** friendly.
we, you, they	are	They **are** friendly.

Simple Present: *Be* (negative)		
Subject	***Be*** **(Negative)**	**Example sentence**
I	am not	I **am not** friendly.
he, she, it	is not	She **is not** friendly.
we, you, they	are not	They **are not** friendly.

> friendly   helpful   careful   cheerful

D Write the *be* verb.

1. Emilio ____is____ friendly with the customers.
2. Carolina ____is____ not cheerful.

3. We ____are____ helpful.
4. They ____are____ not careful.

 E Listen and circle.

CD 2
TR 42

Work Evaluation

Name: _Chan Chin_

Is careful	Yes	(No)
Is friendly	(Yes)	No
Is helpful	Yes	(No)
Is cheerful	(Yes)	No

Manager Signature: _Jim Brown_

GOAL ➤ **Read evaluations**

F **Read.**

    Vache Deluse is a salesperson. He works every day, Monday through Friday. He always helps customers and he is always friendly. Sometimes he is not careful with clothing, and sometimes he doesn't come to work on time.

G **Complete the evaluation.**

Work Evaluation

Name: _Vache Deluse_

Helps customers	(Yes)	No
Comes to work on time	Yes	(No)
Is friendly	(Yes)	No
Is careful	Yes	(No)

Manager Signature: _Calvin Carter_

H **Complete an evaluation for yourself at school.** (Answers will vary.)

My Evaluation

I come to school on time.	Yes	No
I follow directions.	Yes	No
I do my homework.	Yes	No
I am cheerful and friendly.	Yes	No

Presentation 3   10-15 mins. ■■■□

Ask students to close their books. Read the paragraph to them. By now students have probably learned *sometimes* and *always,* but make sure they understand what the two words mean. Write *Vache Deluse* on the board. Explain to them that this is a name.

Write the following words on the board: *works, helps, friendly,* and *careful.*

Read the paragraph out loud again. Ask students to raise their hands and put them down again immediately every time they hear one of the words.

Teaching Tip

Kinesthetic learners

Learners can be predominantly visual, auditory, tactile, global, or analytic. The *Stand Out* approach addresses each learning style and suggests a variety of teaching methods so students with different needs and learning styles can better benefit from instruction.

Kinesthetic learners learn better when they move around or manipulate things. They tend to remember more when they act something out. In the ESL classroom, kinesthetic learners learn better if they are asked to physically respond to questions or information. This can be as simple as following TPR commands or raising their hands or as complicated as acting out a play.

F **Read.**

Go over the reading. If you have time, leave the information you have written on the board and give a quick dictation. While students are doing this activity, you might ask them to cover Exercise G so they don't do the practice activity before you ask them to.

For shorter classes, ask students to do Exercise G for homework.

Practice 3   7-10 mins. ■

G **Complete the evaluation.**

Ask students to circle the correct answers based on the reading.

Evaluation 3   5-7 mins. ■

Check students' book work.

Application   20-30 mins. ■■■

H **Complete an evaluation for yourself at school.**

In this activity, students write about themselves.

Activity Bank

Lesson 4, Worksheet 1: Reading Evaluations

 Refer students to *Stand Out Basic Grammar Challenge,* Unit 7, Challenge 4 for more practice with the *be* verb and characteristics.

Instructor's Notes

_____

_____

_____

_____

_____

_____

_____

_____

_____

_____

_____

_____

_____

_____

_____

_____

Objective: Read signs and follow directions
Grammar: Imperatives
Academic Strategy: Focused listening
Vocabulary: *don'ts, dos, answer, wash, type*

RESOURCES

Activity Bank: Lesson 5, Worksheet 1
Reading and Writing Challenge: Unit 7
Grammar Challenge: Unit 7, Challenge 5

Audio: CD 2, Track 43
Heinle Picture Dictionary: Factory, pages 156-157

■ 1.5 hour classes   ■ 2.5 hour classes   ■ 3+ hour classes

AGENDA

Make awards for cheerful and helpful students.
Read signs.
Practice following directions.
Read a job description.
Write classroom dos and don'ts.

Warm-up and Review   10–15 mins.

As a class, prepare awards for the most cheerful and the most helpful students. Have an election and give out the awards.

Introduction   15–20 mins.

Pantomime the signs and messages on this page. The students should have their books closed. Write each direction on the board as students call it out. Then ask a student to say each direction and react by pantomiming as if he/she is commanding you. State the objective: *Today we will read signs and follow directions.*

Presentation 1   15–20 mins.

(A) Listen and point.

Do this activity as a class. You may introduce the terms *negative* and *affirmative* to the students if you think they will understand. Write the two word pairs *negative* and *no,* and *affirmative* and *yes.*

 Listening Script   *CD 2, Track 43*

The listening script matches the items in Exercise A.

Look around the room for any signs. Identify any other safety signs that may be on campus. Ask them what other messages a manager or supervisor might leave for employees.

Practice 1   10–15 mins.

(B) Read the signs and notes. Circle *Yes* or *No.*

Have students circle *yes* or *no* based on the signs and notes.

Ask students to pantomime to a group the different verbs and have them say the commands listed in Exercise B, either negative or affirmative. Ask students to form groups and play charades.

Evaluation 1   3–5 mins.

Observe students as they play charades.

STANDARDS CORRELATIONS

CASAS: 4.4.4, 4.8.1, 4.8.3 (See CASAS Competency List on pages 167–173.)
SCANS: **Basic Skills** Reading, writing, listening, speaking
Resources Allocate human resources
Information Acquire and evaluate information, organize and maintain information, interpret and communicate information

Interpersonal Participate as a member of a team
EFF: **Communication** Read with understanding, convey ideas in writing, speak so others can understand, listen actively, observe critically
Decision Making Solve problems, make decisions, plan
Interpersonal Cooperate with others, advocate and influence, resolve conflict and negotiate, guide others

Please type this letter.

GOAL ➤ **Read signs and follow directions**

 A Listen and point.

CD 2
TR 43

1. Don't smoke.

2. Wash your hands.

3. File the papers.

4. Fred, please answer the phones.

5. Fred, please type these letters.

6. Don't eat in the office.

 B Read the signs and notes. Circle *Yes* or *No*.

1. Smoke.	Yes	**No**	
2. Wash hands.	**Yes**	No	
3. File.	**Yes**	No	
4. Answer the phones.	**Yes**	No	
5. Type letters.	**Yes**	No	
6. Eat.	Yes	**No**	

LESSON 5 **GOAL** ➤ **Read signs and follow directions**

C Read.

Affirmative Commands			
	Verb		**Example sentence**
~~You~~	wash	your hands	Wash your hands.
	answer	the phones	Answer the phones.
	type	letters	Type the letters.

Negative Commands				
	Verb			**Example sentence**
~~You~~	don't	wash	your hands	Don't wash your hands.
		answer	the phones	Don't answer the phones.
		type	letters	Don't type the letters.

wash	answer	type	clean
file	eat	smoke	

D Complete the sentences.

1. Wash **your hands.**
2. Clean your desk.
3. Answer the phones.
4. Don't eat in the office.

E Read and practice the conversations. Use the commands in Exercise C.

Manager: How are you, Isabel?
Isabel: I'm fine, thank you.
Manager: Please, <u>clean your desk today</u>.
Isabel: Yes, of course.

Manager: How are you, Isabel?
Isabel: I'm fine, thank you.
Manager: Please, <u>don't eat in the office</u>.
Isabel: No, of course not.

Presentation 2　　　20–30 mins.

C Read.

Read the charts with students. Help them understand that we don't say the subject pronoun *you* with commands. Review words that are associated with the actions. For example, *wash* can be associated with *hands, the table, the car,* etc.

Review the other vocabulary words and associate them with actions.

D Complete the sentences.

Do this activity together with students as reinforcement.

Prepare students for the practice by going over the two dialogs in Exercise E. Show students how they might substitute information.

Practice 2　　　7–10 mins.

E Read and practice the conversations. Use the commands in Exercise C.

Evaluation 2　　　5–7 mins.

Ask volunteers to present the conversations for the class.

Presentation 3   7-10 mins. ■■■

F Read.

Go over the job description with students. Ask them questions about it, including the following: *What is the job title? When does the receptionist work? What are some of the duties?*

Practice 3   10-15 mins. ■

G Look at the job descriptions in Exercise F. Write the commands.

Ask students to write the information in the spaces provided. Then, in groups, ask students to determine what responsibilities are most important.

Evaluation 3   10 mins. ■

Check students' book work.

Application   10-15 mins. ■■■

H In groups, write classroom *do's* and *don'ts.*

When they finish, ask groups to report to the class.

Refer students to *Stand Out Basic Grammar Challenge*, Unit 7, Challenge 5 for more practice with the imperative.

Activity Bank

Lesson 5, Worksheet 1: Commands

GOAL ➤ **Read signs and follow directions**

F Read.

RECEPTIONIST JOB DESCRIPTION
WINTER HOLIDAY HOTEL
2900 W. EDEN BLVD.
SACRAMENTO, CA 94203

Position: #33
Job Title: Receptionist
Hours: 9:00 A.M– 6:00 P.M.

1. Answer phones.
2. Talk to customers.
3. File.
4. Don't come to work late!
5. Don't eat in the office.
6. Don't smoke in the office.

G Look at the job description in Exercise F. Write the commands.

Do's	Don'ts
Answer phones.	Don't come to work late.
Talk to customers.	Don't eat in the office.
File.	Don't smoke in the office.

H In groups, write classroom *do's* and *don'ts*. (Answers will vary.)

Classroom Do's	Classroom Don'ts
Listen.	

Review

(A) Write the name of the job. (Lesson 1)

1.

custodian

2.

teacher

3.

receptionist

4.

salesperson

5.

cashier

6.

bus driver

7.

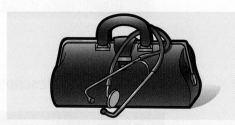

doctor

8.

manager

(B) Point to a picture in Exercise A. Ask a partner about the job. (Lesson 1)

EXAMPLE: *A:* What does he do?
           B: He's a custodian.

AT-A-GLANCE PREP

Objective: All unit objectives
Grammar: All unit grammar
Academic Strategies: Focused listening,
  reviewing, evaluating, developing study skills
Vocabulary: All unit vocabulary

AGENDA

Discuss unit objectives.
Complete the review.
Do My Dictionary.
Evaluate and reflect on progress.

 1.5 hour classes   2.5 hour classes   3⁺ hour classes

Warm-up and Review   7–10 mins.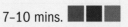

With their books closed, ask students to help you make a list on the board of all the vocabulary they can come up with from the unit. Then have a competition where students in groups find and write the page number for each item on the list. The first group to have the correct page number for each item wins.

Introduction   5 mins.

Write all the objectives on the board from Unit 7. Show students the first page of every lesson so they understand that today will be review. Complete the agenda.

Note: Depending on the length of the term, you may decide to have students do Presentation and Practice 1 for homework and then review student work as the warm-up for another class meeting.

Presentation 1   10–15 mins.

This presentation and practice will cover the first three pages of the review. Quickly go to the first page of each lesson. Discuss the objective of each. Ask simple questions to remind students what they have learned.

Practice 1   15–20 mins.

A Write the name of the job. (Lesson 1)

B Point to a picture in Exercise A. Ask a partner about the job. (Lesson 1)

Teaching Tip

Recycling/Review

The review process and the project that follows are part of the recycling/review process. Students at this level often need to be reintroduced to concepts to solidify what they have learned. Many concepts are learned and forgotten while learning other new concepts. This is because students learn, but are not necessarily ready to acquire language concepts.

Therefore, it becomes very important to review and to show students how to review on their own. It is also important to recycle the new concepts in different contexts.

STANDARDS CORRELATIONS

CASAS: 4.1.3, 4.1.8, 4.4.1, 4.8.1, 4.8.3, 7.4.1, 7.4.2, 7.4.3 (See CASAS Competency List on pages 167–173.)
SCANS: Basic Skills Reading, writing, listening, speaking
Information Acquire and evaluate information, organize and maintain information, interpret and communicate information

Thinking Skills See things in the mind's eye
EFF: Communication Speak so others can understand
Lifelong Learning Take responsibility for learning, reflect and evaluate

Practice 1 (continued)

C Match the job with the duty. Draw a line.
(Lessons 1 and 3)

D Write *when, where, what,* or *who.* (Lesson 2)

C Match the job with the duty. Draw a line. (Lessons 1 and 3)

1.

    a. types letters

2.

    b. makes change

3.

    c. mops the floor

4.

    d. talks to customers

D Write *when, where, what,* or *who.* (Lesson 2)

1. <u>When</u>   does the store open? The store opens at 10:00 A.M.
2. <u>Where</u>   do you take a break? I take a break in the cafeteria.
3. <u>Where</u>   do you work? I work in Sacramento.
4. <u>Who</u>   is your manager? His name is Martin.
5. <u>What</u>   does she do? She's a nurse.

Identify the signs. (Lesson 5)

1. __Don't smoke.__

2. __Don't eat.__

3. Wash your hands.

F **Talk to a partner. Write. (Lessons 3 and 4)** (Answers will vary.)

EXAMPLES: I can speak English well.
I can follow directions.
I am friendly, helpful, careful, and cheerful.

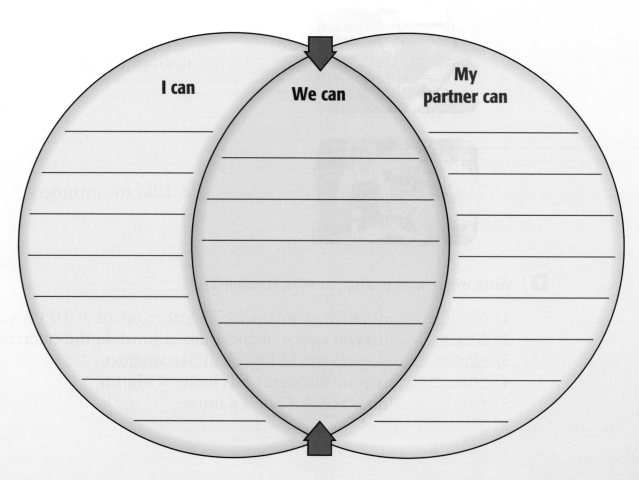

I can

We can

My
partner can

Practice 1 (*continued*)

(**E**) Identify the signs. (Lesson 5)

(**F**) Talk to a partner. Write. (Lesson 3)

Evaluation 1

15 mins. ■■■■

Go around the room and check on students' progress. Help individuals when needed. If you see consistent errors among several students, interrupt the class and give a mini lesson or review to help students feel comfortable with the concept.

Presentation 2   5-7 mins.

My Dictionary

Review with students what My Dictionary is and help them see the value of it.

Practice 2   7-10 mins.

Ask students to complete My Dictionary.

Evaluation 2   3 mins.

Have students share their cards with the class.

Presentation 3   5 mins.

Learner Log

Review the concepts of the Learner Log. Make sure students understand the concepts and how to do the log including the check marks.

Teaching Tip

Learner Logs

Learner Logs function to help students in many different ways.

1. They serve as part of the review process.

2. They help students to gain confidence and document what they have learned. In this way, students see that they are progressing and want to move forward in learning.

3. They provide students with a tool that they can use over and over to check and recheck their understanding. In this way, students become independent learners.

Practice 3   10-15 mins.

Ask students to do the Learner Log.

Evaluation 3   2 mins.

Go over the log with students.

Application

Ask students to write down their favorite lesson or page in the unit.

My Dictionary

Make flash cards to improve your vocabulary.

1. Choose four new words from this unit.
2. Write each word on an index card or on a piece of paper.
3. On the back of the index card or paper, draw a picture, find and write a sentence from the book with the word, and write the page number.
4. Study the words.

I'm a manager.

page 125

Learner Log

Write the page number(s).

	Page Number	I can do it. ✓
1. Identify occupations.	121–123	
2. Ask questions with *when* and *where*.	124–126	
3. Talk about job duties.	127–129	
4. Use *can* and *can't*.	130–132	
5. Discuss do's and don'ts.	133–135	

My favorite page in this unit is (Answers will vary.).

Team Project

Start a company.

1. Form a team with four or five students. In your team, you need:

POSITION	JOB	STUDENT NAME
Student 1: Team Leader	See that everyone speaks English. See that everyone participates.	
Student 2: Writer	Write job descriptions.	
Student 3: Artist	Make a cover page with the name of your company and a logo.	
Students 4/5: Spokespeople	Prepare a presentation.	

2. What is the name of your company?
   What is your company logo? Make a cover page.

3. What are the occupations in the company?

4. Write three job descriptions for jobs in your company.

5. Present your company to the class.

Introduction

In this project, students will work in teams to create a company, incorporating the vocabulary they have learned from this unit.

Stage 1   15–20 mins.

Form a team of four or five students.

Discuss the art on the Student Book page.

Help students to assign positions in their groups. On the spot, students will have to choose who will be the leader of their group. Review the responsibility of a leader and ask students to write the name of their leader in their books. Do the same with the remaining positions: artist, writer, and spokesperson.

Stage 2   3–5 mins.

What is the name of your company? What is your company logo? Make a cover page.

Help students as needed. Bring in some logos from companies in your community for students to look at.

Stage 3   40–50 mins.

What are the occupations in the company?

Make sure students distinguish between their roles on the team and their jobs in the company.

Stage 4   10–30 mins.

Write three job descriptions for jobs in your company.

You can use Activity Bank worksheets for this project.

Stage 5   10–30 mins.

Present your company to the class.

Ask teams to practice their presentations before they give it to the class. Videotaping the presentations can greatly enhance the learning experience.

Instructor's Notes

_____

_____

_____

_____

_____

_____

_____

_____

_____

_____

_____

_____

_____

_____

STANDARDS CORRELATIONS

CASAS: 2.2.3, 4.8.1 (See CASAS Competency List on pages 167–173.)
SCANS: **Basic Skills** Reading, writing, listening, speaking
Resources Allocate time, allocate money, allocate materials and facility resources, allocate human resources
Information Acquire and evaluate information, organize and maintain information, interpret and communicate information, use computers to process information
Interpersonal Participate as a member of a team, teach others, serve clients and customers, exercise leadership, negotiate to arrive at a decision, work with cultural diversity
Systems Understand systems, monitor and correct performance, improve and design systems

Thinking Skills Think creatively, make decisions, solve problems, see things in the mind's eye
Personal Qualities Responsibility, sociability, self management
EFF: **Communication** Read with understanding, convey ideas in writing, speak so others can understand, listen actively, observe critically
Decision Making Solve problems, make decisions, plan
Interpersonal Cooperate with others, advocate and influence, resolve conflict and negotiate, guide others
Lifelong Learning Take responsibility for learning, reflect and evaluate

Objective: Organize study materials

Grammar: *Be* verb

Academic Strategies: Focused listening, test-taking skills, organization skills

Vocabulary: *binder, inch, sheet, divider, lined paper, personal profile*

RESOURCES

Activity Bank: Lesson 1, Worksheet 1

Reading and Writing Challenge: Unit 8

Grammar Challenge: Unit 8, Challenge 1

 1.5 hour classes ▮ 2.5 hour classes ▮ 3⁺ hour classes

Audio: CD 2, Tracks 44–45

Heinle Picture Dictionary: Classroom, pages 18–19

Stand Out Basic Assessment CD-ROM with *ExamView®*

AGENDA

Discuss what makes a good student.

Discuss organization materials.

Organize a binder.

Complete a personal profile.

Preassessment *(optional)*   ▮▮▮

Use the Stand Out Basic Assessment CD-ROM with *ExamView®* to create a pretest for Unit 8.

Note: Unit 8 is composed of review lessons that also take students through the development of a study binder, which will help them review concepts in the book after the term is complete.

Warm-up and Review   15-20 mins.   ▮▮▮

Ask: *What makes a good student?* Make a list on the board of the students' answers. To get them started, you may wish to write some of your ideas on the board such as: *Come to school every day. Study at home.* Ask students to rank the ideas from the most important to the least important, first individually and then as a class.

Introduction   3-7 mins.   ▮▮▮

Tell students that to be a good student, you should be organized. Help them understand the meaning of *organized* by writing the word on the board. To make it clearer, show them some examples of organization and disorganization, like a messily organized binder and a neat orderly one with dividers. State the objective: *Today we will identify ways to organize study materials.*

Presentation 1   20-30 mins.   ▮▮▮

A Listen and repeat.

Ask students questions about the items in the picture such as: *What is this? Who has this? What's it for?*

🎧 **Listening Script**   CD 2, Track 44

The listening script matches the list of items in Exercise A.

B Write more items you use to organize your study materials.

Help students think of things to write in this activity. Get them started by giving them some suggestions such as *file cabinet* and *pencils.*

Prepare students to do the listening activity by going over the pictures they see in the exercise items.

Note: Practice 1 and Evaluation 1 appear on the next page.

Lifelong Learning and Review

GOALS

➤ **Organize study materials**
➤ **Make purchases**
➤ **Give and follow directions**

➤ **Make goals**
➤ **Develop a study schedule**

Let's get organized!

GOAL ➤ Organize study materials

A Listen and repeat.

CD 2
TR 44

binder

dividers

sheets of lined paper

B Write more items you use to organize your study materials. (Answers will vary.)

_____   _____

_____   _____

_____   _____

 C Listen and bubble in.

CD 2
TR 45

1. What size binder do they need?
   - ○ 1 inch
   - ● 1 ½ inches
   - ○ 3 inches

2. How many dividers do they need?
   - ○ 1 divider
   - ○ 3 dividers
   - ● 5 dividers

3. How many sheets of lined paper do they need?
   - ○ 50 sheets
   - ○ 100 sheets
   - ● 200 sheets

D Look through Units 1–7 of your book. Write the page numbers and two words for each section in your binder.

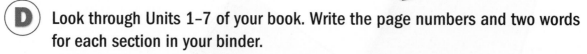

Section	Reference pages	Example vocabulary
Personal Information	1–40	(Answers will vary.)
Consumer Economics (FOOD / CLOTHING)	41–80	
Community Resources	81–100	
Health	101–120	
Occupational Knowledge	121–140	

Practice 1

7-10 mins.

C Listen and bubble in.

Play the recording two times and allow students to discuss their answers between listenings.

 Listening Script   CD 2, Track 45

1. A: *The teacher wants us to make special binders to study after school is finished.*
    B: *Yes, I know. We have to go to the store and buy some things. I don't think it will be expensive.*
    A: *We need binders first.*
    B: *What size do we need?*
    A: *I think we need 1½" binders.*
    B: *That sounds right. They shouldn't be too big.*

2. A: *We need dividers, too.*
    B: *What are dividers?*
    A: *You know, the heavy paper to make sections in your binder.*
    B: *Oh, yeah. How many do we need?*
    A: *We need a set of five dividers.*

3. A: *What else do we need?*
    B: *We need paper for each section.*
    A: *How many sheets do we need?*
    B: *Two hundred sheets, I think.*
    A: *That sounds right.*

Evaluation 1

3 mins.

Check students' book work.

Presentation 2

10-15 mins.

Ask students to refer to the table of contents in their books. Go over it with them. Show them where the page numbers are. Then ask them to go to the appendix in the book and look at the vocabulary lists. Ask them what two words are most important to them in the first two units. Refer them back to Exercise D and ask them to write those two words in the space provided. Explain to students that each divider in the binder represents a different section in the book. Point out the tabs.

Practice 2

8-10 mins.

D Look through Units 1–7 of your book. Write the page numbers and two words for each section in your binder.

Remind students to check the vocabulary list in the appendix.

Evaluation 2

3 mins.

Ask students to share their answers and display their dividers if possible.

Presentation 3   10–15 mins. ▪▪□

Remind students of all the questions they learned in Units 1 and 2. Walk around the room and ask students questions as review.

Go over each question in Exercise E. Explain to students that this activity will prepare them to start their own binders.

Help students with pronunciation and question intonation. If your students are ready, you might write key words on the board, have them close their books, and ask them for the questions based solely on the key words. You may also have them use the grid that is available on the Activity Bank CD-ROM for this unit.

Review the *be* verb in preparation for Practice 3.

Practice 3   10–15 mins. ▪

(E) Interview and write about your partner. Report to a group.

Ask students to report to their groups about their partners.

Evaluation 3   5–7 mins. ▪

Ask volunteers to present their interviews in front of the class.

Application   15–20 mins. ▪▪▪

(F) Make the first page in your binder on a sheet of paper.

Ask students to create their own Personal Profile like in the introductory page of a date planner using the sample provided, or ask them to complete the form provided on the Activity Bank CD-ROM.

📖 Refer students to *Stand Out Basic Grammar Challenge*, Unit 8, Challenge 1 for more practice with the *be* verb.

Activity Bank 💿

Lesson 1, Worksheet 1: Personal Profile

GOAL ➤ Organize study materials

E Interview and write about your partner. Report to a group. (Answers will vary.)

1. What's your name? _____

2. Where do you live? _____

3. What is your phone number? _____

4. What is your birth date? _____

5. Are you married? _____

6. Where are you from? _____

Be Verb
I am . . .
My phone number is . . .

F Make the first page in your binder on a sheet of paper.

PERSONAL PROFILE

PHOTO

_____
SCHOOL

_____
TEACHER

NAME _____
        First   Middle   Last

ADDRESS _____

CITY _____ STATE _____ ZIP _____

COUNTRY _____

MARITAL STATUS *(Circle)*   Single   Married   Divorced

I need paper.

GOAL ➤ Make purchases

A Read the advertisements.

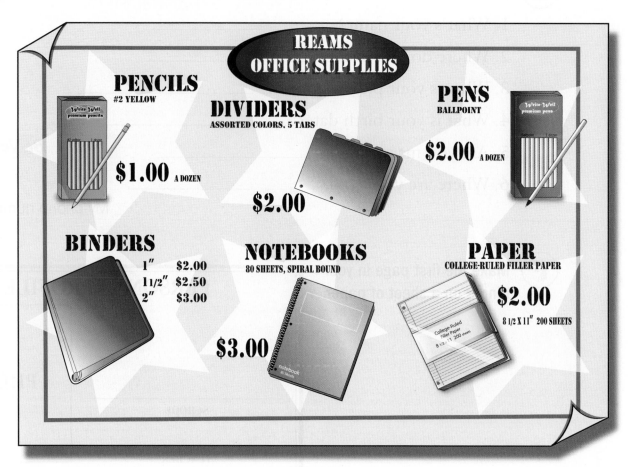

REAMS OFFICE SUPPLIES

PENCILS
#2 YELLOW

Write Well premium pencils

$1.00 A DOZEN

DIVIDERS
ASSORTED COLORS, 5 TABS

$2.00

PENS
BALLPOINT

$2.00 A DOZEN

Write Well premium pens

BINDERS

1″	$2.00
1 1/2″	$2.50
2″	$3.00

NOTEBOOKS
80 SHEETS, SPIRAL BOUND

$3.00

notebook

PAPER
COLLEGE-RULED FILLER PAPER

$2.00

8 1/2 X 11″ 200 SHEETS

College-Ruled Filler Paper
8 1/2 : 1 200 sheets

> How much **is** the paper?   How much **are** the notebooks?

B Listen to the conversation and practice.

CD 2
TR 46

Customer: Excuse me, how much are the dividers?
Salesperson: They are $2.00 for a set of five.
Customer: Thanks. I need one set, please.

Objective:
Make purchases
Grammar: *How much is, How much are*
Academic Strategy: Focused listening
Vocabulary: *package, set, dozen, ballpoint pen, colored, box*

AGENDA

Talk about places to shop.
Read an ad.
Complete a receipt.
List food and clothing you buy.
Make a section for Consumer Economics in your binder.

RESOURCES

Activity Bank: Lesson 2, Worksheet 1
Reading and Writing Challenge: Unit 8
Grammar Challenge: Unit 8, Challenge 2

Audio: CD 2, Tracks 46–47
Heinle Picture Dictionary: Money and Shopping, pages 8–9; Food, pages 82–103; Clothing, pages 104–117

■ 1.5 hour classes   ■ 2.5 hour classes   ■ 3⁺ hour classes

Warm-up and Review   15-20 mins. ■■■

Ask students to work in groups and share the information they wrote on their personal profiles from the previous class.

Introduction   5-7 mins. ■■■

Ask students where they buy food, clothing, and other items. Write the names of the stores on the board and take an informal poll to see what the most popular stores are. State the objective: *Today we will review making purchases.* Help students understand what a *purchase* is. Use the word *buy* and give some examples.

Presentation 1   30-40 mins. ■■■

 Read the advertisements.

Go over the ads with students. There is a lot of "extra" vocabulary that they may not need, but since they will be confronted by these words when they go off to make real purchases, help them discern what is important.

Review questions with *How much is* and *How much are.*

 Listen to the conversation and practice.

Help students understand the basic format of the question and the words that may be unknown to them, such as *set.*

 Listening Script   *CD 2, Track 46*

The listening script matches the conversation in Exercise B.

 Listen and repeat.

Go over each sentence with students. Help them with new vocabulary.

Listening Script   *CD 2, Track 47*

The listening script matches the list of statements in Exercise C.

Note: Practice 1 and Evaluation 1 appear on next page.

STANDARDS CORRELATIONS

CASAS: 1.1.6, 1.2.1, 1.3.1, 1.6.4, 7.1.4 (See CASAS Competency List on pages 167-173.)
SCANS: **Basic Skills** Reading, writing, listening, speaking
Resources Allocate money
Information Acquire and evaluate information, organize and maintain information, interpret and communicate information
Interpersonal Participate as a member of a team, teach others

Thinking Skills Think creatively, make decisions
Personal Qualities Responsibility, sociability, self-management
EFF: **Communication** Read with understanding, convey ideas in writing, speak so others can understand, listen actively, observe critically
Decision Making Solve problems and make decisions, plan
Interpersonal Cooperate with others, guide others
Lifelong Learning Take responsibility for learning, reflect and evaluate

Practice 1   5-7 mins. ■■□

D What do you need? Write.

Ask students to complete the receipt by using the information on page 144, Exercise A, and on page 145, Exercise C.

Evaluation 1

Check students' book work.

Presentation 2   15-20 mins. ■■□

Practice the conversation in Exercise E with a volunteer. Make sure they understand how to substitute information from Exercises A and C.

Practice 2   10-15 mins. ■□

E Practice the conversation. Use the information from Exercise A on page 144.

Do the conversation with students one time so that they understand what to do before you ask them to work in pairs.

Evaluation 2   3-5 mins. ■□

Ask volunteers to present their conversations in front of the class.

F Active Task. Go to a store in your community and buy office supplies.

If possible, take the class on a field trip to a local office supply store.

GOAL ➤ **Make purchases**

 C Listen and repeat.

CD 2
TR 47

I need …
 a box of pencils.
 a two-inch binder.
 a set of five colored dividers.
 a package of paper.
 a box of ballpoint pens.
 a notebook.

> a two-inch binder = a 2" binder

 D What do you need? Write.

REAMS OFFICE SUPPLIES

Item	Quantity	Price
2" Binder	1	$3.00
box of pencils	1	$1.00
set of dividers	1	$2.00
package of paper	1	$2.00
box of ballpoint pens	1	$2.00
notebook	1	$3.00
	Total	$13.00

Customer Copy

 E Practice the conversation. Use information from Exercise A on page 144.

Salesperson: What do you need?
Customer: I need a <u>two-inch binder</u>.
Salesperson: They are over here.
Customer: How much are they?
Salesperson: They are <u>$3.00</u> each.

F Active Task. Go to a store in your community and buy office supplies.

Vocabulary | Grammar
Life Skills
Academic | Pronunciation

G In a group, make a list of food you buy in the supermarket.

Food	Price
(Answers will vary.)	

H In a group, make a list of clothing you buy in a clothing store.

Clothing	Price
(Answers will vary.)	

I Look at Exercise E on page 145. Write and practice new conversations about food and clothing.

J Prepare a section in your binder for Consumer Economics.

Consumer Economics

Stand Out Basic Page Numbers
_____

Important Vocabulary

Food:
apples
_____ _____ _____ _____
_____ _____ _____ _____

Clothing:
shoes
_____ _____ _____ _____
_____ _____ _____ _____

Sentences and Questions

What's for lunch?
I need a blue shirt.
_____ _____
_____ _____
_____ _____
_____ _____

Consumer Economics

Grammar
Prepositions of Location   Page Number: _____

[   ]

Singular and Plural   Page Number: _____

[   ]

Simple Present - *like*   Page Number: _____

[   ]

Presentation 3   10–15 mins. ■■□

Again ask students where they buy food and clothing. Make a list on the board of different places they go.

Practice 3   30–40 mins. ■■

(G) In a group, make a list of food you buy in the supermarket.

Help as needed.

(H) In a group, make a list of clothing you buy in a clothing store.

Help as needed.

(I) Look at Exercise E on page 145. Write and practice new conversations about food and clothing.

Help as needed.

Evaluation 3   3–5 mins. ■■

Ask for volunteers to present their conversations in front of the class.

Application   10–15 mins. ■■■

(J) Prepare a section in your binder for Consumer Economics.

Ask students to create their own Consumer Economics summary page for their binder, using the sample provided, or ask them to complete the forms provided on the Activity Bank CD-ROM for this unit.

📖 Refer students to *Stand Out Basic Grammar Challenge*, Unit 8, Challenge 2 for more practice with *How much is* and *How much are*.

Activity Bank 💿

Lesson 2, Worksheet 1: Consumer Economics

Objective: Give and follow directions
Grammar: Prepositions
Academic Strategy: Focused listening
Vocabulary: Office supplies

AGENDA

Make conversations about shopping.
Practice giving directions.
Read a phone directory.
Draw a map.
Make a section for Community
in your binder.

RESOURCES

Activity Bank: Lesson 3, Worksheet 1
Reading and Writing Challenge: Unit 8
Grammar Challenge: Unit 8, Challenge 3

Audio: CD 2, Track 48
Heinle Picture Dictionary: Community, pages 46–61

■ 1.5 hour classes   ■ 2.5 hour classes   ■ 3⁺ hour classes

Warm-up and Review   15–20 mins.

Ask students to share some of the conversations they completed in Exercise I on page 146.

Introduction   3–5 mins.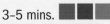

Ask students where an office supply store is near the school. Help them understand that an office supply store is a store where they can buy all the materials they need for their binders. State the objective: *Today we will review how to give and follow directions.*

Presentation 1   40–50 mins.

A Look at the picture.

Ask students to look at the picture and tell you what is happening in it. Have them guess what the woman is asking. It's fine if students look at the conversation in Exercise B at this stage.

Go over the conversation with students in Exercise B. Explain to them that they will be listening to the conversation and filling in the missing information.

Practice 1   5–10 mins.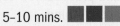

B Listen to the conversation. Write.

 Listening Script   CD 2, Track 48

The listening script matches the conversation in Exercise B.

Evaluation 1   5–7 mins.

Check students' book work. Review *right, left,* and *straight.* Have two students perform the dialog with gestures in front of the class.

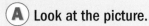

STANDARDS CORRELATIONS

CASAS: 2.1.1, 2.2.1, 7.1.4 (See CASAS Competency List on pages 167–173.)
SCANS: Basic Skills Reading, writing, listening
Information Acquire and evaluate information, organize and maintain information, interpret and communicate information

Interpersonal Participate as a member of a team, teach others
Personal Qualities Responsibility, sociability, self-management
EFF: Communication Read with understanding, convey ideas in writing, speak so others can understand, listen actively, observe critically
Lifelong Learning Take responsibility for learning, reflect and evaluate

Where's the office supply store?

GOAL ➤ Give and follow directions

A Look at the picture.

 B Listen to the conversation. Write.

CD 2
TR 48

Linda: Excuse me, where is Reams Office Supplies?

Officer: It's on First Street.

Linda: On First Street?

Officer: Yes, go straight on this street. Turn ____right____ on Main Street

and ____left____ on First. It's ____next to____ the video store.

Linda: Thanks.

GOAL ➤ **Give and follow directions**

C Read.

City Phone Directory

Nursing Schools

Ace Nursing Schools
8237 Beachnut Ave. ············555-6732
Metropolitan Nursing
2467 Apple Lane ············ 555-3472

Office Supply

Pencil Head Stationers
11 Broadway ···················· 555-3411
Nottingham Paper
23400 Portland Ave ············555-0045
Reams Office Supply
1717 First St. ····················555-2762

Optometrists

Dr. Michael's Eye Exams
1723 First St. ····················555-3310
Quick Check Glasses
3456 W. Circle Ave. ············ 555-6776

Painting Supplies

Bill's Painting Supply
5678 First St.····················555-1301
Paint for Less
15 Broadway ···················· 555-3737
Picture Perfect

D Read the conversation.

Linda: Excuse me, where is <u>Reams Office Supplies</u>?
Officer: It's on <u>First Street</u>.
Linda: What's the address?
Officer: It's <u>1717 First Street</u>.
Linda: Thanks.

E Practice new conversations with the information in Exercise C.

Presentation 2   20-30 mins. ■■■□

C Read.

Help students find the phone number and address for Reams Office Supply. Ask other questions about other places in the directory.

D Read the conversation.

Prepare students to do Exercise E.

Practice 2   10-15 mins. ■■□

E Practice new conversations with the information in Exercise C.

Help as needed.

Evaluation 2   7-10 mins. ■■□

Ask for volunteers to present their conversations in front of the class. There are many opportunities for students to perform unique conversations. Try to get all students in class to perform at least once.

Presentation 3   15–20 mins. ■■■□

F Draw a map from your school to an office supply store in your community.

Do this exercise with the class. Use the board to draw a map to a local office supply store or another store where students can buy the materials for their binders. Remind students of the prepositions they might use in Practice 3.

Practice 3   7–10 mins. ■

G Write directions to the office supply store.

Help as needed.

Evaluation 3   5–7 mins. ■

Have students write their directions on the board.

Application   7–10 mins. ■■□

H Prepare a section in your binder for Community.

Ask students to create their own Community Resource summary page for their binder, using the sample provided, or ask them to complete the forms provided in the Activity Bank CD-ROM for this unit.

📖 Refer students to *Stand Out Basic Grammar Challenge*, Unit 8, Challenge 3 for more practice with prepositions of location.

Activity Bank 💿

Lesson 3, Worksheet 1: Community

LESSON 3

GOAL ➤ Give and follow directions

F Draw a map from your school to an office supply store in your community.

(Answers will vary.)

Prepositions
It's *next to* the bank.
It's *between* the bank and the store.
It's *on* the corner.

G Write directions to the office supply store.

(Answers will vary.)

H Prepare a section in your binder for Community.

Community
Stand Out Basic Page Numbers
Important Vocabulary
left
Sentences and Questions
What's for lunch?
I need a blue shirt.

Community
Grammar
in/on   Page Number: _____
Simple Present   Page Number: _____
_____   Page Number: _____

Sleep eight hours a day.

GOAL ➤ Make goals

A Read Liang's goals.

> **My Goals**
> ☑ Sleep eight hours a day.
> ❏ Go to school every day.
> ❏ Exercise one hour a day.
> ☑ Eat three good meals a day.
> ❏ Study English at home one hour a day.
> ☑ Read the newspaper in English fifteen minutes a day.
> ❏ Watch TV fifteen minutes a day.

B Listen and check Carina's three goals.

CD 2
TR 49

☑ Sleep eight hours a day.

❏ Go to school every day.

☑ Exercise one hour a day.

❏ Eat three good meals a day.

☑ Study English at home one hour a day.

❏ Read the newspaper in English fifteen minutes a day.

❏ Watch TV fifteen minutes a day.

C Talk about Liang's and Carina's goals.

EXAMPLE: Liang's goal is to sleep eight hours a day.

AT-A-GLANCE PREP

Objective: Make goals
Grammar: Simple present
Academic Strategies: Focused listening, study skills
Vocabulary: *goals, a day, a week, every, study, watch, poll*

RESOURCES

Activity Bank: Lesson 4, Worksheet 1
Reading and Writing Challenge: Unit 8
Grammar Challenge: Unit 8, Challenge 4

Audio: CD 2, Track 49
Heinle Picture Dictionary: Health, pages 132–145

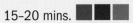 1.5 hour classes 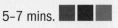 2.5 hour classes 3+ hour classes

Warm-up and Review   15–20 mins.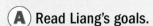

Take a poll and determine how many hours students sleep a day. Make the results into a bar graph.

Introduction   5–7 mins.

Ask students how many hours of sleep is healthy, and write it down as a goal. State the objective: *Today we will make goals, including study goals.*

Presentation 1   15–20 mins.

A Read Liang's goals.

Go over each goal with the class. Prepare students for focused listening. They will hear Carina talk about three goals. Students should put a check by the goals they hear.

Practice 1   10–15 mins.

B Listen and check Carina's three goals.

Play the recording three times. Let students discuss answers. Ask groups to rank the goals.

🎧 Listening Script   CD 2, Track 49

I have many goals. There are a lot of things that I want to accomplish. Right now, I'm focusing on daily goals. First, I need to exercise every day. I want to get up early and exercise one hour a day. It's important to be physically fit. I suppose that it's important to be prepared for school every day, too, so I'm going to study a lot. I plan to study for one hour every day, even if I'm tired after work. I need to learn English, and studying will help me do it faster. Somehow, I need to get plenty of sleep, too. Right now, I only sleep six hours a night, but my goal is to get eight hours of sleep. I hope I can do it. That's my goal. With all these goals, I will be healthy and have great success at school.

C Talk about Liang's and Carina's goals.

Evaluation 1   3–5 mins.

Check students' answers. Ask the class to rank Liang's and Carina's goals.

STANDARDS CORRELATIONS

CASAS: 0.2.1, 3.5.9, 6.7.2, 7.1.1, 7.1.2, 7.1.4 (See CASAS Competency List on pages 167–173.)
SCANS: Basic Skills Reading, writing, listening, speaking
Resources Allocate time, allocate materials and facility resources, allocate human resources
Information Acquire and evaluate information, organize and maintain information, interpret and communicate information

Interpersonal Participate as a member of a team, teach others
Personal Qualities Responsibility, sociability, self-management
EFF: Communication Read with understanding, convey ideas in writing, speak so others can understand, listen actively, observe critically
Lifelong Learning Take responsibility for learning, reflect and evaluate

Presentation 2　　　　　15–20 mins. ■■■

D Read about Liang's class.

Go over the graphs with students and make sure they understand the information by asking them information questions.

Practice 2　　　　　15–20 mins. ■■■

E Take a class poll. Make a bar graph.

Evaluation 2　　　　　5–7 mins. ■■

Check students' book work.

D Read about Liang's class.

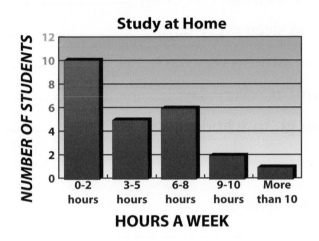

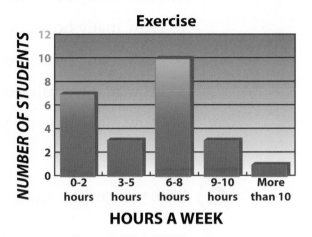

E Take a class poll. Make a bar graph. (Answers will vary.)

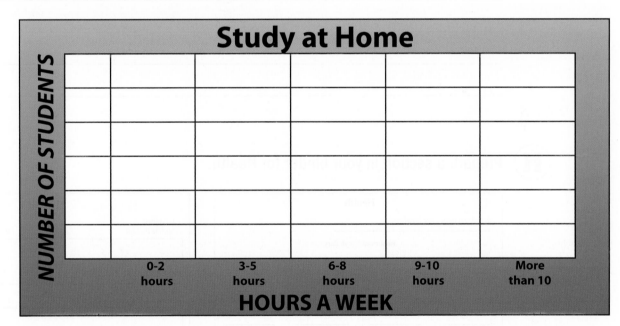

GOAL ➤ **Make goals**

F Interview a partner. Write his or her answers. (Answers will vary.)

1. How many hours do you exercise every day? _____

2. How many hours do you sleep every day? _____

3. How many hours do you study every day? _____

4. How many meals do you eat every day? _____

5. How many days do you go to school a week? _____

G Write your goals. (Answers will vary.)

_____

_____

_____

_____

_____

_____

H Prepare a section in your binder for Health.

Health

Stand Out Basic Page Numbers
_____

Important Vocabulary

___	___	___	___
___	___	___	___
___	___	___	___
___	___	___	___

Sentences and Questions

_____   _____
_____   _____
_____   _____
_____   _____

Health

Grammar
Simple Present   Page Number: _____

Negative Simple Present   Page Number: _____

Present Continuous   Page Number: _____

Presentation 3   10–15 mins. ■■□□

Ask students to close their books and discuss their personal goals. Ask them how many hours they sleep and how many hours they wish they could sleep. Help them to see that what they do and their goals can be the same or different. Ask the class as a whole each of the questions in Exercise F.

Ask students to open their books and go over each question with them. Review information-question intonation and the simple present.

Practice 3   15–20 mins. ■

(F) Interview a partner. Write his or her answers.

Help as needed.

Evaluation 3   5–7 mins. ■

Ask volunteers to report their partners' answers to the class.

Application   15–20 mins. ■■□

(G) Write your goals.

Help as needed.

(H) Prepare a section in your binder for Health.

Ask students to create their own Health summary page for their binder, using the sample provided, or ask them to complete the form provided in the Activity Bank CD-ROM for this unit.

Refer students to *Stand Out Basic Grammar Challenge*, Unit 8, Challenge 4 for more practice with the simple present.

Activity Bank 💿

Lesson 4, Worksheet 1: Health

Objective: Develop a study schedule
Grammar: Simple present
Academic Strategies: Focused listening, study skills
Vocabulary: *homework, prepare, evaluation, at home, schedule, organize*

RESOURCES

Activity Bank: Lesson 5, Worksheet 1
Reading and Writing Challenge: Unit 8
Grammar Challenge: Unit 8, Challenge 5
Audio: CD 2, Track 50
Heinle Picture Dictionary: School, pages 22–23

■ 1.5 hour classes   ■ 2.5 hour classes   ■ 3⁺ hour classes

AGENDA

Make a list of characteristics
 for good workers.
Discuss what teachers and students do.
Read a schedule.
Complete a schedule.
Read an evaluation.
Complete an evaluation.
Add a section for Occupational
 Knowledge in your binder.

Warm-up and Review   10-15 mins.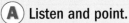

Ask students what makes a good worker. Make a list of their ideas on the board.

Introduction   15-20 mins.

Ask students if they study at home. Explain that it is best to study the same time every day. State the objective: *Today we will develop a study schedule.*

Presentation 1   7-10 mins.

(A) Listen and point.

Ask students to listen and identify which duty is being spoken about. Go over the duties and make sure students understand them.

 Listening Script   CD 2, Track 50

Teachers and students share many duties, or responsibilities. Among them are several very important things. For example, teachers and students should come to class on time. Students don't like to come early and find that the teacher is late. The teacher should come with a prepared lesson every day. That's also very important. Students have more confidence in a teacher who is prepared. The teacher teaches the students, but students can also teach each other. Students should study at home. There is a lot that they can study. For example, they can study new words at home. Sometimes the teacher gives homework. Students who do their homework learn English faster.

Practice 1   10-15 mins.

(B) Write.

Ask students to work in groups or pairs. Help them see that some duties fit in both categories.

(C) Add more duties to the list in Exercise B.

Ask students in groups to add to the lists.

Evaluation 1   3-5 mins. ■■■

Discuss the lists with students.

STANDARDS CORRELATIONS

CASAS: 4.1.1, 4.4.4, 7.1.1, 7.1.4 (See CASAS Competency List on pages 167-173.)
SCANS: Basic Skills Reading, writing, listening
Resources Allocate human resources
Information Acquire and evaluate information, organize and maintain information, interpret and communicate information

Interpersonal Participate as a member of a team, teach others
Personal Qualities Responsibility, sociability, self-management
EFF: Communication Read with understanding, convey ideas in writing, speak so others can understand, listen actively, observe critically
Lifelong Learning Take responsibility for learning, reflect and evaluate

When can I study?

GOAL ➤ Develop a study schedule

 A Listen and point.

CD 2
TR 50

Teacher and Student Duties

help students	study at home	come to class on time
study new words	prepare lessons	do homework

B Write.

Student duties	Teacher duties
help students	help students
study at home	come to class on time
come to class on time	prepare lessons
study new words	
do homework	
(Additional answers will vary.)	

C Add more duties to the list in Exercise B.

GOAL ➤ Develop a study schedule

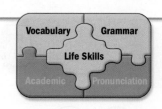

D Read and talk about the schedule. When does Liang work?

LIANG'S SCHEDULE

	Sunday	Monday	Tuesday	Wednesday	Thursday	Friday	Saturday
6:00 A.M.	Breakfast	Breakfast	Breakfast	Breakfast	Breakfast	Breakfast	Breakfast
9:00 A.M.		School	School	School	School	Study	Study
11:00 A.M.	Lunch	Lunch	Lunch	Lunch	Lunch	Lunch	Lunch
1:00 P.M.		Study	Study	Study	Study	Study	Study
3:00 P.M.							
5:00 P.M.		Work	Work	Work	Work	Work	
7:00 P.M.	Dinner	Dinner	Dinner	Dinner	Dinner	Dinner	Dinner
9:00 P.M.							

E Answer the questions. (Answers will vary.)

1. When do you study at school?

   _____

2. When do you study at home?

   _____

3. When do you work? _____

4. When do you eat breakfast, lunch,

   and dinner? _____

Simple Present

I **study** one hour.

You **study** one hour.

We **study** one hour.

They **study** one hour.

He **studies** one hour.

She **studies** one hour.

F Complete your schedule. (Answers will vary.)

MY SCHEDULE

	Sunday	Monday	Tuesday	Wednesday	Thursday	Friday	Saturday

Presentation 2   15–20 mins. ■■■

D **Read and talk about the schedule. When does Liang work?**

Read the chart with students. Help them to understand what a schedule is. Ask them questions about Liang's schedule. For example: *When does Liang eat lunch?* Help students see that Liang studies at the same time every day.

Review the simple present and show students the spelling for *studies*.

E **Answer the questions.**

Go over the questions with students.

Practice 2   15–20 mins. ■■

F **Complete your schedule.**

Ask students to use Liang's schedule in Exercise D as a model.

Evaluation 2   10 mins. ■■

Ask students questions about their schedules.

Presentation 3   10–15 mins. ■■■

(G) **Read and talk about Liang's evaluation.**

Go over Liang's evaluation with students. This evaluation is about whether Liang is a good student or not.

(H) **Ask questions about Liang.**

Help as needed.

Practice 3   10–15 mins. ■■■

(I) **Complete an evaluation about yourself. Ask your teacher to sign it.**

Evaluation 3   5–7 mins. ■■■

Ask students about their evaluations and observe their book work.

Application   20–30 mins. ■■■

(J) **Prepare a section in your binder for Occupational Knowledge.**

Ask students to create their own Occupational Knowledge summary page for their binder, using the sample provided, or ask them to complete the form provided on the Activity Bank CD-ROM.

Refer students to *Stand Out Basic Grammar Challenge*, Unit 8, Challenge 5 for more practice with the simple present.

Activity Bank

Lesson 5, Worksheet 1: Occupational Knowledge

GOAL ➤ **Develop a study schedule**

G **Read and talk about Liang's evaluation.**

Name: Liang Ochoa

studies at home	(Yes)	No
comes to class on time	Yes	(No)
speaks English in class	Yes	(No)
is organized	(Yes)	No

Teacher's signature: _Jennifer Douglas_

H **Ask questions about Liang.**

EXAMPLE: Does Liang study at home?

I **Complete an evaluation about yourself. Ask your teacher to sign it.** (Answers will vary.)

Name: _____

studies at home	Yes	No
comes to class on time	Yes	No
speaks English in class	Yes	No
is organized	Yes	No

Teacher's signature: _____

J **Prepare a section in your binder for Occupational Knowledge.**

Occupational (Work) Knowledge

Stand Out Basic Page Numbers _____

Important Vocabulary

_____ _____ _____ _____
_____ _____ _____ _____
_____ _____ _____ _____
_____ _____ _____ _____
_____ _____ _____ _____

Sentences and Questions

_____ _____
_____ _____
_____ _____
_____ _____

Occupational (Work) Knowledge

Grammar
when/where   Page Number: _____

can/can't   Page Number: _____

Affirmative and negative instructions   Page Number: _____

Review

A Match. Draw a line.

1. January, _____, March
2. This person answers phones in an office.
3. It is at the end of your arm.
4. your home
5. milk, cheese, butter
6. not sunny
7. medicine for a headache
8. a place for money
9. food for a sandwich
10. ten cents
11. This person can work in a hospital.
12. May, _____, July
13. clothing for winter
14. a place to buy food
15. You wear them on your feet.
16. You _____ a bicycle.

a. dairy
b. address
c. aspirin
d. bank
e. bread
f. dime
g. doctor
h. February
i. hand
j. June
k. cloudy
l. receptionist
m. ride
n. shoes
o. supermarket
p. sweater

B Practice with a partner.

A: It is at the end of your arm.
B: hand

C Find the page number for the words. (You can look at the Vocabulary List on page 161.)

Word(s)	Page number	Word(s)	Page number
divorced	7	broccoli	51
application	17	cash register	70
foggy	33	healthy	101
sit	24	mop	127

Objective: All unit objectives
Grammar: All unit grammar
Academic Strategies: Focused listening, reviewing, evaluating, developing study skills
Vocabulary: All unit vocabulary

AGENDA
Discuss unit objectives.
Complete the review.
Do My Dictionary.
Evaluate and reflect on progress.

■ 1.5 hour classes ■ 2.5 hour classes ■ 3+ hour classes

Warm-up and Review   7–10 mins.

With their books closed, ask students to help you make a list on the board of all the vocabulary from the unit. Then have a competition where students in groups find and write the page number for each item on the list. The first group to have the correct page number for each item wins. Explain that this review will also include going through the entire book for information.

Introduction   5 mins. ■■■

Write all the objectives on the board from Unit 8. Show students the first page of every lesson so they understand that today will be review. Complete the agenda.

Note: Depending on the length of the term, you may decide to have students do Presentation and Practice 1 for homework and then review as the warm-up for another class.

Presentation 1   10–15 mins. ■■■

This presentation and practice will cover the first three pages of the review. Quickly go to the first page of each lesson. Discuss the objective of each. Ask simple questions to remind students what they have learned.

Practice 1   15–20 mins.

A Match. Draw a line.

B Practice with a partner.

Show students how to substitute information from Exercise A.

C Find the page number for the words. (You can look at the Vocabulary List on page 161.)

Make sure students understand that they can find these words throughout *Stand Out Basic*. If students find the word in a sentence, encourage them to read it to a partner or to the class.

Teaching Tip

Recycling/Review

The review and the project that follows are part of the recycling/review process. Students at this level often need to be reintroduced to concepts to solidify what they have learned. Many concepts are forgotten while learning other new concepts. This is because students are not necessarily ready to acquire language concepts.

Therefore, it is very important to review and to show students how to review on their own. It is also important to recycle new concepts in different contexts.

STANDARDS CORRELATIONS

CASAS: 7.4.2, 7.4.3 (See CASAS Competency List on pages 167–173.)
SCANS: **Basic Skills** Reading, writing, listening, speaking
Information Acquire and evaluate information, organize and maintain information, interpret and communicate information

Thinking Skills See things in the mind's eye
***EFF:* Communication** Speak so others can understand
Lifelong Learning Take responsibility for learning, reflect and evaluate

Practice 1 (continued)

D Find the page number from the Vocabulary List on page 161 and write the sentence.

Additional Task: Choose a nearby market as a class. Create a map on the board to practice giving directions and map-reading skills.

E Find two new words from the Vocabulary List on page 161.

D Find the page number from the Vocabulary List on page 161 and write the sentence.

Phrase: marital status

Page number: _7_

Sentence: What's your marital status?

Phrase: extra large

Page number: _68_

Sentence: (Answers will vary.)

Phrase: go straight

Page number: _94_

Sentence: (Answers will vary.)

Word: checkup

Page number: _110_

Sentence: (Answers will vary.)

E Find two new words from the Vocabulary List on page 161. (Answers will vary.)

Word: _____

Page number: ____

Sentence: _____

Word: _____

Page number: ____

Sentence: _____

Review

F Use the Grammar Reference on pages 163–165 and fill in the blanks.

1. a. I _____ am _____ married.

   b. We _____ are _____ students.

   c. You _____ are _____ hungry.

   d. They _____ are _____ thirsty.

   e. She _____ is _____ single.

2. a. I _____ milk.

   b. We _____ a bowl of soup.

   c. You _____ vegetables.   } (Answers will vary.)

   d. They _____ tacos.

   e. She _____ a sandwich.

3. a. _____ Wash _____ your hands.

   b. _____ Answer _____ the phones.

   c. _____ Type _____ letters.

4. a. I can _____.

   b. They can _____.

   c. We can't _____.   } (Answers will vary.)

   d. She can't _____.

G Write the plural forms.

Singular	Plural
pear	pears
cookie	cookies
banana	bananas
egg	eggs
tomato	tomatoes

Practice 1 (continued)

F Use the Grammar Reference on pages 163–165 and fill in the blanks.

G Write the plural forms.

You might want to extend the task by reviewing the singular and plural forms of articles of clothing or other foods studied.

Evaluation 1   15 mins. ■ ■ ■

Go around the room and check on students' progress. Help individuals when needed. If you see consistent errors among several students, interrupt the class and give a mini lesson or review to help students feel comfortable with the concept.

Presentation 2　　　　5-7 mins.

My Dictionary

Review with students what My Dictionary is and help them see the value of it.

Practice 2　　　　7-10 mins.

Ask students to complete My Dictionary.

Evaluation 2　　　　3 mins.

Have students share their cards.

Presentation 3　　　　5 mins.

Learner Log

Review the concepts of the Learner Log. Make sure students understand the concepts and how to do the log including the check marks.

Practice 3　　　　10-15 mins.

Ask students to do the Learner Log.

Evaluation 3　　　　2 mins.

Go over the log with students.

Application　　　　

Ask students to write down their favorite lesson or page in the unit.

My Dictionary

Make flash cards to improve your vocabulary.

1. Choose four new words from this unit.
2. Write each word on an index card or on a piece of paper.
3. On the back of the index card or paper, draw a picture, find and write a sentence from the book with the word, and write the page number.
4. Study the words.

I need a two-inch binder.
page 145

Learner Log

Write the page number(s).

	Page Number	I can do it. ✓
1. Personal information	141–143	
2. How much is the binder?	144–146	
3. Where is the store?	147–149	
4. Goals	150–152	
5. Schedules	153–155	

My favorite page in this unit is (Answers will vary.) .

Team Project

Create a study guide.

1. Form a team with four or five students. In your team, you need:

POSITION	JOB	STUDENT NAME
Student 1: Team Leader	See that everyone speaks English. See that everyone participates.	
Student 2: Writer	Organize and add sections to the study guide.	
Student 3: Artist	Decorate the study guide.	
Students 4/5: Spokespeople	Prepare a presentation.	

2. Complete your binder from this unit. Share the information from your binder with your group.

3. Use your binders to make a team binder. This will be a study guide for new students.

4. Decorate the study guide.

5. Present your study guide to the class.

Introduction

In this project, students will work as a team to create a study guide for new students. They will present their binders to the class as a final class project.

Stage 1   15-20 mins.

Form a team with four or five students.

Discuss the art on the Student Book page.

Help students to assign positions in their groups. On the spot, students will have to choose who will be the leader of their group. Review the responsibility of a leader and ask students to write the name of their leader in their books. Do the same with the remaining positions: artist, writer, and spokesperson.

Stage 2   20-30 mins.

Complete your binder from this unit. Share the information from your binder with your group.

Ask students individually to complete the sections of the binders they developed in this unit and to share what they have completed with the group.

Stage 3   40-50 mins.

Use your binders to make a team binder. This will be a study guide for new students.

Ask students in groups to design a sample binder for new students who might come into the class late in the term. It will be used as a study guide. They will use the worksheets on the Activity Bank CD-ROM for this unit.

Stage 4   10-30 mins.

Decorate the study guide.

Ask students to decorate the binder pages and add pages that the team thinks might be helpful.

Stage 5   10-30 mins.

Present your study guide to the class.

Ask teams to practice their presentation before they give it. Recording student presentations on video can greatly enhance the learning experience.

Instructor's Notes

_____
_____
_____
_____
_____
_____
_____
_____
_____
_____
_____
_____
_____
_____
_____
_____

STANDARDS CORRELATIONS

CASAS: 2.2.3, 4.8.1 (See CASAS Competency List on pages 167-173.)
SCANS: Basic Skills Reading, writing, listening, speaking
Resources Allocate time, allocate money, allocate materials and facility resources, allocate human resources
Information Acquire and evaluate information, organize and maintain information, interpret and communicate information, use computers to process information
Interpersonal Participate as a member of a team, teach others, serve clients and customers, exercise leadership, negotiate to arrive at a decision, work with cultural diversity
Systems Understand systems, monitor and correct performance, improve and design systems

Thinking Skills Think creatively, make decisions, solve problems, see things in the mind's eye
Personal Qualities Responsibility, sociability, self management
EFF: Communication Read with understanding, convey ideas in writing, speak so others can understand, listen actively, observe critically
Decision Making Solve problems and make decisions, plan
Interpersonal Cooperate with others, advocate and influence, resolve conflict and negotiate, guide others
Lifelong Learning Take responsibility for learning, reflect and evaluate

Stand Out Basic Vocabulary List

Pre-Unit
Greetings
bye P1
goodbye P1
hello P1
hi P1
Study verbs
bubble in P9
circle P5
listen P17
point P4
practice P8
read P7
repeat P8
write P7

Unit 1
Calendar
date 14
day 14
month 13
week 13
year 13
Days
Sunday 13
Monday 13
Tuesday 13
Wednesday 13
Thursday 13
Friday 13
Saturday 13
Months
January 13
February 13
March 13
April 13
May 13
June 13
July 13
August 13
September 13
October 13
November 13
December 13
Marital status
divorced 7
married 7
single 7
Personal information
address 10
application 13
birth date 14
birthplace 5
city 10
name 1

state 10
zip code 10

Unit 2
from 4
live 6
phone number 28
schedule 30
time 31
Weather
cloudy 33
cold 33
foggy 33
hot 33
rainy 33
snowy 33
sunny 33
windy 33
Classroom words
book 24
board 24
bookcase 24
computer 24
desk 24
file cabinet 24
CD 24
notebook 24
pen 24
pencil 24
pencil sharpener 24
plant 24
sit 29
stand 29
table 24
trash can 24
Location
between 25
in 25
in the back 25
in the front 25
next to 25
on 25

Unit 3
hungry 45
thirsty 45
Food
apple 42
banana 42
bread 42
broccoli 51
butter 42
cake 53
candy 53
carrot 46

cheese 42
chicken 42
chips 44
chocolate 53
cookie 46
egg 42
fries 44
fruit 49
ground beef 47
ham 41
hamburger 44
ice cream 53
lettuce 42
mayonnaise 42
milk 42
onion 47
orange 42
pear 48
pepper 48
pie 53
potato 42
rice 44
salt 47
sandwich 41
spaghetti 47
taco 44
tomato 42
tuna fish 41
turkey 42
vegetables 44
water 42
yogurt 53
Meals
breakfast 43
dinner 43
lunch 43
Containers
and measurements
bag 48
can 48
jar 47
package 47
pound 47
Supermarket
dairy 50
fish 50
meat 50

Unit 4
Clothing
blouse 61
coat 62
dress 62
pants 61
shirt 61

shoes 61
shorts 61
socks 61
sweater 62
Colors
black 68
blue 68
green 68
red 68
white 68
yellow 68
Shopping
cash register 67
receipt 72
sale 73
size 68
small 68
medium 68
large 68
extra large 68
Money
dime 71
dollar 71
nickel 71
penny 71
quarter 71

Unit 5
Places in the community
bank 93
bookstore 93
bus stop 82
clothing store 81
convenience store 81
department store 81
fast food 82
hospital 93
hotel 82
pharmacy 81
post office 93
restaurant 82
shoe store 81
supermarket 81
telephone 82
video store 81
Housing
apartment 84
condominium 85
house 84
mobile home 84
Transportation
car 89
bicycle 89
bus 89
taxi 89

train 89
walk 89
come 89
drive 91
go 89
ride 91
take 91
Directions
go straight 94
stop 94
turn left 94
turn right 94

Unit 6
checkup 110
exercise 110
healthy 110
smoke 110
Parts of body
arm 102
back 102
ear 103

eye 103
foot 102
hand 102
head 102
leg 102
mouth 103
neck 102
nose 102
Ailments
backache 104
cold 104
cough 104
fever 104
headache 104
runny nose 104
sore throat 110
stomachache 104
Medicine
antacid 108
aspirin 108
cough syrup 108

Unit 7
Occupations
administrative
    assistant 127
bus driver 122
cashier 122
cook 123
custodian 124
doctor 122
employee 127
mail carrier 123
manager 123
nurse 123
receptionist 124
salesperson 122
student 122
teacher 122
worker 128
Work verbs
answer the phone 127
file 128
mop 127

type 127
make change 127
manage employees 127
take breaks 128
talk to customers 127
Evaluations
careful 121
cheerful 121
friendly 121
helpful 121

Unit 8
binder 141
divider 141
goal 150
notebook 145
paper 141
pencil 145
pen 145

Simple Present		
Subject	**Verb**	**Example sentence**
I, you, we, they	live take ride walk	I **live** in Mexico. We **take** the bus. You **ride** a bicycle. They **take** a train.
he, she, it	live**s** take**s** ride**s** walk**s**	He **takes** the bus. She **rides** a bicycle.

Simple Present		
Subject	**Verb**	**Example sentence**
I, you, we, they	eat	I **eat** three meals a day.
he, she, it	sleep**s**	She **sleeps** seven hours a night.

Negative Simple Present			
Subject	**Verb**		**Example sentence**
I, you, we, they	**don't**	eat	We **don't eat** three meals a day.
he, she, it	**doesn't**	sleep~~s~~	He **doesn't sleep** seven hours a day.

Simple Present: *Be*		
Subject	*Be*	**Example sentence**
I	am	I **am** friendly.
he, she, it	is	She **is** friendly.
we, you, they	are	They **are** friendly.

Simple Present: *Be* (negative)		
Subject	*Be* **(Negative)**	**Example sentence**
I	am not	I **am not** friendly.
he, she, it	is not	She **is not** friendly.
we, you, they	are not	They **are not** friendly.

Simple Present: *Have*		
Subject	*Have*	**Example sentence**
I, you, we, they	have	I **have** two shirts.
he, she	has	She **has** a dress.

Possessive Adjectives

Subject	Possessive adjective	Example sentence
I	my	**My** phone number is 555-3456.
you	your	**Your** address is 2359 Maple Drive.
he	his	**His** name is Edgar.
she	her	**Her** name is Julie.
we	our	**Our** last name is Perez.
they	their	**Their** teacher is Mr. Jackson.

Prepositions of Location

a. It's **in the front of** the store.

b. It's **in the corner of** the store.

c. It's **in the middle of** the store.

d. It's **in the back of** the store.

e. It's **on the left side of** the store.

f. It's **on the right side of** the store.

How much and How many

Question		Answer
How much	(money) is the sweater?	It is $33.00.
How many	coats do you want?	I want three coats.

Yes/No Questions

Question	Answer
Do you buy clothing at a department store?	Yes, I do.
Do you buy food at a supermarket?	No, I don't.
Do you buy shoes at a shoe store?	

Imperatives

	Subject	Verb
Please	~~you~~	read
		open
		let me (look)
		sit down
		stand up

Present Continuous (right now)

Subject	*Be* verb	Base + *ing*	Example sentence
I	am	talking	I **am talking**.
he, she, it	is	sleeping	He **is sleeping**.
we, you, they	are	waiting	They **are waiting**.

Information Questions

Question word	Type of answer
What	information (receptionist)
Where	a place (Johnson Company)
When	a time or day (9–6) (Monday–Friday)
Who	a person (Martin)

Can

Subject	*Can*	Verb (base)	Example sentence
I, you, he, she, it, we, they	can	type	I can type.
		mop	He can mop floors.

Can't

Subject	*Can't*	Verb (base)	Example sentence
I, you, he, she, it, we, they	can't	type	I can't type.
		mop	He can't mop floors.

Affirmative Commands

	Verb		Example sentence
~~You~~	wash	your hands	Wash your hands.
	answer	the phones	Answer the phones.
	type	letters	Type the letters.

Negative Commands

		Verb		Example sentence
~~You~~	don't	wash	your hands	Don't wash your hands.
		answer	the phones	Don't answer the phones.
		type	letters	Don't type the letters.

CASAS Competencies

0. Basic Communication

0.1 Communicate in interpersonal interactions
0.1.1 Identify or use appropriate non-verbal behavior in a variety of situations (e.g., handshaking)
0.1.2 Identify or use appropriate language for informational purposes (e.g., to identify, describe, ask for information, state needs, command, agree or disagree, ask permission)
0.1.3 Identify or use appropriate language to influence or persuade (e.g., to caution, request, advise, persuade, negotiate)
0.1.4 Identify or use appropriate language in general social situations (e.g., to greet, introduce, thank, apologize, compliment, express pleasure or regret)
0.1.5 Identify or use appropriate classroom behavior
0.1.6 Clarify or request clarification

0.2 Communicate regarding personal information
0.2.1 Respond appropriately to common personal information questions
0.2.2 Complete a personal information form
0.2.3 Interpret or write a personal note, invitation, or letter
0.2.4 Converse about daily and leisure activities and personal interests

1. Consumer Economics

1.1 Use weights, measures, measurement scales, and money
1.1.1 Interpret recipes
1.1.2 Use the metric system (see also 1.1.4, 6.6.1, 6.6.2, 6.6.3, 6.6.4)
1.1.3 Interpret maps and graphs (see also 1.9.4, 2.2.1, 2.2.5)
1.1.4 Select, compute, or interpret appropriate standard measurement for length, width, perimeter, area, volume, height, or weight (see also 1.1.2, 6.6.1, 6.6.2, 6.6.3, 6.6.4, 6.6.5)
1.1.5 Interpret temperatures (see also 6.6.4)
1.1.6 Count, convert, and use coins and currency, and recognize symbols such as ($) and (.) (see also 6.1.1, 6.1.2, 6.1.3, 6.1.4, 6.1.5)
1.1.7 Identify product containers and interpret weight and volume
1.1.8 Compute averages (see also 6.7.5)
1.1.9 Interpret clothing and pattern sizes and use height and weight tables

1.2 Apply principles of comparison-shopping in the selection of goods and services
1.2.1 Interpret advertisements, labels, charts, and price tags in selecting goods and services
1.2.2 Compare price or quality to determine the best buys for goods and services
1.2.3 Compute discounts (see also 6.4.1)
1.2.4 Compute unit pricing
1.2.5 Interpret letters, articles, and information about consumer-related topics

1.3 Understand methods and procedures used to purchase goods and services
1.3.1 Compare different methods used to purchase goods and services
1.3.2 Interpret credit applications and recognize how to use and maintain credit
1.3.3 Identify or use various methods to purchase goods and services, and make returns and exchanges
1.3.4 Use catalogs, order forms, and related information to purchase goods and services
1.3.5 Use coupons to purchase goods and services
1.3.6 Use coin-operated machines
1.3.7 Interpret information or directions to locate merchandise (see also 2.5.4)
1.3.8 Identify common food items
1.3.9 Identify common articles of clothing

1.4 Understand methods and procedures to obtain housing and related services
1.4.1 Identify different kinds of housing, areas of the home, and common household items
1.4.2 Select appropriate housing by interpreting classified ads, signs, and other information
1.4.3 Interpret lease and rental agreements
1.4.4 Interpret information to obtain, maintain, or cancel housing utilities
1.4.5 Interpret information about tenant and landlord rights
1.4.6 Interpret information about housing loans and home-related insurance
1.4.7 Interpret information about home maintenance, and communicate housing problems to a landlord (see also 1.7.4)
1.4.8 Recognize home theft and fire prevention measures

1.5 Apply principles of budgeting in the management of money
1.5.1 Interpret information about personal and family budgets
1.5.2 Plan for major purchases (see also 1.5.1)
1.5.3 Interpret bills (see also 2.1.4)

1.6 Understand consumer protection measures
1.6.1 Interpret food packaging labels (see also 1.2.1, 3.5.1)
1.6.2 Identify consumer protection resources available when confronted with fraudulent practices
1.6.3 Identify procedures the consumer can follow if merchandise or service is unsatisfactory
1.6.4 Check sales receipts

1.7 Understand procedures for the care, maintenance, and use of personal possessions

1.7.1 Interpret product guarantees and warranties
1.7.2 Interpret clothing care labels
1.7.3 Interpret operating instructions, directions, or labels for consumer products (see also 3.4.1)
1.7.4 Interpret maintenance procedures for household appliances and personal possessions
1.7.5 Interpret information to obtain repairs

1.8 Use banking and financial services in the community

1.8.1 Demonstrate the use of savings and checking accounts, including using an ATM
1.8.2 Interpret the procedures and forms associated with banking services, including writing checks
1.8.3 Interpret interest or interest-earning savings plans
1.8.4 Interpret information about the types of loans available through lending institutions
1.8.5 Interpret information on financial agencies and financial planning

1.9 Understand methods and procedures for the purchase and maintenance of an automobile and interpret driving regulations

1.9.1 Interpret highway and traffic signs (see also 2.2.2)
1.9.2 Identify driving regulations and procedures to obtain a driver's license (see also 2.5.7)
1.9.3 Compute mileage and gasoline consumption
1.9.4 Interpret maps related to driving (see also 1.1.3, 2.2.1, 2.2.5)
1.9.5 Interpret information related to the selection and purchase of a car
1.9.6 Interpret information related to automobile maintenance
1.9.7 Recognize what to do in case of automobile emergencies
1.9.8 Interpret information about automobile insurance

2. Community Resources

2.1 Use the telephone and telephone book

2.1.1 Use the telephone directory and related publications to locate information
2.1.2 Identify emergency numbers and place emergency calls (see also 2.5.1)
2.1.3 Interpret information about time zones (see also 2.3.1)
2.1.4 Interpret telephone billings
2.1.5 Interpret telegram rates and procedures
2.1.6 Interpret information about using a pay telephone
2.1.7 Take and interpret telephone messages, leave messages on answering machines, and interpret recorded messages (see also 4.5.4)

2.1.8 Use the telephone to make and receive routine personal and business calls

2.2 Understand how to locate and use different types of transportation and interpret related travel information

2.2.1 Ask for, give, follow, or clarify directions (see also 1.1.3, 1.9.4, 2.2.5)
2.2.2 Recognize and use signs related to transportation (see also 1.9.1)
2.2.3 Identify or use different types of transportation in the community, and interpret traffic information
2.2.4 Interpret transportation schedules and fares
2.2.5 Use maps relating to travel needs (see also 1.1.3, 1.9.4, 2.2.1)

2.3 Understand concepts of time and weather

2.3.1 Interpret clock time (see also 2.1.3, 6.6.6)
2.3.2 Identify the months of the year and the days of the week
2.3.3 Interpret information about weather conditions

2.4 Use postal services

2.4.1 Address letters and envelopes
2.4.2 Interpret postal rates and types of mailing services
2.4.3 Interpret postal service forms and instructions on returned mail
2.4.4 Purchase stamps and other postal items and services
2.4.5 Interpret procedures for tracing a lost letter or parcel
2.4.6 Interpret a postal money order form

2.5 Use community agencies and services

2.5.1 Locate and utilize services of agencies that provide emergency help
2.5.2 Identify how and when to obtain social and governmental services (e.g., low-income housing, Social Security, Medicare), and how to interact with service providers
2.5.3 Locate medical and health facilities in the community (see also 3.1.3)
2.5.4 Read, interpret, and follow directions found on public signs and building directories (see also 1.3.7)
2.5.5 Locate and use educational services in the community, including interpreting and writing school-related communications
2.5.6 Use library services
2.5.7 Interpret permit and license requirements (see also 1.9.2)
2.5.8 (unassigned)
2.5.9 Identify child care services in the community (see also 3.5.7)

2.6 Use leisure time resources and facilities

2.6.1 Interpret information about recreational and entertainment facilities and activities

2.6.2 Locate information in TV, movie, and other recreational listings

2.6.3 Interpret information in order to plan for outings and vacations

2.6.4 Interpret and order from restaurant and fast food menus, and compute related costs

2.7 Understand aspects of society and culture

2.7.1 Interpret information about holidays

2.7.2 Interpret information about ethnic groups, cultural groups, and language groups

2.7.3 Interpret information about social issues (see also 2.7.2)

2.7.4 Interpret information about religion

2.7.5 Interpret literary materials such as poetry and literature

2.7.6 Interpret materials related to the arts, such as fine art, music, drama, and film

3. Health

3.1 Understand how to access and utilize the health care system

3.1.1 Describe symptoms of illness, including identifying parts of the body; interpret doctor's directions

3.1.2 Identify information necessary to make or keep medical and dental appointments

3.1.3 Identify and utilize appropriate health care services and facilities, including interacting with providers (see also 2.5.3)

3.2 Understand medical and dental forms and related information

3.2.1 Fill out medical health history forms

3.2.2 Interpret immunization requirements

3.2.3 Interpret information associated with medical, dental, or life insurance

3.2.4 Ask for clarification about medical bills

3.3 Understand how to select and use medications

3.3.1 Identify and use necessary medications (see also 3.3.2, 3.3.3)

3.3.2 Interpret medicine labels (see also 3.3.1, 3.4.1)

3.3.3 Identify the difference between prescription, over-the-counter, and generic medications (see also 3.3.1)

3.4 Understand basic health and safety procedures

3.4.1 Interpret product label directions and safety warnings (see also 1.7.3, 3.3.2)

3.4.2 Identify safety measures that can prevent accidents and injuries

3.4.3 Interpret procedures for simple first-aid

3.4.4 Interpret information about AIDS and other sexually transmitted diseases (see also 3.1.1)

3.4.5 Recognize problems related to drugs, tobacco, and alcohol and identify where treatment may be obtained

3.5 Understand basic principles of health maintenance

3.5.1 Interpret nutritional and related information listed on food labels (see also 1.6.1)

3.5.2 Select a balanced diet

3.5.3 Interpret food storage information

3.5.4 Identify practices that promote dental health

3.5.5 Identify practices that promote cleanliness and hygiene

3.5.6 Interpret information and identify agencies that assist with family planning (see also 2.5.3, 3.1.3)

3.5.7 Identify child-rearing practices and community resources that assist in developing parenting skills (see also 2.5.9)

3.5.8 Identify practices that promote mental well being

3.5.9 Identify practices that promote physical well being

4. Employment

4.1 Understand basic principles of getting a job

4.1.1 Interpret governmental forms related to seeking work, such as applications for Social Security (see also 2.5.2)

4.1.2 Follow procedures for applying for a job, including interpreting and completing job applications, résumés, and letters of application

4.1.3 Identify and use sources of information about job opportunities such as job descriptions, job ads, and announcements, and about the workforce and job market

4.1.4 Identify and use information about training opportunities (see also 2.5.5)

4.1.5 Identify procedures involved in interviewing for a job, such as arranging for an interview, acting and dressing appropriately, and selecting appropriate questions and responses

4.1.6 Interpret general work-related vocabulary (e.g., experience, swing shift)

4.1.7 Identify appropriate behavior and attitudes for getting a job

4.1.8 Identify common occupations and the skills and education required for them

4.1.9 Identify procedures for career planning, including self-assessment

4.2 Understand wages, benefits, and concepts of employee organizations

4.2.1 Interpret wages, wage deductions, benefits, and timekeeping forms

4.2.2 Interpret information about employee organizations

4.2.3 Interpret employment contract and union agreements

4.2.4 Interpret employee handbooks, personnel policies, and job manuals

4.3 Understand work-related safety standards and procedures

4.3.1 Interpret safety signs found in the workplace (see also 3.4.1)

4.3.2 Interpret work safety manuals and related information

4.3.3 Identify safe work procedures and common safety equipment, including wearing safe work attire

4.3.4 Report unsafe working conditions work-related accidents, injuries, damages

4.4 Understand concepts and materials related to job performance and training

4.4.1 Identify appropriate behavior, attire, attitudes, and social interaction, factors that affect job retention advancement

4.4.2 Identify appropriate skills and education for keeping a job and getting a

4.4.3 Interpret job-related signs, charts, diagrams, forms, and procedures, record information on forms, charts, checklists, etc. (see also 4.2.1, 4.3.4)

4.4.4 Interpret job responsibilities and performance reviews (see also 4.4.2)

4.4.5 Identify job training needs and goals

4.4.6 Interpret work specifications and standards

4.4.7 Demonstrate the ability to apply skills learned in one job situation another

4.4.8 Interpret job-related technical information, such as from service manuals and classes

4.5 Effectively utilize common workplace technology and systems

4.5.1 Identify common tools, equipment, machines, and materials required one's job

4.5.2 Demonstrate simple keyboarding

4.5.3 Demonstrate ability to use a filing or other ordered system (e.g., coded numbered)

4.5.4 Demonstrate use of common business machines (see also 2.1.7, 2.1.8)

4.5.5 Demonstrate basic computer skills use of common software programs, including reading or interpreting computer generated printouts

4.5.6 Demonstrate ability to select, set use tools and machines in order accomplish a task, while operating a technological system

4.5.7 Demonstrate ability to identify resolve problems with machines follow proper maintenance procedures

4.6 Communicate effectively in the workplace

4.6.1 Follow, clarify, give, or provide feedback to instructions; give and respond appropriately to criticism

4.6.2 Interpret and write work-related correspondence, including notes, memos, letters, and e-mail (see also 4.4.3)

4.6.3 Interpret written workplace announcements and notices (see also 4.4.1, 4.4.3)

4.6.4 Report progress on activities, status of assigned tasks, and problems and other situations affecting job completion (see also 4.3.4)

4.6.5 Select and analyze work-related information for a given purpose and communicate it to others orally or in writing

4.7 Effectively manage workplace resources

4.7.1 Interpret or prepare a work-related budget, including projecting costs, keeping detailed records, and tracking status of expenditures and revenue

4.7.2 Identify or demonstrate effective management of material resources, including acquisition, storage, and distribution

4.7.3 Identify or demonstrate effective management of human resources, including assessing skills, making appropriate work assignments, and monitoring performance

4.7.4 Identify, secure, evaluate, process, and/or store information needed to perform tasks or keep records

4.8 Demonstrate effectiveness in working with other people

4.8.1 Demonstrate ability to work cooperatively with others as a member of a team, contributing to team efforts, maximizing the strengths of team members, promoting effective group interaction, and taking personal responsibility for accomplishing goals

4.8.2 Identify ways to learn from others and to help others learn job-related concepts and skills

4.8.3 Demonstrate effective communication skills in working with customers and clients

4.8.4 Demonstrate initiative and resourcefulness in meeting the needs and solving the problems of customers

4.8.5 Demonstrate leadership skills, including effectively communicating ideas or positions, motivating and respecting others, and responsibly challenging existing policies

4.8.6 Demonstrate negotiation skills in resolving differences, including presenting facts and arguments, recognizing differing points of view, offering options, and making compromises

4.8.7 Identify and use effective approaches to working within a multicultural workforce, including respecting cultural diversity, avoiding stereotypes, and recognizing concerns of members of other ethnic and gender groups

4.9 Understand how social, organizational, and technological systems work, and operate effectively within them

4.9.1 Identify the formal organizational structure of one's work environment

4.9.2 Demonstrate how a system's structures relate to its goals

4.9.3 Identify sources of information and assistance, and access resources within a system

4.9.4 Assess the operation of a system or organization and make recommendations for improvement, including development of new systems

5. Government and Law

5.1 Understand voting and the political process

5.1.1 Identify voter qualifications

5.1.2 Interpret a voter registration form

5.1.3 Interpret a ballot

5.1.4 Interpret information about electoral politics and candidates

5.1.5 Interpret information about special interest groups

5.1.6 Communicate one's opinions on a current issue

5.2 Understand historical and geographical information

5.2.1 Interpret information about U.S. history

5.2.2 Identify or interpret U.S. historical documents

5.2.3 Interpret information about world history

5.2.4 Interpret information about U.S. states, cities, geographical features, and points of interest

5.2.5 Interpret information about world geography

5.3 Understand an individual's legal rights and responsibilities and procedures for obtaining legal advice

5.3.1 Interpret common laws and ordinances, and legal forms and documents

5.3.2 Identify individual legal rights and procedures for obtaining legal advice (see also 5.3.1)

5.3.3 Interpret basic court procedures

5.3.4 Interpret laws affecting door-to-door sales (see also 1.6.2)

5.3.5 Interpret information about traffic tickets

5.3.6 Interpret information or identify requirements for establishing residency and/or obtaining citizenship

5.3.7 Identify common infractions and crimes, and legal consequences

5.3.8 Identify procedures for reporting a crime

5.4 Understand information about taxes

5.4.1 Interpret income tax forms

5.4.2 Compute or define sales tax

5.4.3 Interpret tax tables (see also 5.4.1, 5.4.2)

5.4.4 Interpret tax information from articles and publications

5.5 Understand governmental activities

5.5.1 Interpret information about international affairs

5.5.2 Interpret information about legislative activities

5.5.3 Interpret information about judicial activities

5.5.4 Interpret information about executive activities

5.5.5 Interpret information about military activities

5.5.6 Interpret information about law enforcement activities

5.5.7 Interpret information about local policymaking groups

5.5.8 Identify local, state and federal government leaders

5.6 Understand civic responsibilities and activities

5.6.1 Interpret information about neighborhood or community problems and their solutions

5.6.2 Interpret information about civic organizations and public service groups

5.6.3 Interpret civic responsibilities, such as voting, jury duty, taxes

5.7 Understand environmental and science-related issues

5.7.1 Interpret information about environmental issues

5.7.2 Interpret information related to physics, including energy

5.7.3 Interpret information about earth-related sciences

5.7.4 Interpret information about new technologies and scientific issues

5.8 Understand concepts of economics

5.8.1 Interpret economic information and statistics

5.8.2 Interpret information on economic issues and trends

5.8.3 Interpret information on world economic systems

6. Computation

6.0 Demonstrate pre-computation skills

6.0.1 Identify and classify numeric symbols

6.0.2 Count and associate numbers with quantities, including recognizing correct number sequencing

6.0.3 Identify information needed to solve a given problem

6.0.4 Determine appropriate operation to apply to a given problem

6.0.5 Demonstrate use of a calculator

6.1 Compute using whole numbers

6.1.1 Add whole numbers

6.1.2 Subtract whole numbers

6.1.3 Multiply whole numbers
6.1.4 Divide whole numbers
6.1.5 Perform multiple operations using whole numbers

6.2 Compute using decimal fractions
6.2.1 Add decimal fractions
6.2.2 Subtract decimal fractions
6.2.3 Multiply decimal fractions
6.2.4 Divide decimal fractions
6.2.5 Perform multiple operations using decimal fractions
6.2.6 Convert decimal fractions to common fractions or percents

6.3 Compute using fractions
6.3.1 Add common or mixed fractions
6.3.2 Subtract common or mixed fractions
6.3.3 Multiply common or mixed fractions
6.3.4 Divide common or mixed fractions
6.3.5 Perform multiple operations using common or mixed fractions
6.3.6 Convert common or mixed fractions to decimal fractions or percents
6.3.7 Identify or calculate equivalent fractions

6.4 Compute with percents, rate, ratio, and proportion
6.4.1 Apply a percent to determine amount of discount (see also 1.2.3)
6.4.2 Apply a percent in a context not involving money
6.4.3 Calculate percents
6.4.4 Convert percents to common, mixed, or decimal fractions
6.4.5 Use rate to compute increase or decrease
6.4.6 Compute using ratio or proportion (see also 6.4.5)

6.5 Use expressions, equations, and formulas
6.5.1 Recognize and evaluate simple consumer formulas
6.5.2 Recognize and apply simple geometric formulas
6.5.3 Recognize and apply simple algebraic formulas
6.5.4 Recognize and evaluate logical statements

6.6 Demonstrate measurement skills (see also 1.1)
6.6.1 Convert units of U.S. standard measurement and metric system (see also 1.1.2, 1.1.4)
6.6.2 Recognize, use, and measure linear dimensions, geometric shapes, or angles (see also 1.1.2, 1.1.4)
6.6.3 Measure area and volume of geometric shapes (see also 1.1.2, 1.1.4)
6.6.4 Use or interpret measurement instruments, such as rulers, scales, gauges, and dials (see also 1.1.2, 1.1.4, 1.1.5, 4.3.3, 4.4.3)
6.6.5 Interpret diagrams, illustrations, and scale drawings (see also 1.1.4, 4.4.3)
6.6.6 Calculate with units of time

6.6.7 Solve measurement problems in stipulated situations
6.6.8 Interpret mechanical concepts or spatial relationships
6.6.9 Use or interpret switches and controls

6.7 Interpret data from graphs and compute averages
6.7.1 Interpret data given in a line graph (see also 1.1.3)
6.7.2 Interpret data given in a bar graph (see also 1.1.3)
6.7.3 Interpret data given in a picture graph
6.7.4 Interpret data given in a circle graph (see also 1.1.3)
6.7.5 Compute averages, medians, or modes (see also 1.1.8)

6.8 Use statistics and probability
6.8.1 Interpret statistical information used in news reports and articles
6.8.2 Interpret statements of probability

6.9 Use estimation and mental arithmetic
6.9.1 Use computation short cuts
6.9.2 Estimate answers

7. Learning to Learn

7.1 Identify or practice effective organizational and time management skills in accomplishing goals
7.1.1 Identify and prioritize personal, educational, and workplace goals (see also 4.4.5)
7.1.2 Demonstrate an organized approach to achieving goals, including identifying and prioritizing tasks and setting and following an effective schedule
7.1.3 Demonstrate personal responsibility and motivation in accomplishing goals
7.1.4 Establish, maintain, and utilize a physical system of organization, such as notebooks, files, calendars, folders, and checklists (see also 4.5.3)

7.2 Demonstrate ability to use thinking skills
7.2.1 Identify and paraphrase pertinent information
7.2.2 Analyze a situation, statement, or process, identifying component elements and causal and part/whole relationships
7.2.3 Make comparisons, differentiating among, sorting, and classifying items, information, or ideas
7.2.4 Identify or make inferences through inductive and deductive reasoning to hypothesize, predict, conclude, and synthesize; distinguish fact from opinion, and determine what is mandatory and what is discretionary

7.2.5 Evaluate a situation, statement, or process, assembling information and providing evidence, making judgements, examining assumptions, and identifying contradictions

7.2.6 Generate ideas using divergent (brainstorming) and convergent (focus) approaches, and also through creative imagination

7.2.7 Identify factors involved in making decisions, including considering goals, constraints, and consequences, and weighing alternatives

7.3 Demonstrate ability to use problem-solving skills

7.3.1 Identify a problem and its possible causes

7.3.2 Devise and implement a solution to an identified problem

7.3.3 Evaluate the outcome of an implemented solution and suggest modifications to the solution as needed

7.3.4 Utilize problem-solving strategies, such as breaking down the problem into component parts and generating alternative or creative solutions

7.4 Demonstrate study skills

7.4.1 Identify or utilize effective study strategies

7.4.2 Take notes or write a summary or an outline

7.4.3 Identify, utilize, or create devices or processes for remembering information

7.4.4 Identify or utilize appropriate informational resources, including the Internet (see also 4.9.3)

7.4.5 Use reference materials, such as dictionaries and encyclopedias

7.4.6 Use indexes and tables of contents

7.4.7 Identify or utilize test-taking skills

7.4.8 Interpret visual representations, such as symbols, blueprints, flowcharts, and schematics (see also 6.6.5)

7.4.9 Identify personal learning style

7.5 Understand aspects of and approaches to effective personal management

7.5.1 Identify personal values, qualities, interests, abilities, and aptitudes

7.5.2 Identify or use strategies to develop a positive attitude and self-image, and self-esteem

7.5.3 Identify or use strategies to cope with negative feedback

7.5.4 Identify sources of stress, and resources for stress reduction

7.5.5 Identify personal, family, and work responsibilities, and ways to accommodate them and deal with related problems

7.5.6 Identify or use strategies for communicating more successfully

7.5.7 Identify constructive ways of dealing with change, including showing flexibility and adaptability, and updating skills

8. Independent Living

8.1 Perform self-care skills

8.1.1 Recognize and/or demonstrate hygiene and grooming skills (see also 3.5.5)

8.1.2 Recognize and/or demonstrate dressing skills

8.1.3 Recognize and/or demonstrate dining skills and manners

8.1.4 Recognize and/or demonstrate selection and care of clothing and personal property

8.2 Perform home-care skills

8.2.1 Recognize and/or demonstrate meal and snack preparation tasks and activities (see also 1.1.1, 3.5.2)

8.2.2 Recognize and/or demonstrate dishwashing and meal clean-up activities (see also 3.5.5)

8.2.3 Recognize and/or demonstrate housekeeping and house cleaning tasks

8.2.4 Recognize and/or demonstrate laundry skills and related clothing-care skills (see also 1.7.2, 1.7.3)

8.2.5 Recognize and/or demonstrate yard and garden tasks and activities

8.2.6 Recognize and/or demonstrate general household repair and maintenance (see also 1.4.7, 1.7.4)

8.3 Use support services to assist in maintaining independence and achieving community integration

8.3.1 Identify and interact with persons in the home environment who can provide support in achieving goals (e.g., family, friends, caregivers)

8.3.2 Identify and interact with persons in the community who can provide support in achieving goals (e.g., neighbors, contacts from human service agencies and recreation facilities)

Photo Credits

ACADEMIC SKILLS

Bubbling in
Ailments, 106
Housing, 85
Instructions, P9
Organizing study materials, 142
Purchases and money, 70
Telling time, 31

Charts, graphs, and maps, 11, 23, 43, 48, 54, 55, 64, 68, 69, 84, 87, 89, 93, 94, 98, 105, 106, 107, 111, 114, 117, 123, 126, 127, 128, 149, 151

Grammar
a/an, 84
Affirmative and negative commands, 134
can and *can't*, 129
Contractions, P3, 9, 15
How much and *How many*, 74
Information questions, 125–126
Negative simple present, 111–112
on/in, 84
Plurals, 48
Possessive adjectives, 22
Prepositions, 25, 43, 65
Present continuous, 29
Pronouns, 22
Simple present, 6, 35, 52, 54, 57, 63, 91, 92, 105, 109
Singular and plural nouns, 48–49
Subject pronouns, 1–3
Verbs, P8
be, 8–9, 12, 45, 69, 72, 92, 131
have, 63
Yes/No questions, 83

Group activities, 26, 35, 123, 135, 146

Listening
Addresses, 10, 11
Affirmative and negative commands, 133
Ailments, 104
Body parts, 101
Classroom activities, 27
Clothing, 61, 66, 67, 68
Colors, 68
Conversations, 113, 147
Dates, 13
Directions, 95, 147
Food, 41–42, 44, 46, 47, 50, 51, 53
Goals, 150
Greetings, P1–P3
Healthy habits, 111
Housing, 84, 85, 86

Information questions, 124, 126
Instructions, P7–P9
Introductions, 21
Locations, 81, 82, 84, 86
Making purchases, 144, 145
Money, 71, 72
Names, 2–3
Nationality, 4, 5
Numbers, P4
Occupations, 121, 122
Organizing study materials, 141
Personal information, 2, 7, 8
Study schedules, 153
Telling time, 30, 32
Transportation, 87, 90
Weather, 33
Work information, 124

Matching
Classroom activities, 28, 38
Directions, 93
Job duties, 137
Marital status, 17
Matching, 71
Meanings, 156
Questions and answers, 125

Partner activities, 3, 15, 17, 86, 114, 138, 143, 152

Pronunciation
can and *can't*, 129
Final *s* sound, 48
/g/ sound, 114
Introductions, 23
/m/ sound, P2
/t/ sound, P8
Yes/No questions, 67, 83, 128

Reading
Addresses, 10, 12
Affirmative and negative commands, 134
Ailments, 104
Body parts, 102, 103
Charts, 48, 54, 105, 111, 114, 117
Clothing, 63, 65, 67, 75
Colors, 67, 69
Conversations, 123, 148
Dates, 14
Directions, 95, 148
Evaluations, 130, 132
Food, 43, 44, 45, 46, 47, 51, 52
Goals, 151
Graphs, 89
Healthy habits, 110, 112
Housing, 85, 86
Information questions, 125, 126
Introductions, 36
Job descriptions, 135

Locations, 85, 89
Maps, 94, 98
Money, 71
Nationality, 4
Present continuous, 29
Signs, 133–135
Simple present, 35, 105, 109
Study schedules, 154, 155
Telling time, 30, 37
Transportation, 87, 91, 92
Weather, 34, 35

Speaking
Addresses, 11
Ailments, 106
Asking questions, 24, 67, 83
Body parts, 102, 103
Colors, 67
Conversations, 55, 70, 75, 86, 89, 103, 104, 110, 123, 134, 145
Dates, 13–15
Directions, 148
Food, 48, 49, 55, 58
Greetings, P1–P3
Housing, 84
Information questions, 125
Introductions, 23
Locations, 83
Names, 1–3
Numbers, P4
Occupations, 122, 123
Shopping, 65
Study schedules, 154, 155
Transportation, 88, 89

Studying
Goals, 150, 151
Organizing study materials, 141–143
Study schedules, 153–155

Vocabulary
Addresses, 10
Ailments, 104–106
Body parts, 101–103
Classroom, 24, 28
Clothing, 61–63, 73
Colors, 67–69
Dates, 14
Directions, 94
Doctor's appointments, 113–115
Evaluations, 131
Flash cards, P10, 19, 39, 59, 79, 99, 119, 139, 159
Food, 42, 44, 46, 48, 53
Greetings, P1
Housing, 84–86
Job duties, 127–129
Locations, 81–83, 84, 93

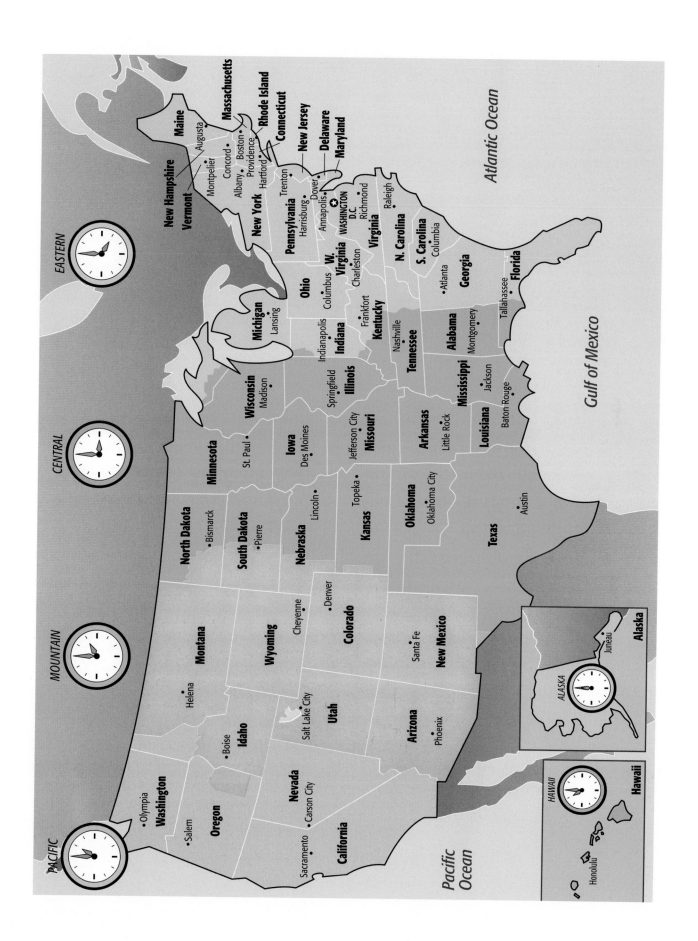

Activity Bank Contents (available on the enclosed CD-ROM)

Unit	Lesson	CD-ROM Folder	Worksheets*	Skill
Pre-Unit	1	Pre-unit	1. Say *Hello* and *Goodbye* 🎧	Practice saying *hello* and *goodbye* and listening.
		Templates	Table – 2 columns	Use two-column template to record student names (Application).
		Literacy	Literacy Worksheets 1–6	The literacy folder includes worksheets for writing letters and names.
	2	Pre-unit	1. Write Phone Numbers	Write phone numbers based on given information.
		Literacy	Literacy Worksheets 1–6	The literacy folder includes worksheets for writing numbers.
	3	Pre-unit	1. Classroom Instructions 🎧	Listen and match classroom activity and associated object.
Unit 1	1	Templates	Table – 2 columns	Use two-column template to record student names and phone number (Warm-up).
		Unit 1	1. Say *Hello!* 2. Use Subject Pronouns	1. Practice a conversation and read a paragraph. 2. Write subject pronouns and sentences.
	2	Unit 1	1. Write About Countries and Cities	Write sentences about countries and cities from given information
	3	Unit 1	1. Marital Status 🎧 2. *Be* Verb	1. Read and listen to identify marital status. 2. Use *be* to write sentences.
	4	Templates	Table – 4 columns	Use four-column template to record student name, marital status, residence, and native country (Warm-up).
		Unit 1	1. Write Addresses 2. Personal Information	1. Write addresses from given information. 2. Ask for and record personal information.
		Internet	1.1 Zip and Area Codes	Template allows students to use the Internet to find zip and area codes.
	5	Unit 1	1. Calendars and Dates 2. Ordinal Numbers	1. Identify dates. 2. Identify and write ordinal numbers.
	Project	Unit 1	1. Student Profile 2. Class Phone Book	1. Write personal information. 2. Complete a class phone directory.
		Computer	1.1 Class list	Inputting data about classmates on to Excel template.
	Ext.	Unit 1	1. Application Forms	Complete the personal information on rental and job application.
Unit 2	1	Unit 2	1. Introductions 2. Possessive Adjectives	1. Practice conversations with new vocabulary. 2. Complete sentences and a paragraph with possessive adjectives.
	2	Unit 2	1. Prepositions of Location	Complete sentences by looking at a floor plan.
	3	Unit 2	1. Classroom Activities	Identify and read about classroom activities.
	4	Unit 2	1. Telling Time 2. Schedules and Times 3. Daily Planner	1. Read clocks. 2. Practice information gap activities.
		Computer	2.1/2.2 Complete the Schedule	Imputing data and saving information about schedules on Excel.
		Internet	2.1 Time	Template allows students to look up time zones and the current time online.
	5	Unit 2	1. How's the Weather?	Write sentences about schedules.
	Project	Unit 2	1. How to Organize Your Team Collage	Record personal information.
	Ext.	Templates	Daily Planner	Write about a classmate on the template.
		Computer	2.3 Classroom Inventory / 2.4 Daily Schedule	Printing, copying and pasting in Excel on an inventory of items in the classroom.

Unit	Lesson	CD-ROM Folder	Worksheets*	Skill
Unit 3	1	Templates	Table – 2 column	Use two-column template to record food preferences (Practice 1).
		Unit 3	1. Food 🎧	Identify food vocabulary and listen.
		Computer	3.1 Food Ads	Changing font size and styles.
	2	Templates	Table – 2-column	Use two-column template to record fruits and vegetables (Warm-up).
		Unit 3	1. I'm Hungry!	Practice the *be* verb in an information gap activity expressing hunger.
	3	Templates	Table – 4-column	Use four-column template to classify foods (Warm-up).
		Unit 3	1. Singular and Plural	Identify singular and plural and write a recipe.
	4	Templates	Venn Diagram	Use Venn diagram for additional practice.
		Unit 3	1. Simple Present: *Want* 🎧	Complete sentences with the simple present using *want*.
	5	Unit 3	1. Simple Present: *Like*	Complete sentences and a Venn diagram using the simple present of *like*.
	Project	Templates	1. Meal Template	Plan templates.
		Computer	3.2 Shopping Lists	Sorting data in Excel to make shopping lists.
	Ext.	Unit 3	1. Taking an Order	Practice a conversation with given information.
		Internet	3.2 Food Groups/3.3 Grocery Shopping	Templates allow students to explore the Internet.
Unit 4	1	Unit 4	1. Clothing	Practice clothing vocabulary through an information gap activity.
	2	Templates	Venn Diagram	Ask students to complete a Venn diagram with information from their closets (Warm-up).
		Unit 4	1. Sections in a Store 2. Locations	1. Practice new vocabulary through answering questions and conversations. 2. Complete a floor plan and use prepositions.
	3	Unit 4	1. Colors and Clothing 🎧	Read and listen to conversations and identify colors and clothing.
		Computer	4.1 Clothing Ads	Changing font size and styles for clothing ad.
	4	Unit 4	1. Money and Totals 2. Counting Money	Add up amounts from receipts. Determine denominations.
	5	Unit 4	1. Asking Questions 2. Create an Advertisement	1. Write a conversation and practice it using *how much* and *how many*. 2. Complete a template to make an advertisement.
	Project	Unit 4	1. Newspaper Advertisement Template 2. Inventory Template	1. Complete a template to make an advertisement. 2. Complete a template to record quantity, item, size, color, and price.
		Computer	4.2 Clothing Data	Copy and paste or sort data in Excel describing clothing.
	Ext.	Unit 4	1. Writing Checks	Write checks based on information in receipts.
		Internet	4.1/4.2/4.3	Use the Internet to shop for clothes.

Unit	Lesson	CD-ROM Folder	Worksheets*	Skill
Unit 5	1	Unit 5	1. Locations in the Community	Answer questions and make answers into a paragraph.
		Computer	5.1 My Neighborhood	Write a paragraph.
	2	Unit 5	1. Housing	Complete an information gap activity about housing.
	3	Templates	Table – 3-column	Use a three-column template to record housing information (Warm-up).
		Unit 5	1. Transportation Vocabulary 2. Transportation Prices	1. Match vocabulary and verbs and make a graph. 2. Identify prices through an information gap activity.
	4	Templates	Bar Graph	Use a bar graph template to record transportation data from the class (Warm-up).
	5	Unit 5	1. Simple Present	Complete sentences using the simple present tense including *be*.
		Unit 5	1. Following Directions	Follow directions and identify locations while listening.
		Computer	5.2 Directions	Input data and sort in Excel.
	Project	Unit 5	1. Types of Transportation 2. Conversations about Directions	1. Complete the chart of transportation. 2. Practice two conversations.
	Ext.	Unit 5	1. Places in Your Community 2. Information Questions	1. Complete a chart about your community. 2. Answer and ask personal information questions.
		Internet	5.1/5.2/5.3	Use the Internet to explore transportation options.
Unit 6	1	Unit 6	1. Body Parts	Write and unscramble body part vocabulary.
	2	Unit 6	1. Symptoms and Illnesses 2. Simple Present	1. Complete sentences and practice conversations with symptoms and illnesses. 2. Use the simple present to complete sentences.
	3	Unit 6	1. Medicine 2. Medicine for Ailments 3. Simple Present: *Need, Have*	1. Write sentences and listen and identify medications. 2. Use the template to interview people about medications. 3. Complete sentences with *need* and *have*.
		Internet	6.1 Pharmacy	Use the template to shop online for medicines.
	4	Templates	Table – 2-column	Record illnesses and medicines in a two-column template.
		Unit 6	1. Personal Inventory 2. Negative Simple Present	1. Write sentences and make them into a paragraph about health habits. 2. Complete sentences with the negative simple present.
	5	Unit 6	1. Present Continuous	Complete and write sentences with the present continuous.
	Project	Unit 6	1. Appointment Book Page 2. Appointment Conversations	1. Complete a template of an appointment book page. 2. Conversation about making an appointment.
	Ext.	Unit 6	1. Making Appointments 2. Warning Labels	1. Information gap conversations making appointments. 2. Interpret medicine labels.
		Computer	6.1 My Health Habits	Edit and write a paragraph.
		Computer	6.2 Sleep Habits	Make a bar graph.

Unit	Lesson	CD-ROM Folder	Worksheets*	Skill
Unit 7	1	Unit 7	1. Occupations	Practice conversations about occupations.
	2	Templates	Bar Graph	Create a bar graph with the graph template of occupations (Warm-up).
		Unit 7	1. *When*, *Where*, and *What*	Match questions with answers. Ask classmates questions.
	3	Unit 7	1. Duties 🎧 2. Using *can* and *can't*	1. Listen and identify job duties. 2. Use *can* and *can't* to write sentences.
	4	Unit 7	1. Reading Evaluations	Interpret evaluations and practice a conversations.
	5	Unit 7	1. Commands	Write affirmative and negative commands.
	Project	Unit 7	1. Company Information	Describe a company with the template.
	Ext.	Unit 7	1. Job Interviews 2. Interviews	1. Create a conversation and practice. 2. Answer personal questions.
		Internet	7.1 Job Search	Use the Internet to search for classified ads.
		Computer	7.1 My Job 7.2 Salaries	Writing a paragraph and adding clip art. Make a pie chart in Excel.
Unit 8	1	Unit 8	1. Personal Profile	Complete the personal profile using the template.
		Computer	8.1 Making a Table	Creating a table in Word.
	2	Unit 8	1. Consumer Economics	Identify important vocabulary and grammar from Units 3–4.
		Computer	8.2 Make Purchases	Totaling data in Excel.
		Internet	8.1 Office Supplies	Use the Internet to buy office supplies.
	3	Unit 8	1. Community	Identify important vocabulary and grammar from Units 5–6.
	4	Unit 8	1. Health	Identify important vocabulary and grammar from Unit 6.
	5	Unit 8	1. Occupational (Work) Knowledge	Identify important vocabulary and grammar from Unit 7.

* Unit worksheets include low, mid-level, and high multilevel versions.
🎧 Audio scripts included on worksheets.